ACRL PUBLICATIONS IN LIBRARIANSHIP NO. 66

Interdisciplinarity and Academic Libraries

Edited by Daniel C. Mack
and Craig Gibson

Association of College and Research Libraries
A Division of the American Library Association
Chicago 2012

The paper used in this publication meets the minimum requirements of American National Standard for Information Sciences–Permanence of Paper for Printed Library Materials, ANSI Z39.48-1992. ∞

Library of Congress Cataloging-in-Publication Data

Interdisciplinarity and academic libraries / editors, Daniel C. Mack and Craig Gibson.
    pages cm. -- (ACRL publications in librarianship ; no. 66)
    Includes bibliographical references and index.
    ISBN 978-0-8389-8615-8 (pbk. : alk. paper) 1. Academic libraries--Relations with faculty and curriculum. 2. Interdisciplinary research. 3. Area specialist librarians. I. Mack, Daniel C. II. Gibson, Craig, 1954-
    Z675.U5I578 2012
    027.7--dc23
                    2012018651

Printed in the United States of America.

16 15 14 13 12   5 4 3 2 1

Cover photo, "Tapestry" © 2011 by Marc Falardeau and made available under a Creative Commons license.

Table of Contents

The Role of the Academic Library as an Interdisciplinary Knowledge Hub

Daniel C. Mack

Interdisciplinarity is not merely a buzzword in the academy. Rather, it is a defining concept that is shaping many institutions' curricula, research agendas, and policies. But what exactly is interdisciplinarity, and how does it affect the academic library as we develop collections and programs for the twenty-first-century university? The term *interdisciplinarity* and its variations *multidisciplinarity, cross-disciplinarity,* and *transdisciplinarity* cover a range of methodological approaches, all of which involve the use of multiple disciplines or fields of inquiry. Some of these issues are explored in depth within this volume, but a few working definitions are in order. *Multidisciplinary research* generally investigates a problem from the viewpoints of several different disciplines. For example, a multidisciplinary panel discussion on the prevention and treatment of HIV/AIDS in developing countries might include researchers in medicine, public health, sociology, public policy, and law. Each of these disciplines contributes a unique perspective on the issue at hand. The individual contributors may focus on the methods and approaches of a particular field of inquiry, but the panel as a whole is an example of multidisciplinarity. *Cross-disciplinary research* involves the analysis of one field of study using the methods of another. A work on optics analyzing perspective and color for art historians is an example of cross-disciplinarity. In this case, the methods of physics, particularly the physics of light, offer new insight into the study of art history. *Transdisciplinary research* refers to holistic approaches that seek a unity of knowledge beyond both traditional disciplinary boundaries and the approaches of multidisciplinarity and cross-disciplinarity.[1] Within the academy, *interdisciplinarity* often carries both a specific and a general meaning. In a precise sense, interdisciplinary research involves approaching a problem from several disciplinary perspectives simultaneously. *Interdisciplinarity* is also often used in a more general sense to refer to any research that involves more than one discipline. In this sense *multidisciplinarity, cross-disciplinarity,* and *transdisciplinarity* are subsets of *interdisciplinarity,* and this is how the term is generally used throughout this volume.

Institutions of higher education now frequently foster a wide range of formal and informal partnerships among and between the humanities, the social sciences, the fine and performing arts, science, technology, and medicine. These collaborations increasingly require participation by scholars from across the curriculum. Regardless of the various fields of study involved, all interdisciplinary research has one thing in common: the need for information from multiple disciplinary sources. This need offers today's academic library an unprecedented opportunity to leverage a central role in the academy.

Why is interdisciplinarity so important now? Several factors have contributed to the advancement of interdisciplinary research and teaching throughout academia. One of the most important factors is the internationalization of the academy. Not only has the curriculum become global; international students and faculty have increased significantly throughout institutions of higher education in the United States over the last three decades. Along with this globalization come an increasingly international perspective toward research problems and their solutions and a willingness to try new approaches to research. New students and new faculty bring with them new ways to do research and new bodies of research literature to explore. While most visible in large research universities, this internationalization can be seen in liberal arts and community colleges as well.

Also contributing to the rise of interdisciplinarity is the constant evolution and adoption of new technologies for the storage, retrieval, classification, and dissemination of information. This in turn has led to new means for formal and informal communication among scholars at every level. As researchers adopt new media and formats for scholarship and teach these to a new generation of students, the print monograph and journal article find themselves in increasing competition with new forms of scholarly activity. As academia adopts cloud computing, scholarship will increasingly be born digital. Not only must the future university find ways to store and retrieve this information, it must also develop new and innovative ways to evaluate and vet this research if some form of peer review is to survive.

Another contributing factor to increasing interdisciplinarity is the promotion of new methods, theories, and fields of study. Ethnic, race, and gender studies; queer theory, postcolonial theory, and other identity studies; and the varieties of postmodernism have not only spread throughout the humanities and social science curriculum, but have gained a foothold in science and technology disciplines as well. While some of these new paradigms of scholarship draw intense criticism from some members of the university, they nevertheless do influence research and teaching in the contemporary university. One emerging discipline, disability studies, offers an excellent example. Drawing on fields as diverse as philosophy, medicine, law, public policy, architecture, literature, history, engineering, and industrial design, disability studies combines research with activism to explore the role of persons with disabilities in society. Many other examples of interdisciplinary curricula occur throughout the contemporary academy. Even traditional disciplinary-based programs are now frequently offered as dual-degree programs. Business, law, and medicine have long partnered in joint MBA/JD, MD/MBA, and JD/MD programs, and other fields of study have followed suit at most research universities. Even more important for interdisciplinarity than joint degree programs are the numerous institutes and research centers that have sprung up at many colleges and universities during the past half-century. These institutes by their very nature are often the collaboration of researchers from a variety of disciplinary backgrounds.

Where is the place of the academic library in the twenty-first-century college or university library? The library is, or ought to be, right in the center, as the hub of interdisciplinary activity. Research libraries, at least successful ones, have long since learned that they must go far beyond their traditional image as "warehouses of books." In the academy of the future, not only must libraries provide collections in a wide variety of media and formats; they must also provide both front-end and hidden services to facilitate access to and use of information in all disciplines. This places libraries in the center of scholarly activity, a location that will be difficult to maintain, but vital if the library is to survive as an effective institution within higher education. And while this is especially true at large research universities, there is no reason this model should not also develop at the liberal arts or community college library as well.

As libraries find themselves at the hub of the interdisciplinary academy, so individual librarians will encounter interdisciplinarity in many different activities: during reference and research consultation, while preparing for library instruction sessions, as a part of collection development, and in a variety of other public service activities. Library personnel behind the scenes must also work constantly with interdisciplinary issues while ordering, classifying, cataloging, digitizing, and otherwise processing and providing access to library materials to support the research and teaching needs of the university. The faculty and administrators of today's academic libraries must thoughtfully answer the question, "How do we handle interdisciplinarity?" Whether we are providing research assistance to scholars, teaching the use of library resources, or developing and assessing library collections across subject areas, formats, and media, we must keep this question in mind.

So how can the academic library function as a hub of interdisciplinarity, and what must librarians do to secure this central position? By using library resources to provide background for unfamiliar disciplinary areas and to open up new disciplinary venues to scholars, the library becomes the natural center of interdisciplinary research. As researchers venture beyond their own disciplinary backgrounds to explore other fields of inquiry, the library can act as negotiator among the multiple vocabularies, literatures, methods, and paradigms encountered throughout the curriculum. The interdisciplinary librarian will consult and collaborate with other librarians and collegiate faculty; address issues of interdisciplinarity, multiculturalism, internationalization, and emerging technologies; seek solutions to reference inquiries, library instruction, and collection development that cut across traditional disciplinary boundaries; and work as a collaborative colleague and creative consultant with collegiate faculty and with other librarians.

Note

1.   See Basarab Nicolescu, *Manifesto of Transdisciplinarity,* trans. Karen-Claire Voss (New York: SUNY Press, 2002).

The Structuring Work of Disciplines

Roberta J. Astroff

Academic discourse about interdisciplinarity describes the increasing permeability, or perhaps dissolution, of disciplinary boundaries that were supposedly stable in the field of knowledge of the past. That perceived stability was in fact the result of constant cultural work focused on maintaining those boundaries. The work of maintaining disciplinary boundaries is carried out through common academic processes such as defining curricula and related faculty positions, making hiring decisions, managing the creation of new courses, approving doctoral thesis proposals, and performing peer review of academic writing. In each instance, decisions are made as to what topics and methodologies are appropriate for classes, research, and articles; which texts are received as defining instances of the field; what kind of work is recognized as belonging to that discipline; and, most important in the context of this chapter, which of these disciplinary definitions are institutionalized within the university. Within the field of critical pedagogy, this cultural work has been seen largely through the paradigm Michel Foucault explicated in his book *Discipline and Punish*.[1] Using Foucault's paradigm, analysts such as Henry Giroux in the field of critical pedagogy identified disciplinary structures as closed, undemocratic, and essentially conservative, that is, devoted to the maintenance of existing disciplinary definitions, hierarchies, and privilege through the exclusion of new ideas and new cultural workers. The emphasis in this analysis of disciplinary structure then has been on policing functions.

The structure of disciplines and the structure of contemporary universities appear to be inseparable. Academic departments are named and their fields defined from standard disciplinary documents and according to the requirements of policing disciplinary organizations. Those organizations mandate, though accreditation procedures, the number of courses a department must offer, the nature of those courses, the type of resources that must be available, the number of credits students can take within and outside the discipline. Within those parameters, as mandated by universities, courses are defined and faculty hired by departments. At the next highest university level, colleges bring together and manage departments seen as sharing certain disciplinary characteristics (hard vs. soft, pure vs. applied, hard science vs. life sciences vs. social sciences vs. humanities). The deans of those colleges represent those soft, hard, pure, applied, and life disciplines to the highest management levels of the university, where decisions are made about the allocation of funds and office space, the formation of degree requirements and tenure procedures, and the nature of the statistics gathered by university offices of institutional research (itself another process of definition). All levels of academic activity within a university can be seen as structured by the disciplinary formation of its administration and faculty.

The structural apparatus of disciplines—that is, their institutionalization—shapes the actions of researchers and teachers on other levels as well. Disciplinary processes extend beyond hiring practices and tenure procedures into teaching methods, ways of interaction between students and professors, faculty expectations of students, and students' expectations of faculty. The participation of faculty in graduate student work, for example, varies dramatically from the hard sciences, where dissertation topics might be assigned, to the humanities, where dissertation work is seen as highly individual. The nature of assessing what has been learned varies dramatically from the sciences to the humanities. Further, as Del Favero notes, training within a discipline results in "a system of orderly behavior recognized as characteristic of the discipline. Such behaviors are manifested in scholars' approaches to understanding and investigating new knowledge, ways of working, and perspectives on the world around them."[2]

That is, disciplines function like cultures.

The Cultural Process of (Inter)Disciplinarity

Once we begin to see disciplines as cultures, though, the problems of focusing so heavily on the policing function become visible. As McArthur argues, Giroux posits a need to "escape disciplinary boundaries and build interdisciplinary spaces" in which a public flow of discourse could enable critical thought.[3] Giroux and other writers in the field of critical pedagogy hold a view of culture as active, in flux, and full of contestation and negotiation, but locate this *outside* the boundaries of disciplines. This posits a sort of "epistemological essentialism" in their view of disciplines.[4] It is more useful, and more accurate, to see that academic disciplines are and always have been "complex, permeable and contested spaces" whose boundaries are subject to frequent challenge and negotiation.[5] The processes of cultural agency, the ability to act on and within social structures, exist within disciplines as well as outside them.

If we posit disciplines as active sites of definition, contestation, challenge, and repair even within their institutionalized structures, what then is interdisciplinarity and what role does it play in universities? And if interdisciplinary spaces exist in the interstices between disciplinary structures, what happens when interdisciplinarity gets institutionalized?

We must, of course, define *interdisciplinarity.* Klein develops a taxonomy of interdisciplinarity, distinguishing between *multidisciplinarity* and *interdisciplinarity*, and identifying "species" (methodological interdisciplinarity, theoretical interdisciplinarity, bridge building, and critical interdisciplinarity, etc.) within the larger genus.[6] Significant here is the larger distinction between interdisciplinarity and multidisciplinarity. According to Klein, when disciplines are *integrated and interactive*, we have interdisciplinarity. Multidisciplinarity juxtaposes disciplines, though the "disciplines remain separate, disciplinary elements retain their original identity, and existing structures of knowledge are not challenged. This tendency is evident in conferences, publications, and research projects that present different views of the same topic or problem in serial order."[7] Our focus is interdisciplinarity, whose integration of content, sources, and methodologies challenges disciplinary boundaries.

Much of the popular academic discourse on interdisciplinarity (opinion pieces in the *Chronicle of Higher Education*, for example) focuses on what Steve Fuller calls "deviant interdisciplinarity."[8] Fuller includes dialectical materialism, social feminism, psychoanalysis, and general semantics as examples of this, though with his training in the philosophy and history of science, he notes the history of physics is shaped by this process as well, as in the development of thermodynamics.[9] The popular academic discourse doesn't tend to see scientific fields within this category, however, focusing on those challenges to disciplinarity that emerged, according to this narrative, as part of the culture wars. Fields such as women's studies, racial and ethnic studies, area studies, and other fields heavily influenced by feminism, anticolonialism, and postmodern theory are those most commonly identified as interdisciplinary.

It is easy to see the history of these "deviant" interdisciplinary fields as the storming of the disciplinary castle gates. Their challenges to the disciplinary structure of universities happened at all the levels mentioned above. At the level of teaching, research, and publication, disciplines were challenged to become inclusive, to become aware of their exclusions based on gender, race, ethnicity, economic class, and geopolitics. The canon of each of these disciplines was seen as incomplete attempts at claiming a universal survey of knowledge while excluding vast portions of the world.

In addition to challenges at the level of content, those same challenges revealed the biases inherent in the methodologies that evolved to answer canonical questions. To use history as an example, the methodologies of history were challenged when historians were challenged to include women, outsider cultures, and the losers when history is written by the victors. Many of the methodologies of history (what constituted evidence, for example) were based on the very institutions that were now being challenged. Similarly, in literature, researchers had to consider how to study those who had been excluded from publication. These challenges put researchers of "deviant" interdisciplinarity on a collision course with core disciplines, core journals, accreditation agencies, and the policing function of peer review.

Within the university structure, hiring practices also had to be contested. The relatively closed disciplinary structure tended to reproduce itself, training new researchers to function within the parameters accepted by those already certified as orderly practitioners within their fields. A view of the professoriate revealed a demographic profile that confirmed claims of exclusion based on gender, race, and ethnicity. During the long years of beating at those gates, the newer forms of research and new faculty began to find shaky, uncertain spaces in the university, in the interstices between disciplines. Centers of women's studies, ethnic studies, and area studies were created. But these creations were clearly "in between." Most were clearly labeled as "centers" and "programs," since departments are still disciplinary structures. The tenure home for many of the faculty in these interstices was still located within traditional departments, thus creating situations in which faculty challenging the content, methodologies, and purpose of the disciplines needed to satisfy disciplinary criteria to keep their jobs. With most funding and representation within a university based on departmental structure, these centers and programs were often supported by soft funding. Not only does this mean uncertainty and difficulties in strategic planning, it also signifies the lack of university acceptance.

The future of the uncertain institutionalization of these new fields often depended, ironically, on the discursive success of these challenges to disciplinary canons. As sociology, history, and literature departments began to routinely offer classes addressing formerly excluded populations, cultures, and methodologies, programs and centers were closed and their courses and faculty reabsorbed into disciplinary departments. While at times concern has been expressed that this reabsorption meant cooptation, the changes within disciplines can be seen as demonstrating their nature, as McArthur argued, as "complex, permeable and contested spaces" whose boundaries are subject to frequent challenge and negotiation.[10]

We need to insert another type of interdisciplinarity into the discussion, and that is the inherent interdisciplinarity of some professional fields of study. Most of the academic articles about interdisciplinarity in the university focus either on the challenges from deviant interdisciplinarity to traditional academic disciplines or the development of interdisciplinary scientific research. Social work, for example, appears to fit Klein's definition of interdisciplinarity as integrated and interactive. Graduate students and faculty in social work routinely incorporate into their research not only research and reports produced by and for social workers or researchers in social work, but also peer-reviewed research articles from economics, political science, psychology, counseling, nutrition, cognitive theory, education, ethics, and law. The faculty are publishing in ethics, technology, psychology, and policy journals, as well as social work journals. Similar patterns can be seen in other applied graduate programs, including urban studies and urban planning, counseling, school psychology, and criminal justice.

Applied fields like social work and urban studies are faced with the same disciplinary pressures with the university structure. Funds and teaching positions are allocated to departments, and historically such programs have had to argue for their legitimacy as not only university departments (as opposed to "programs") but as academic research disciplines.[11] The traditional hierarchy of knowledge institutionalized within universities privileges "pure research" and theory over applied practices. Thus despite the inherent interdisciplinarity of these fields, the pressure to establish themselves as disciplines in order to gain legitimacy within universities has been fierce. It has required the creation of disciplinary apparatus such as accrediting organizations and academic research training for practitioners, and has resulted in a vast library of articles struggling to define social work, nursing, library science, or communication as an academic discipline.

Thus disciplines and interdisciplines all are formed, and form themselves, in constant processes of definition and institutionalization. Those processes can also include, of course, redefinition, as in the absorption of ethnic studies and women's studies into sociology, for example, as well as the changing boundaries of established disciplines to include them. It can also include deinstitutionalization via the closing of departments and journals and the defunding of programs.

Contemporary Academic Libraries and the Fluidity of Disciplines

Where is the library in these processes of definition and institutionalization? And where is the library located within the highly disciplinary structure of the university?

On the institutional level, despite the important function of liaison librarians and a mission to support the teaching and research of faculty and students, academic libraries exist outside of the departmental and college structure of universities, even in those institutions where the head of the library holds the position of dean and the librarians have faculty status. In these institutions, the library structure might appear to be homologous, in some ways, to the college structure, with the tenure process occurring first within the library, as it does within an academic department, before proceeding to the dean and then the universitywide committee. But the library, even in this structure, is not subject to the same policing functions of curriculum approval and accreditation. There are two instances in which an academic library comes close to that sort of pressure: when (and if) it attempts to conform to ARL standards (and even under those circumstances the results are not the same as the need to achieve accreditation) and when it contributes to the accreditation reviews of the subject departments. It is in support of academic departments that the library strives to meet external disciplinary requirements. And even these requirements are set by libraries and the academic library community, rather than by the disciplines. In accreditation reports, libraries report statistics: how many titles, how many journals, how much funding is available, even how far the library is from the academic department. While the report may mention the subdisciplines covered, this does not present the same sort of disciplinary policing that manifests itself in curriculum development. The library section of an accreditation report for an academic department will discuss how the library supports—or just that the library supports—the goals, curriculum, and research needs of that department. It is left to the department to defend the way it embodies the discipline.

For the most part, it is left to the library to organize itself within the university structure. Academic departments do not have input into the routine running of the library. The library budget as a whole is not assigned by the university via academic departments. In other words, in a structural sense the library does not depend on academic departments and colleges. Internally, however, libraries have long organized themselves along disciplinary lines and thus have contributed to the institutionalization of disciplines. The three structures that most closely tie libraries to a disciplinary organization are classification systems, the subject specialist/liaison role, and the allocation of collection funds.

Within the "culture wars" that were part of the development of disciplinary interstices, asserting that disciplines used controlled vocabularies was seen as a challenge to disciplinary claims of validity and objectivity. Library systems, on the other hand, used disciplinary languages as tools to organize the published and unpublished texts of the disciplines. In the process, libraries have also wrestled with the issues of those interstices between disciplines. Whose language is codified in those controlled vocabularies? Researchers in the newer, contested interdisciplinary fields such as ethnic studies repeatedly ran into the invisibility of their research subjects in controlled vocabularies, which are necessarily slow to change but do in fact change in response to changing cultures. Researchers in ethnic studies confronted one of the basic search strategy questions—What are the keywords of my search?—in fundamental ways: *Latino, Hispanic,* or *Mexican-American? Negro, Afro-American* or *African American?* The interdisciplinary fields of area studies presented libraries with geographic problems, in both literal and figurative senses. Area studies as an interdiscipline argues that the geography, history, economics, and culture of a place are inextricably entwined and overdetermined. How, then, can a library classify such a book? Where should it be shelved? That decision still often determines where the book physically resides, next to which other texts, and even in which library building.

One result was an attempt to form libraries within libraries organized around (inter)disciplinary definitions. Thus university libraries might have separate Latin American studies libraries, where the geographic category functions as the overarching classification, and the standard cataloging according to the traditional disciplines of political science, economics, literature, and so forth, exists in miniature, so to speak, under that umbrella. This fragmentation, though, is potentially almost infinite. Why not continue to establish separate collections by country? And what of the economics student who must leave the economics library to find titles that have been classed and shelved in the area studies library? Should libraries recognize growing disciplines by creating even more subject libraries? Interdisciplinary studies also push in the other direction: not more separation, but more integration.

A common recourse to problems in the organization of knowledge is to hope that digitizing resources and tools will do away with the issues. And it is true that hypertext has at least alleviated some of the issues. The number of subject headings allowed on catalog records has increased, allowing catalogers to assign a single text to many disciplines. The catalogs themselves have been superseded by discovery tools that allow us to bypass established controlled vocabularies and disciplinary boundaries in our search for materials by searching the texts themselves. Full-text searching, aggregated databases, cross-disciplinary databases, electronic journals, and e-books have helped erase the spatial aspect of disciplinary organization from libraries. We no longer even have to choose which disciplinary database to search, since in many cases we can search many diverse databases at a time.

Questions that remain include whether libraries discard as many disciplinary structures as possible or continue to use them, and how then libraries can support interdisciplinary work. Just as McArthur wants to reclaim disciplines from an essentialist argument that focuses only on their policing function,[12] it is important that we recognize the value of disciplinary structures within the library.

The development of library collections has depended for several decades primarily on the subject specialists and library liaisons, their knowledge of their assigned subjects, curricula, related publishers, and prominent researchers and writers. Important assets in the development of collections that support the work of the faculty and students, they often have degrees in the subjects they are supporting. In other words, they too are formed within the disciplines they support. Going back to Del Favero, they have been trained within a discipline into the "system of orderly behavior" that is "manifested" in approaches to research, knowledge, and world views.[13] The subject specialist is expected to know and consult with the faculty, be familiar with their research and their syllabi, and participate in the education of students into their discipline through instruction in disciplinary resources. Guidelines to selectors on how to spend those funds have often relied on disciplinary tools such as graduate reading lists, lists of "core" journals, and (though this is less common now) having faculty members choose purchases. An experienced and valuable subject selector is conversant with the canonical texts and core journals of their disciplines. Furthermore, subject selectors fluent within their disciplines use the discipline's definitions of validity, importance, and prestige in developing their collection priorities. This creates coherent collections that support the work of the faculty and students. The subject specialists who keep current in their fields can also keep those disciplinary boundaries porous, making sure that challenges and new areas of study are represented in the collection.

In a 1996 article on (hyper)specialization and libraries, Michael Winter speaks to the importance of the specialization of librarians. He identifies it as

> a coping mechanism for dealing with the overwhelming mass of output; by narrowing the focus, it filters out some of the flow and makes the rest easier to manage… Second, it permits the librarian to understand enough of the textual form and content to be of more help to users. Deeper knowledge of content also enables the librarian to understand new knowledge from the inside and to benefit from the filtering mechanisms that experts in the field themselves use. And librarians must also be specialized, otherwise they can not hope to have any semblance of collegial contact and communication with a wide range of their user groups.[14]

The librarian as specialist, Winters argues, also benefits the profession of librarianship, as many tasks earlier performed by librarians are now performed by paraprofessionals. Specialized knowledge makes the profession.

At the same time, Winters argues that the subject specialization is in need of restructuring. In the face of the exponential growth of knowledge, it is no longer enough for subject specialists to be defined by the traditional disciplines of the post–Word War II university, even with the addition of some of the critical newer (inter)disciplines such as women's studies, ethnic studies, and LGBT studies. Librarians needs to colonize those interstices and develop specializations in those "deviant" interdisciplinarities (cultural studies, legal studies, discourse analysis, etc.) as well as the new interdisciplinary areas that cross the broadest disciplinary divisions of hard sciences, soft sciences, arts, and humanities, such as psychoimmunology, ethnopharmacology, sociobiology, and ecofeminism.[15]

Once we can see the development of such interdisciplinarities, the possibilities seem endless. On a practical level, subject specialists can follow the academic researchers into new areas, identify the new structures for the dissemination of knowledge and information that support the new research, and work together with other librarians, so that the life sciences librarians and the social sciences librarians together support the psychoimmunologists and the ethnopharmacologists. What looks like the balkanization of the disciplines thus also provides for integrative and cooperative efforts.

In many libraries, paraprofessionals offer basic reference services. Just-in-time and patron-driven collection development are supplementing and perhaps replacing just-in-case book purchasing by subject specialists, often in response to budget and space limitations. Aggregated purchases of journals and electronic books in disciplinary and cross-disciplinary packages are growing and replacing title-by-title purchases. These circumstances have contributed to seeing the role of the subject specialist as a true, advanced specialist who can assist more advanced work in their disciplines. Ultimately, though, however specialized we become in our disciplines and interdisciplines, librarians are and should be specialists in the distribution and social organization of knowledge. Distribution, Winters says, is the activity of the librarian and covers "selecting, acquiring, gaining access to, collecting, controlling, assessing, evaluating, mediating and all the other functions librarians fulfill in matching texts with their users."[16]

Selection, acquisition, and collection may have changed, but those processes still involve the activities of librarians. The librarian operating in the contemporary field of knowledge production and distribution with its profound and ever-growing interdisciplinarity, is a specialist in tracking and identifying texts across old boundaries, in filtering the information found in cross-disciplinary and cross-platform discovery tools, and in navigating the new structures of knowledge dissemination.

Notes

1. Michel Foucault, *Discipline and Punish: The Birth of the Prison* (New York: Vintage, 1995).
2. Marietta Del Favero, "Academic Disciplines," in *Encyclopedia of Education*, 2nd ed., vol. 1, ed. James W. Guthrie (New York: Macmillian Reference USA, 2003), 10.
3. Jan McArthur, "Time to Look Anew: Critical Pedagogy and Disciplines within Higher Education," *Studies in Higher Education* 35, no. 3 (May 2010): 306.
4. Paul Trowler, "Beyond Epistemological Essentialism: Academic Tribes in the Twenty-First Century," in *The University and Its Disciplines: Teaching and Learning within and beyond Disciplinary Boundaries*, ed. Carolin Kreber (New York: Routledge, 2009), 181–195.
5. McArthur, "Time to Look Anew," 306.

6. Julie Thompson Klein, "A Taxonomy of Interdiscipinarity," in *Oxford Handbook of Interdisciplinarity*, ed. R. Frodeman, J. T. Klein, and Carl Mitcham, (Oxford: Oxford University Press, 2010), 15–30.

7. Ibid., 17.

8. Steve Fuller, "Deviant Interdisciplinarity," in *Oxford Handbook of Interdisciplinarity*, ed. R. Frodeman, J. T. Klein, and Carl Mitcham, (Oxford: Oxford University Press, 2010), 50–64.

9. Ibid., 51.

10. McArthur, "Time to Look Anew," 306.

11. L. C. Green, "Pariah Profession, Debased Discipline? An Analysis of Social Work's Low Academic Status and the Possibilities for Change," *Social Work Education* 25, no. 3 (April 2006): 245–264, EBSCOhost Professional Development Collection, (accessed March 21, 2011); Ian F. Shaw, Hilary Arksey, and Audrey Mullender, "Recognizing Social Work," *British Journal of Social Work* 36 (2006): 227–246.

12. McArthur, "Time to Look Anew."

13. Del Favero, "Academic Disciplines," 10.

14. Michael F. Winter, "Specialization, Territoriality, and Jurisdiction: Librarianship and the Political Economy of Knowledge," *Library Trends* 44, no. 2 (1996): 343–354, Gale Business & Company Resource Center (A18928470), (accessed January 6, 2011).

15. Ibid, 343-354.

16. Ibid, 343-354.

Disciplinary Morphologies, Interdisciplinarities: Conceptualizations and Implications for Academic Libraries

Jean-Pierre V.M. Hérubel

The siren call of interdisciplinary imperatives has been growing since the early 1970s.[1] Interdisciplinary activity is deemed highly desirable, if not the most productive, and indeed most effective, approach to research and pedagogy within the emerging academy of the twenty-first century.[2] Interdisciplinary centers, courses, and faculty appointments, as well as funding of research, have all experienced the vicissitudes of embracing interdisciplinary activities and agendas. Without sounding overly dramatic, for academic libraries, whether situated in small liberal arts colleges or regional or national research universities, interdisciplinarity continues to be a hallmark of advancing the agendas established by libraries struggling to define their position within the academy as they continue to meet the challenges of pedagogy and research. For academic libraries, this poses both opportunities and challenges to be effectively addressed. The first challenge is to understand what constitutes and defines disciplines and their respective morphologies; without such an understanding, interdisciplinarity activities, whether collaborative, instructional-oriented, collection-driven, or research-focused, lack a firm conceptual framework.

This discussion considers the cultures of disciplinary activity and proposes and explicates working definitional configurations of academic disciplinary, subdisciplinary, multidisciplinary, and interdisciplinary approaches to knowledge, especially in selected humanities and social sciences domains of knowledge.[3] Questions of academic professionalization, knowledge generation, and knowledge retrieval will offer a necessary background and contextualized grounding for discussion of the characteristics of interdisciplinarity. Graphical examples will highlight articulated discussion of various morphologies specific to illustrations chosen from various humanities and social sciences. In-depth discussion of the organic nature of disciplinary formation will augment the narrative, concentrating on conceptual characteristics of disciplinary formation, disciplinary specializations, and hyperspecialization. Concluding this presentation, discussion will address implications for academic libraries and librarians as they must interact with the fluid and organically dynamic nature of disciplinary knowledge(s).

The Morphologies of Disciplines: Constellations of Knowledge

Knowledge is not created ex nihilo; it is grounded within the social and temporal context of the evolution of discovery and its various manifestations. Human attempts to understand phenomena, fix them under examination, and situate them within a contextual frame with which to further articulate nuanced examination, are central to scholarly endeavors.[4] Without overstating the importance of these frames, researchers and scholars rely upon frameworks, often epistemological in nature, to further their efforts in advancing knowledge as well as disseminating it. Generally, scholars work within disciplines, attending and adhering to protocols, consensus-driven and normative values derived from disciplines and their respective characteristics. Disciplines are responsible for the training of future scholars, teachers, and researchers and are often the primary focus of pedagogy within contemporary academia, so much so that disciplines form the constellation of subjects within higher education through which most education is pursued. Indeed, the sociological environments within which disciplines are born and evolve reflect the social construction inherent to professionalization and the requirements intrinsic to disciplinary acculturation without which disciplinary knowledge could not appear and be sustained. Since the nineteenth century, academic disciplines have evolved to assume their position within the political economy of higher education, research, and the drive toward pedagogical and research-oriented discoveries so critical to contemporary academics ensconced in departmental structures.[5] Moreover, disciplines yield highly integrated contributions to established consensus-driven scholarship, utilizing honed methodologies and accepted techniques of research. Within well-defined boundaries, disciplines continue to enhance, amplify, and distill the fruits of their activities within normative requirements of individual disciplinary professionalization.[6] Complementing this phenomenon, core literatures are perforce created, animated, and sustained through disciplinary adherence to individual disciplinary prerogatives. Intellectual and groundbreaking discoveries occur within articulated disciplines, continuously building upon previously vetted scholarship, research protocols, and normative standards of scholarly comportment. Throughout the twentieth century, this preoccupation constituted normative practice among academic disciplines.

Disciplinary orientations give form to knowledge, formulate methodologies, engender intellectual perspectives, and vet both knowledge and pedagogy through adherence to disciplinary prerogatives. Without such disciplined approaches to learning or research, most discoveries would in effect be amorphous, if not undifferentiated. To *discipline* knowledge and learning is effectively to frame them within context, that is, an agreed-upon body of vetted knowledge understood by practitioners of that discipline. This is generally still the normative position of higher education and present departmental structures. From undergraduate programs and majors to master's and doctoral programs, where disciplinary acculturation assumes significant influence, disciplines are the accepted animus and cultural capital in academe. In the past thrity-five years, interest in interdisciplinary activities has assumed a larger presence in academic affairs, engendering sustained efforts to decompartmentalize pedagogical and especially research agendas in American institutions of higher learning. Nowhere is this more evident than in programmatic forays into undergraduate curricula, where "studies" approaches have blossomed.[7] Such majors as media studies, women's studies, and gender studies have joined such formerly established majors as area studies (e.g., Latin American studies, African studies, Asian studies, etc.). Even such majors as medieval studies or visual studies have self-defining intellectual and temporal or civilizational orientations and agendas. All have interdisciplinary or multidisciplinary orientations, making them appear less disciplinary and consequently more elastic than traditional disciplinary alignments.

Disciplinary orientations of knowledge reflect a very real principle of disciplinary life and activity: the organic nature of disciplines.

Indeed, if academic disciplines can be identified by their respective characteristics—that is, specific perspectives, objects broached and studied, and/or methodologies pursued—they necessarily exhibit organic characteristics. Since disciplines are ever-changing and subject to paradigmatic influences and intellectual dynamism, they are sensitive to evolutionary conditions.[8] Since the late nineteenth century, academic disciplines were born and have matured, undergoing sustained mutation stemming from professional practice, the exigencies of knowledge discovery, and emerging intellectual trends exerting pressures upon their evolution. Indeed, much as any organic entity, disciplines can emerge, prosper, mature, ossify, and even disappear. Once a vibrant and critical academic discipline in post-1945 western institutions of higher learning, Soviet studies died a quick death after the fall of the Soviet Union. Albeit multidisciplinary in nature, this field, sustained by professional and scholarly journals, undergraduate and graduate programs, and centers and think tanks, experienced sudden demise and disappearance from the academic firmament. So an imperative for interdisciplinary prerogatives must consider the organic nature of the disciplinary enterprise as the call for disciplinary collaboration, if not interdisciplinary and multidisciplinary agendas, grows more pronounced.

An effective way to illustrate disciplinary configurations is to graphically display their contours and general characteristics. Since knowledge is given form via disciplinary alignment, it is useful to ascertain disciplinary positions in relation to each other. Since disciplinary cultures evince demonstrable characteristics, their *morphologies*—that is, their appearance—reveal salient qualities that bear upon how these configurations incorporate methodologies, techniques of research, protocols, and the vetting of knowledge, as well as how consensus may animate core beliefs and comportment.[9] Indeed, scholars recognize each other according to the intellectual characteristics exhibited by previous acculturation. Historians differ from anthropologists, sociologists differ from political scientists, and geographers differ from demographers. In the humanities, the objects of research and knowledge orientation shape the their respective characteristics of disciplines: literary studies focuses on literary objects and production, philosophy upon ideas or ideational phenomena, musicology upon music and its attendant phenomena. Knowledge is undifferentiated until disciplined; that is, until a disciplinary form emerges and animates that particular set of activities and approaches to inquiry and the drive to discover knowledge, let alone its dissemination. Once *disciplined*, disciplinary cultures emerge and form constellations of knowledge as shown in figure 2.1.

Figure 2.1. Morphologies of Disciplinary Alignment and Cultures

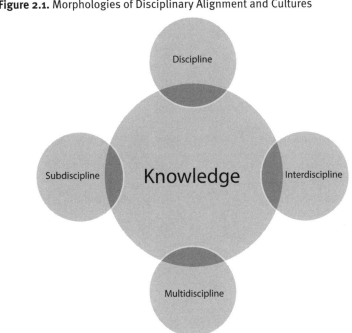

Disciplinary cultures prescribe structures of research, subjects or topics to be pursued, and consensus-driven approaches to what constitutes bona fide research and the vetting of subsequent knowledge. What passes as knowledge in one discipline may not be recognized or vetted by another discipline. Often, this conundrum faces academic ventures when various disciplines attempt to cross-fertilize their efforts. Successful interdisciplinary or multidisciplinary ventures have not always found fruitful resolutions. To understand disciplinary configurations and their respective characteristics, it is imperative to appreciate their morphological natures and how those characteristics animate intellectual, research, and professional features inherent to disciplines. These definitional disciplinarities lay open general contours of what disciplinary cultures are and how they may intellectually appear (see figure 2.2).

Having broached the nature of disciplinary morphologies, examples of what may originate in disciplinary configurations offer ad-

Figure 2.2. Disciplinary Morphology and Typology

Disciplinarity	Subdisciplinarity
• A highly defined and honed approach with focused objectives, and specific methodological and technical characteristics. Specialized nomenclature and consensus-driven protocols and procedures are adhered to and maintained. • *Examples*—History, Philosophy	• A highly specialized approach within a disciplinary framework concentrating on specific objectives, utilizing unique methodologies and techniques. Often, a particularistic area of interest is considered within the greater spectrum of a discipline. • *Examples*— Environmental History, Philosophy of History
Interdisciplinarity	Multidisciplinarity
• Two or more disciplines come together to examine a topic or set of topics and meld into a permanent relationship. • *Examples*—Historical Sociology, Political Communication.	• Two or more disciplines involved, providing their unique perspectives without actually melding. Disciplines come together to explore phenomena and work on stated objectives, while retaining their singular characteristics. • *Examples*—Latin American Studies, American Studies

ditional appreciation for what animates disciplinary alignments and respective orientations to how academic subjects divide the intellectual topography within academia. The rise of departmental structures tightly bound to disciplines demonstrates the power of disciplinary adherence and professional comportment. When such constellations emerge—for example, American studies, Asian studies, or medieval studies—standard disciplinary contours can no longer encompass the boundary shattering occurring with such intellectual ventures. Since World War II, the American academy developed centers for such academic enterprises, often under the auspices of a given disciplinary department, but often remaining a separate programmatic affair. Another way of looking at these morphologies is to see them via a single identifiable discipline, in the case of figure 2.3, history or historical studies in the main.

Figure 2.3. Disciplinary Configurations

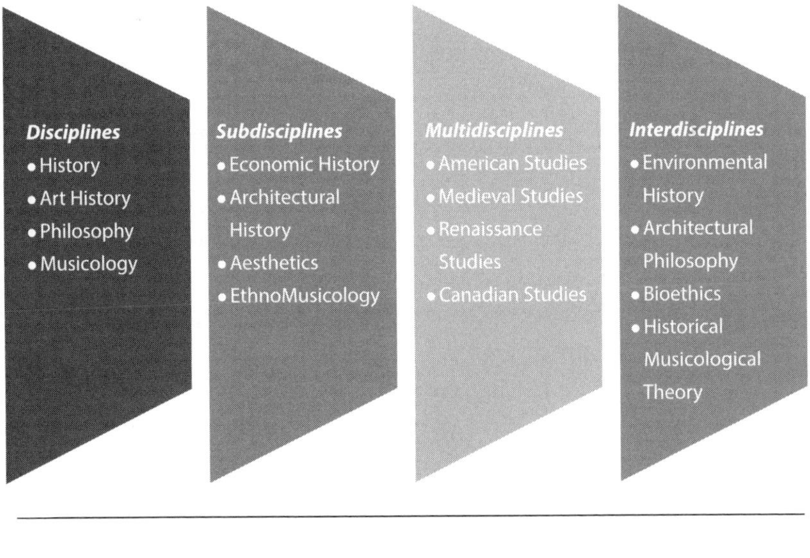

Disciplines	Subdisciplines	Multidisciplines	Interdisciplines
• History	• Economic History	• American Studies	• Environmental History
• Art History	• Architectural History	• Medieval Studies	• Architectural Philosophy
• Philosophy	• Aesthetics	• Renaissance Studies	• Bioethics
• Musicology	• EthnoMusicology	• Canadian Studies	• Historical Musicological Theory

The configurations shown in figure 2.3 illustrate possible disciplinary morphologies that animate specific bodies of knowledge, discovery, and dissemination within the context of academic disciplinary activity. The salient characteristic driving these morphologies is their reliance upon a primary grounding within a broader discipline, in this case, history or historical studies. Perhaps the most critical feature of a disciplinary morphology is its internal coherence—without an epistemic coherence that animates and holds together a specific disciplinary configuration, the center generally does not hold and the disciplinary formation falls apart. This crucial feature is at the foundation of any disciplinary configuration. These disciplinary illustrations serve to highlight the many possible configurations available to the various disciplines found in academia. Whether disciplinary, subdisciplinary, multidisciplinary, or interdisciplinary, disciplinary morphologies constitute the very skeletal structure, body, and nervous system of academia without which academia would possibly not exist in its present manifestation.

Specialization, Fragmentation, or Opportunistic Configurations

Since disciplines are perforce organic and exhibit dynamism, they are subject to possible mutations, or evolutionary changes. Sometimes this leads to a truly new approach or configuration which creates a heretofore unforeseen field unique to a set of research problems, objects of research, or set of mutually inclusive techniques or theoretical perspectives. A good example is sociology of art—although not occupying a center of prominence in sociology per se, it nevertheless has matured and established a niche from which it has generated a core literature as well as identified a spectrum of research objects: for example, museums, artists as sociological actors, art markets, artistic production, art and societal relations, and art as mediation. The melding of aesthetics, sociological theory, and sociological research analysis, including quantification and model generation, have effectively integrated in dynamic tension the prerogatives of artistic activity in its many manifestations with the prerogatives inherent in sociology. Yet what can be said when a discipline begins to include different specializations? What occurs when specializations become established subdisciplines? What if the objectives and natural drive to push research opens fissures within a discipline, leading to fragmentation? These questions pertain to the very nature of disciplinary cultures and their respective morphologies.

The intellectual and scholarly topography of academic disciplines is open to the possibility of disciplinary fragmentation. Established academic disciplines are not immune, nor are they impervious to outside influences or internal questions of systemic cohesion. Sometimes disciplines do begin to exhibit dislocation of subdisciplinary activity and, at times in the evolution of a discipline, fragmentation.[10] In and of itself, fragmentation can lead to communication problems, concerns over professionalization of colleagues in neighboring fields, and concerns over what constitutes legitimate knowledge respective to those subdisciplines.[11] As an illustration, two social science disciplines come to mind—anthropology and geography (see figure 2.4).

Figure 2.4. Primary Divisions in Anthropology and Geography

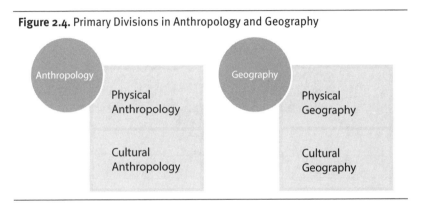

Within these disciplines, many branches have arisen to create a topography not unlike a complex ecology of competing entities oriented toward balance and survival within a larger environment. Additionally, the unique divide between physical and human sciences within each discipline works to generate disciplines open to further divisions; indeed, divisions—in practice, subdisciplines—have emerged over the past century (see figures 2.5 and 2.6).

Both disciplines have experienced profound challenges in maintaining disciplinary cohesion; as subdisciplines continue to emerge and as older subdisciplines continue to mature, insisting upon their particular protocols and so forth, the professionalization of knowledge generated from those subdisciplines will require sustained evaluation and dialogue if disciplines are to represent consensus-driven morphologies. Indeed, the serious divide between human and physical geography illustrates this very concern—that, indeed, the general perspective inherent in geographical training, research, and dissemination of knowledge is seriously pivoted upon this disciplinary axis. Anthro-

Figure 2.5. Possible Constituent Subdisciplines for Cultural Anthropology

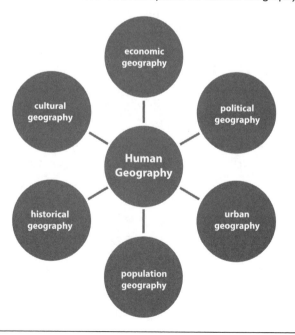

Figure 2.6. Possible Constituent Subdisciplines for Human Geography

pology experiences similar divides between those pursuing physical versus those pursuing cultural anthropology, with possible splintering into more and more subfields—for example, anthropology of art, anthropology of music, or visual anthropology. Unlike anthropology or geography, sociology is not divided into a science of physical and nonphysical dimensions; instead, it has the capacity to generate very discrete fields of interest, easily assuming configurations that possess subdisciplinary characteristics. Consequently, in sociology and its attendant subdisciplines, where quantification versus nonquantification is only one of many major degrees of separation among sociological interests, the drive toward specialization can lead to hyperspecialization.[12] Not immune to quantification and model building, political science and economics have also burgeoned into a multitude of fields of interests, which often mutate into subdisciplinary configurations. A significant factor is the use of technical methodologies and the importation of theoretical insights into the discrete research and pedagogy pursued by researchers in disciplines. When subdisciplines form around or are animated by these importations, new ways of appropriating knowledge and information assume normative status, further separating the subdisciplines from the general disciplinary morphology from which they sprang.[13] As illustrated by anthropology or geography, the drive toward more research is the locomotive for possible disciplinary division, and at times fragmentation.

The Problematic Nature of Interdisciplinarity

Much to the delight of current conversations concerning interdisciplinarity, contemporary academia's celebration of interdisciplinary initiatives and programmatic innovation belies the fact that definitional concerns surrounding what constitutes institutional interdisciplinarity may conflate what is actually occurring.[14] Most institutions may be referring to the more ubiquitous notion inherent in multidisciplinarity rather than the more synthetic interdisciplinarity so often propounded by higher education administrators. When examined closely, most "interdisciplinary" ventures are actually more likely multidisciplinary in nature. This does not mean that conflation is intentional; rather, the contrary is indicated—it is easier to pursue multidisciplinary initiatives than the more intrinsically difficult synthesizing imperatives demanded of interdisciplinary engagement. Among concerns leveled at interdisciplinary initiatives is the manner in which interdisciplinary activity should be institutionalized and made accountable to established academic structures, departmental structures often predicated upon individual disciplinary lines. A perennial concern is how best to accommodate disciplinary faculty who embark upon interdisciplinary research and pedagogy, or how are scholars, once trained in interdisciplinary graduate programs, effectively integrated within existing individual disciplinary departments? These and other concerns are not easily broached, nor are they successfully treated or navigated in hierarchical research infrastructures.

Even with institutional and cultural challenges to interdisciplinarity, academia's interest in championing its prerogatives leaves interdisciplinarity in an especially privileged position. Rather than marginalizing interdisciplinary possibilities, academia has not only embraced the idea of interdisciplinarity, it has fostered a growing appreciation for its protean possibilities which may evade more established, yet still effective, disciplinary morphologies. Often, critical teamwork composed of various branches of learning has revealed the potential of disciplinary collaborations, especially in the medical sciences, sciences, and technologies. Area studies initiatives, first concertedly inaugurated in post–World War II academia, laid the fertile matrix in which interdisciplinary forays in the social sciences and the humanities could grow and prosper. Along the spectrum of possible combinations open to interdisciplinary activity, only one principal criterion need be addressed—without qualification, critical to knowledge exploration and discovery is achieving balance between the drive for creative research and the demands of available disciplinary borrowings that can effectively enhance that research. Unbridled interdisciplinary or multidisciplinary experimentation or excess may only cloud the benefits open to researchers, leading to the suspicion that so often has cast a shadow on interdisciplinary enterprises in the past.

An especially instructive approach to gaining a sense of how interdisciplinary motivations, interests, and objectives have gained serious credibility over time is to consult the scholarly literature indexed in various databases. Among the databases available, JSTOR serves to highlight those humanities and social science disciplines that reflect the respective core literature appearing in vetted mainline and recognized scholarly journals.[15] When JSTOR is searched for examples of interdisciplinary occurrence among a selected and representative set of disciplines and then the data organized by decades to gain a longitudinal and evolutionary sense of how much interest appears in the literature, the pattern revealed is one When decennial years are used to indicate a longitudinal and evolutionary approach to gaining a sense of how much interest appears in the literature, searching JSTOR for examples of interdisciplinary occurrence among a selected and representative set of disciplines reveals a pattern of increasing discussion and growing acknowledgment that interdisciplinary initiatives and reflection have been critical to the disciplines of art history, archaeology, architecture and architectural history, geography history, and history of science (figure 2.7).[16]

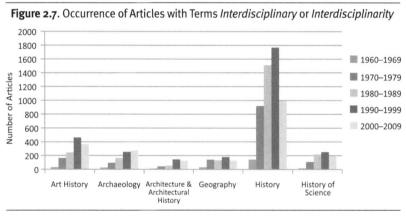

Figure 2.7. Occurrence of Articles with Terms *Interdisciplinary* or *Interdisciplinarity*

The academic discipline of history has experienced the greatest acceleration of interest in interdisciplinary activity; however, each selected discipline has also expressed considerable growth, even while acknowledging the moving wall for 2000–2009. Were the JSTOR moving wall eliminated, indication of continued growth seems self-evident.

History and Historical Scholarship and Disciplinary Morphologies and Interdisciplinary Configurations

Appreciation of the fluidity of disciplinary membranes and contours may be approached by examining mechanisms of how a scholarly discipline actually functions. As an example, history as a scholarly discipline is large enough and capable of protean transformation—indeed, its purview entertains all phenomena originating in the past.[17] For this reason, it offers salient examples of how disciplines function as well as how disciplines are composed of various disciplinary morphologies. Focusing on history as an academic discipline will further illustrate how introduction of methodological approaches or techniques can exert significant changes, if not intellectual transformations, within the context of how a discipline may react to borrowings from other disciplines. Since the past presents a diverse, nuanced spectrum of possible subjects under examination, historians generally attempt to frame their research and pedagogy to the necessity of using primary sources. As historical analysis of discrete subjects generates specializations, historians employ consensus-driven approaches that frame and reframe their subjects as scholarship adding to the body of historical knowledge. Historiographic knowledge and contextualization further articulate the historian's task of addressing questions of evidential and epistemological veracity—an attempt not to recreate the past, but to comprehend it in all its richness. As academic history has undergone many changes since the 1960s, when discussion of how to better undertake historical research started, interest in interdisciplinary initiatives has broached both the theoretical and the practical demands of research methods and techniques, if not philosophical ruminations.[18]

Perusal of several databases permits an open window on the interdisciplinary landscape of academic history, especially as it is indexed by two canonical databases—Historical Abstracts and America: History and Life. Again, using decennial years and searching only peer-reviewed articles with the terms *interdisciplinary* and *interdisciplinarity* revealed a growing interest in interdisciplinary ventures in both hypothetical historiographical discussions and actual research articles utilizing interdisciplinary approaches and methodological techniques. Interest in interdisciplinary approaches cannot be overestimated, as it continues to gain momentum, as the sharp increase between 1990 and 2000-2009 offers ample proof that both Americanist and non-Americanist historical research demonstrate a significant critical mass (figures 2.8 and 2.9).[19]

Figure 2.8. Articles focusing on interdisciplinary or interdisciplinarity in Historical Abstracts

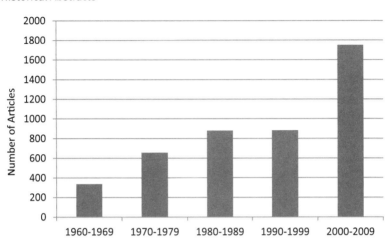

Figure 2.9. Articles focusing on interdisciplinary or interdisciplinarity in America: History and Life

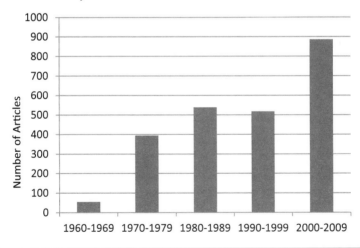

An additional permutation considered was the incidence of inter-disciplinary activity reflected in monographic literature. Since academic historians and historical scholarly professionalization consider the book or its close cousin, the highly honed monograph, the gold standard of historical scholarship, JSTOR was used to examine book reviews for their acknowledgement of interdisciplinary activity (figure 2.10).[20]

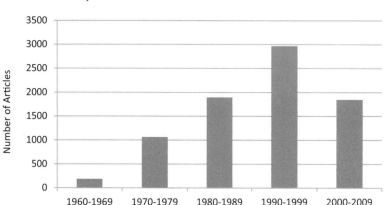

Figure 2.10. Articles focusing on interdisciplinary or interdisciplinarity in book reviews in history

Data revealed that attention to interdisciplinarity is a growing concern with historians who wish to broach new approaches to established and newly emerging subjects of historical interest.[21] Still another very important aspect of academic history is historiography; an examination of historiographic scholarship offers an additional entrée into interdisciplinarity's effect on the academic historical enterprise. To further contextualize historical research across several historically grounded disciplines, JSTOR was searched for the term *interdisciplinary* or *interdisciplinarity* appearing with *historiography*, again revealing increasing interest in applying interdisciplinary initiatives, techniques, or emerging methodological perspectives to historical research (figure 2.11).[22]

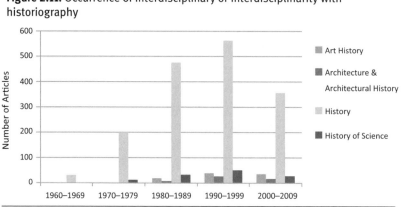

Figure 2.11. Occurrence of interdisciplinary or interdisciplinarity with historiography

In relation to this sample of historical disciplinary literature, it is evident that art history, architecture and architectural history, and history of science are increasing their engagement with interdisciplinarity but are still not as critically engaged as is mainline academic history. Even if one accounts for the larger literature of history vis-à-vis the other historical disciplines, historians engaged in social, cultural, gender, and environmental studies are more likely to consider interdisciplinary connections to their research.[23] Speaking to this phenomenon, the drive to entertain and indeed pursue new subjects, such as history of the family, gender, sexuality, cultural mediation, violence, human comportment, and so on perforce invites interdisciplinary considerations.[24]

What happens when historical research encounters medieval studies, Renaissance studies, eighteenth-century studies, or Canadian studies, let alone Reformation studies? What phenomena should be entertained if area studies are broached? These questions and other similar questions are open to a myriad of possible responses.[25] Often subjects requiring complex approaches demand equally complex configurations of knowledge derived from various possible morphologies. From utilizing a technique, to informed philosophical insights that lay open the foundational conditions of inquiry regarding a given subject under examination, disciplinary alignments often gain from meshing with encounters with such multidisciplinary configurations as medieval, Renaissance, or American studies.[26] If one wishes to examine musical culture, one can certainly adhere to musicological approaches and seasoned techniques, yet perhaps to adequately appropriate musical culture in nineteenth-century Montreal or Toronto may require insights from both musicological knowledge and disciplinary procedures, as well as insights from Canadian studies research and literature. If one is examining advertising in 1920s America, especially as it intersects with the rise of modern marketing techniques and professionalization of advertising, the insights of American studies approaches may offer greater amplitude. Familial structure in thirteenth-century Burgundy may require approaches and insights from medieval studies or Renaissance studies in the main, with their broadly based approaches to historical sociological models of group formation and dynamics essential to comprehending families in evolution within a given historical era. To adequately map the evolution of the idea of paganism in eighteenth-century European intellectual circles may require more than the contributions of philosophy, such as the breadth of eighteenth-century studies, as well the history of communication systems as developed by historical geography.[27]

Two Morphological Examples of Interdisciplinarity

To further illustrate and contextualize discussion by using historical approaches to knowledge, two examples of specialization frame the phenomenon animating historical analysis: the history of science and the history of photography. Among the various historical specializations, history of science early on developed its specialization to include science in all its possible relationships to knowledge and to human society. Over time, the history of science has encompassed a growing dynamic spectrum of subjects, if not discrete topics. No longer an arcane historical enterprise, history of science is entertaining more sophisticated approaches to research and seeking greater articulation of topics to be pursued.[28] Among research interests and subjects, the role of the scientist in society—science and its relationship to societies, politics, religion, and many other nonscientific aspects—is complemented by framing the place of science and its enterprise within the context of human history. A cursory enumeration of indexing rubrics contained among the subject terminologies in the *Isis* Annual Bibliographies accompanying *Isis*, the organ for the Society for the History of Science, reveals the extent to which large thematic considerations animate the history of science. They include, but are not fixed to, the following themes as history of science continues to enlarge its purview: *science and art, science and civilization, science and culture, science and economics, science and ethics, science and gender, science and government, science and ideology, science and industry, science and law, science and literature, science and music, science and politics, science and race, science and religion, science and society, science and sports, science and the military, science education and teaching.*[29]

Because the subdisciplinary morphology of the history of science is replete with concerns for historical narrative, technical and methodological procedures, contextualization, and explication of how science is situated within human society, broader perspectives demand more and more interdisciplinary considerations (figure 2.12).

Figure 2.12. History of science configuration

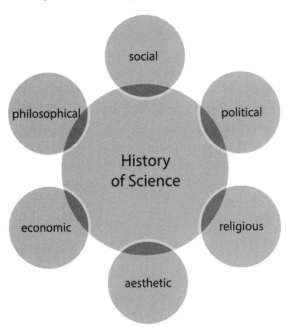

Indeed, as historians of science expand upon their imperative to understand the history of science in its entirety, scientific discovery, institutionalization, professionalization, societal interactions, and other interconnective phenomena will gain greater presence in history of science, making it an incredibly richly layered and intellectually textured historical field of scholarship.

Another interesting example of interdisciplinary and multidisciplinary ferment is the study of photography, especially the history of photography. Since the early 1980s, the history of photography has gained scholarly gravitas among historians of art, so much so that it represents a dynamic and fertile area for sustained research and pedagogy in institutions of higher education. Currently, history of photography embraces various perspectives, continuously enhancing techniques, methodological approaches, and insights increasingly borrowed from various disciplines in the humanities and social sciences.[30] Whether technical—that is, actual production of photography—or interpretative, as is generally the case, history of photography challenges the disciplines that engage within its critical examination.

Apart from historical narrative, historians of photography borrow from anthropology, aesthetics and its sister philosophical approaches, art history, and sociology, to name primary disciplines utilized to explicate photography as cultural phenomenon. From close textual readings of photographic imagery to sociohistorical examination of photographic meaning within time and space, photography is open to many disciplinary approaches and explications. Given its ubiquitous nature, photography as cultural mediator can be explored for its cultural, economic, and political dimensions as well as explicated through traditional narrative historical analysis. Indeed, when several disciplinary vectors are applied to photography, its richly nuanced reconstruction of human, scientific, or aesthetic realities assumes subtle explication, leading to richer textures of scholarly activity (figure 2.13).

Figure 2.13. Disciplinary vectors for history of photography

An intriguing permutation occurs when subdisciplinary activity is introduced—for example, visual anthropology or visual sociology applied to history of photography. Depending upon the theoretical perspective or methodologies and techniques utilized, these subdisciplines can exert transformative influence upon photography. The examination of late-nineteenth-century British or French colonial photography of indigenous cultures or the sociological construction of Jacob Reiss's tenement housing and poverty studies may not be fully understood or appreciated without the insights of these subdisciplines (figure 2.14).

Figure 2.14. Subdisciplinary permutations for history of photography

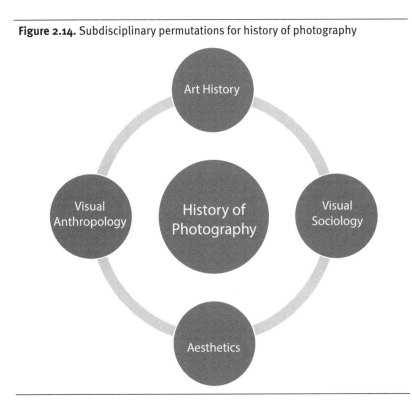

The fine line between discipline and subdiscipline cannot be easily discerned, but nuances provided by such subdisciplinary insights can effectively probe research subjects that formally may not always be entertained or fully articulated by the parent disciplines—in this case, anthropological or sociological analysis. The subdisciplines of visual anthropology and visual sociology offer honed techniques and perspectives creatively addressed and proved over time.

Further illustration serves to increase the awareness of the protean nature of interdisciplinary and multidisciplinary melding when confronted with complex subjects, their differentiation, and their multidimensional possibilities for researchers (figure 2.15).

Figure 2.15. Examples of disciplinary morphologies and multidimensional configurations

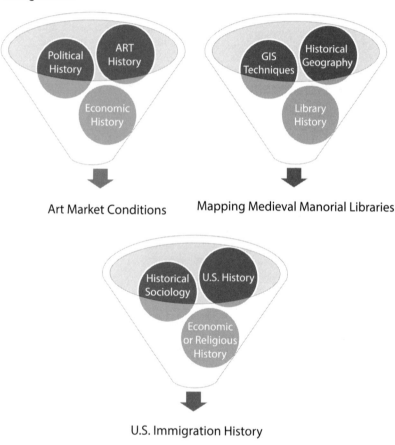

Art markets and their actors, artists, dealers, collectors, and patrons do not act in isolation from each other or from society at large—in fact, they function within dynamic relationships. To adequately examine historical art markets, contextualization of past conditions, and societal interactions requires the possible melding of the disciplines of art history and the subdisciplines of political and economic history, among possible combinations. Examining library collections in time and space, and ownership patterns, as well as literacy, education levels, and so forth, may require innovative use of mapping originating from geographical information systems, insights from established library historical scholarship pertaining to medieval ecclesiastical and secular libraries and reading culture, as well as perspectives derived from and informed by the subdiscipline of historical geography. Explanation of US immigration as historical phenomenon may include techniques and insights judiciously borrowed from the subdisciplines of historical sociology contextualized within established scholarship in US history further articulated by insights and substantive borrowing from religious or economic history subdisciplines. The above examples serve to illustrate possible permutations available to the interdisciplinary paradigm; further examples would produce more permutations as subjects become more and more complex and multilayered.

Disciplinary and Interdisciplinary Morphologies: Conceptual Implications for Libraries

Discussion of disciplinary formations and their respective characteristics cannot be separated from the larger concerns of libraries, especially academic libraries. As libraries continue to meet the challenges of a transforming and evolving academy, they too must address their critical approaches to knowledge, disciplinary and otherwise. Indeed, academic libraries occupy the nexus through which configurations of knowledge and disciplinary morphologies are given further articulation through collections, reference, and instruction. Since library science is itself a configuration of practice as well as intellectually grounded in multidisciplinary activity, it is perhaps more open to and capable of adjusting to the exigencies of professional practice. How should academic librarians respond to growing interest in interdisciplinary initiatives? How should college and especially research libraries interact with ever-evolving disciplinary cultures as they reflect configurations of knowledge and disciplinary morphologies impacting upon infrastructure, services, budgetary concerns, and personnel requirements and issues, as well as nurture the dynamic tension between library, librarians, academic departments, and disciplinary faculty? Among possible considerations, librarians need to incorporate into their professional consciousness an appreciation and understanding of disciplinary morphologies and their respective cultures and configurations. An additional permutation is how configurations of knowledge discovery, examination, and eventual dissemination reflect the myriad specializations inherent to academic cultures in the main.

Provision and fulfillment of library services entails a rededication of effort and commitment to anticipating emerging present and future user needs. However, academic librarians need to become cognizant of and versed in understanding disciplinary cultures, their transformations, and their evolutionary characteristics as they too undergo morphological transitions. Libraries and librarians can effectively meet multidisciplinary and interdisciplinary challenges and opportunities as they arise.[31] Although seemingly revolutionary or disruptive, academic rhetoric aside, multidisciplinary and interdisciplinary initiatives are presently occurring and will continue. Neither cataclysmic nor glacial, the nature of multidisciplinary and interdisciplinary research and pedagogy is currently met through librarian efforts to accommodate emerging collections needs, instruction, and enhanced reference services. Questions of emphasis—for example, from budgeting allocations for multidisciplinary and interdisciplinary collections vis-à-vis departmental disciplinary needs, to changes to information literacy and instruction programming, to dynamic and agile requisites of reference services—are and continue to be addressed by libraries. Looming large on the horizon are questions and perceptions of readiness and adaptability and whether professional training and education can meet these perceived challenges. Does allegiance to subject specialization, so strongly entrenched in research libraries, preclude participation in multidisciplinary and interdisciplinary investigations and ways of thinking and approaching librarianship? These questions and concerns can be effectively appropriated by library science, both as a body of theory and as professional practice.

Unlike other professions, librarianship is capable of transformation when necessity or exigency demands a re-evaluation of services, and practice is predicated upon library science's body of knowledge. Library science is especially constituted and equipped to undertake the demands of increasing changes in disciplinary morphologies, so much so that libraries may be in a privileged position to survey the disciplinary landscapes as they emerge from practitioners in those fields of research and pedagogy. As library science is itself an amalgam of multidisciplinary and interdisciplinary confluence of theory and practice, its own protean nature stands it in good stead within changing academic information environments.[32] Library science has the capacity to function within and along the edges of disciplines, attesting to what may be termed *creative marginality*.[33] As a firm example of creative multidisciplinary and interdisciplinary activity, library science in practice can appreciate the vast and changing topography of disciplinary morphologies, not always so easily perceived or acknowledged by adherents to established disciplines. As disciplinary morphologies and information-rich ecologies invite new relationship to knowledge and information, library science, with its concentration on theories of knowledge, classification, dissemination, and so forth, can effectively throw light on how these shall interact with disciplinary configurations.

Intellectual fermentation arises when seemingly disparate elements meld, inducing productive interpretative insights, if not unforeseen results which can reconfigure or reconceptualize research hypotheses or provide clarification of methodological tools and procedures when disciplines interact—so too with library science. Needless to say, pedagogy and delivery of library services must complement changing disciplinary morphologies and information-rich ecologies. As information and knowledge meld and creatively mix, so too will libraries discover intersections and confluences where they can be most effective. Complementing these adaptations, librarians' evolving roles will create opportunities to participate in partnerships with departmental faculty. Among possible scenarios, integration of information literacy, whatever its definitional role and institutionalized configuration, as well as wider and enriched participation in possible research, campus governance, or data curation, especially in the humanities or social sciences, can only firmly recontextualize essential theoretical and practical library science principles within larger research and pedagogical issues. As data curation assumes critical importance and significance, especially in research libraries and other campus venues, libraries will perforce establish critical interventions.[34]

The Case of Visual Studies

An instructive illustration of library/librarian interaction with an emerging disciplinary morphology is considering visual studies as a potentially rich field for collections, instruction, and reference, as well as faculty partnerships. In the last twenty years, visual studies has evolved into a vital and burgeoning enterprise within the academy, establishing departments, majors, and minors within art history departments proper and assuming a significant presence within schools of art, where foundational appreciation and theory courses are taught.[35] Visual studies represents a confluence of distinctive disciplinary morphologies: art history, anthropology, and sociology, among disciplines animated and informed by cultural studies, philosophy, and critical theory. Primarily but not exclusively, visual studies examines all aspects pertaining to visual culture, potentially all expressions of visual phenomena.[36] From advertising to art, scientific visualization, architectural plans, presentation of textual matter, photography, and so forth, visual studies attempts to capture the mediating forms of visual life. Since visual studies as disciplinary morphology is at the intersection of theoretical and methodological synergy, it is informed by many disciplinary influences (figure 2.16).

Figure 2.16. Potential constituent disciplinary morphologies for visual studies

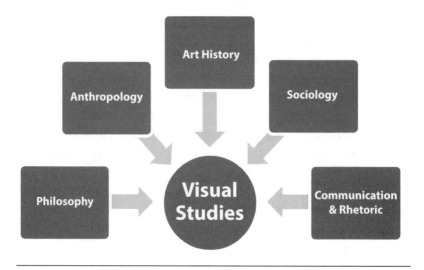

The configuration in figure 2.16 of disciplinary formations potentially incorporated into visual studies offers only one spectrum among others. As subdisciplines offer highly articulated perspectives, methodologies, techniques, and insights useful for in-depth examination of visual phenomena, other configurations of disciplinary morphologies can lay bare discoveries not always available to established disciplines such as art history (figure 2.17).

Figure 2.17. Subdisciplinary configurations influencing visual studies

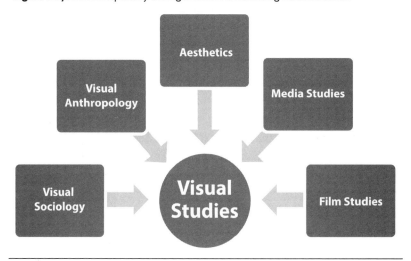

Objects under examination through visual studies may require such borrowings as opposed to more canonical techniques provided by art historical consensus, especially when contemporary subjects pose difficult methodological problems not readily broached by seasoned art historical protocols and vetted approaches used for other historical periods.[37] Successfully addressing visual studies needs may require librarians to move beyond traditional and readily identifiable art historical primary sources and resources and accompanying methodologies and techniques governing art historical research and instruction to incorporate more fluid and intellectually dynamic approaches available from such subdisciplines as visual anthropology or visual sociology, replete with their own set of methods, techniques, and protocols. When specific theoretical perspectives or critical conceptualizations are employed, results can be more creative, encouraging librarians to consider expanding the purview of information literacy and subject-oriented instruction to managing more fluid collections in support of research and pedagogy.

The Case of Magazine Studies

Contrary to received wisdom, disciplines and specializations are not synonymous; rather, they constitute identifiable configurations within the constellations of undifferentiated knowledge. Moreover, specialization reflects specific interests centered upon defined objects of research and an articulated intellectual circumference. Additionally, within identifiable contours, specializations can be very individualized, even idiosyncratic. A representative example of discrete specialization is the field of magazine studies. Magazines represent a very active and especially multifaceted object of interest, as many disciplines and perspectives can be effectively utilized for magazine studies.[38] Magazine research encompasses various formats of serialized literature and publication. Since magazines constitute major spheres of publishing activity as well as content orientation, magazines are especially ubiquitous as a medium and are found virtually throughout society, forming a natural primary source of examination for students and scholars alike. As a specialization, magazine studies is focused on magazines as phenomenon, intellectually, culturally, and sociologically, as well as economic enterprise. Moreover, magazines and magazine culture situate themselves within the nexus of multidisciplinary and interdisciplinary studies: American studies or any configuration of disciplinary research and scholarship. For this reason, magazine studies offers another illustration of how to approach a given specialization of interest through multidisciplinary or interdisciplinary approaches.

Any attempt to ascertain the characteristics of magazine studies invites creative approaches to how best to study magazines as well as how to approach them pedagogically. Creative multidisciplinary and interdisciplinary morphologies would yield methodologies and techniques unique to magazine studies (figure 2.18).

Judicious use of other disciplines can elucidate aspects of magazine readership, economics of publishing, and content analysis, as well as providing insights useful for examining magazines. Sociology pro-

Figure 2.18. Possible constituent disciplinary configurations for magazine studies

vides content analysis; journalism provides a necessary framework and context; economics, the business of publishing; art history, the nature of aesthetic representation of material; literary studies, the textual analysis; history, temporal context; political science, the political intersection with journalism and information; and communication and rhetoric, the study narrative and content analysis. These gross disciplinary influences can be valuable to the user, since no one discipline alone (e.g., journalism) can account for magazine studies. However, in keeping with the benefits of considering multidisciplinary or interdisciplinary approaches to research and pedagogy, librarians can introduce and direct users to more subtle configurations of disciplinary morphologies (figure 2.19).

The benefits of using these subdisciplines and their respective highly refined approaches—that is, methodologies and techniques—yields results not generally available to the more general disciplinary applications. If a librarian directs students and researchers to multidisciplinary approaches as exemplified by studies approaches, the following can yield even more perspectives useful to situating magazines studies within large constructs (figure 2.20).

Insights, perspectives, techniques, and methodological procedures originating from these diverse studies approaches can be complemented by permutations such as gender studies, media studies, or

Figure 2.19. Possible constituent subdisciplinary configurations for magazine studies

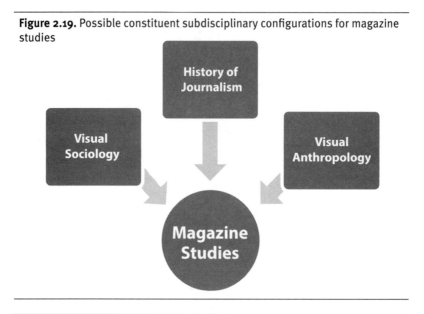

Figure 2.20. Possible constituent multidisciplinary configurations for magazine studies

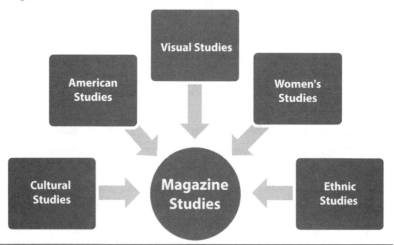

more defined specialties such as comparative history, or the history of the book and print culture, and can contribute to greater analytical power to the user's research or pedagogy.[39] Of course, depending upon geographical, temporal, or other characteristics, magazine studies can be approached creatively by considering other disciplinary orientations for the most effective research or pedagogical results. Each of these illustrations capitalizes upon the central notion that there are options to objects of research and pedagogy that can benefit from venturing beyond the known disciplinary morphologies generally relied upon and utilized.

Concluding Observations

The future is now, and its presence is being felt across academia—as disciplines continue to mutate, transforming themselves again and again, their protean natures continue to offer new configurations of knowledge and learning in a kaleidoscope of ever-changing morphologies and constellations of disciplinary cultures. The disciplines established in the late nineteenth century will continue to exist for the foreseeable future, and their dominance of academic departmental structures will be one manifestation of disciplinary morphologies in higher educational institutions. Operating within this environment, multidisciplinary and interdisciplinary manifestations of knowledge, research, and learning will generate more configurations of knowledge discovery, interpretation, dissemination, and pedagogy. Within this information-rich ecology, academic libraries will have situated their services, repurposed their physical environments, and generated new relationships with the academy and disciplinary cultures. Knowledge and intimate comprehension of the fluidity of knowledge and information will be complemented by judicious stewardship of existing and emerging collections, knowledge transference, teaching, and participation in the continuum that is the merging knowledge and information ecologies.

Celebrating obvious advantages of multidisciplinary and interdisciplinary approaches to library services demands certain qualifications. Disciplinary approaches to knowledge and information are tried and tested, working within intellectually and culturally comfortable parameters not always easily discernible in multidisciplinary and especially interdisciplinary situations. This is within reason, as such practice and operational philosophies have yielded great advances in knowledge and learning. Yet there are real dangers to multidisciplinary and interdisciplinary forays if they are not judiciously considered. Simply pursuing an intellectual smorgasbord with every given pursuit or inquiry may provide only an open display of disconnected perspectives, methodologies, and unresponsive techniques yielding a panoply of findings that are erroneous or incomprehensible and incommensurable with previous hypotheses and vetted knowledge. Previous experiences encountered by area studies can serve to balance necessity with what works and can be efficacious to librarians and users—even American studies, Canadian studies, or film studies and interdisciplinary humanities programs revolve around core principles of inquiry and instruction. This said, libraries and librarians as mediators of information ecologies are in a privileged position, central to the nexus which is represented by disciplinary morphologies, classifications of knowledge, and the critical necessity of services required to make intellectual sense, enlightened instruction, and stewardship of scholarly communication. As library science is itself capable of multidisciplinary and interdisciplinary morphologies, it can provide the necessary perspectives required for multidisciplinary and interdisciplinary engagement.

Notes

1.   Léo Apostel, Guy Berger, Asa Briggs, and Guy Michaud, eds., *Interdisciplinarity: Problems of Teaching and Research in Universities*, Seminar on Interdisciplinarity in Universities, 1970, University of Nice (Paris: Organisation for Economic Cooperation and Development, 1972); Joseph J. Kockelmans, ed., *Interdisciplinarity and Higher Education* (State College: Pennsylvania State University Press, 1979); Julie Thompson Klein, *Interdisciplinarity: History, Theory, and Practice* (Detroit, MI: Wayne State University, 1990); Julie Thompson Klein, *Crossing Boundaries: Knowledge, Disciplinarities, and Interdisciplinarities* (Charlottesville: University Press of Virginia, 1996); for an early conference on interdisciplinary interests held at Pennsylvania State University, consult Sherif Muzafer and Carolyn W. Sherif, eds., *Interdisciplinary Relationships in the Social Sciences* (Chicago: Aldine, 1969).

2.   For a very instrumental and enlightening discussion of how terminologies and the political economy of research universities have entertained disciplinary and interdisciplinary activities, see William B. Dunbar, "Disciplinarily and Interdisciplinary: Rhetoric and Context in the American Research University" (PhD thesis, University of California, Los Angeles, 2008).

3.   For an interesting exploration and discussion, see Ylva Lindholm-Romantschuk, *Scholarly Book Reviewing in the Social Sciences and Humanities: The Flow of Ideas within and among Disciplines* (Westport, CT: Greenwood Press, 1998).

4.   Jean-Pierre V. M. Hérubel, "Being *Undisciplined*; or Traversing Disciplinary Configurations in Social Science and Humanities Databases: Conceptual Considerations for Interdisciplinarity and Multidisciplinarity" (paper, International Federation of Library Associations, Social Science Libraries Section, Satellite

Conference, University of Toronto, Toronto, Canada 6August 6–7, 2008), http://www.ideals.illinois.edu/bitstream/handle/2142/8846/herubel.pdf

5. Alexandra Oleson and John Voss, eds., *The Organization of Knowledge in Modern America, 1860–1920* (Baltimore, MD: Johns Hopkins University Press, 1979).

6. Thomas Bender, *Intellect and Public Life: Essays on the Social History of Academic Intellectuals in the United States* (Baltimore, MD: Johns Hopkins University Press, 1993).

7. For instructive reading, see William Nelson Fenton, *Area Studies in American Universities*, for the Commission on Implications of Armed Services Educational Programs (Washington: American Council on Education, 1947); Wendell Clark Bennett, *Area Studies in American Universities* (New York: Social Science Research Council, 1951); Tsuen-hsuin Tsien and Howard W. Winger, *Area Studies and the Library* (Chicago: University of Chicago Press, 1966); Martin Howard Sable, *International and Area Studies Librarianship: Case Studies* (Metuchen, NJ: Scarecrow Press, 1973); Neil L. Waters, ed., *Beyond the Area Studies Wars: Toward a New International Studies* (Middlebury, VT: Middlebury College Press and University Press of New England, 2000).

8. For general discussions and overarching concerns, consult Robert Frodeman, Julie Thompson Klein, and Carl Mitcham, eds., *The Oxford Handbook of Interdisciplinarity* (Oxford: Oxford University Press, 2010).

9. For a discussion of disciplinary morphologies, see Jean-Pierre V. M. Hérubel, "Musings on Disciplinary Morphology and Nomenclature in the Humanities and Social Sciences: Implications for Book Selection," *Journal of Scholarly Publishing* 39 (2007): 318–326. Although not broached here, another manifestation of disciplinary morphology is *transcendent disciplinarity*, or transcendent fluidity, which characterizes a higher order of multiple disciplines melding and in continuous fluid relationships. When this occurs, various disciplinary strengths join to form a synthesis that is greater than the sum of its parts, leading to a meta-disciplinary approach to knowledge. Rarely can this state be achieved without recourse to utilization of insights, methodologies, techniques, and perspectives, while dissolving constituent disciplinary morphologies themselves. Difficult to achieve, *transcendent disciplinarity* offers examination of phenomena without rigid disciplinary constructions and epistemological boundaries.

10. For further treatment, see Michael F. Goodchild and Donald G. Janelle, "Specialization in the Structure and Organization of Geography," *Annals of the Association of American Geographers* 78 (March 1988): 1–28; Ron Johnston, "Geography: A Different Sort of Discipline?" *Transactions of the Institute of British Geographers* 28 (2003): 133–141; D. L. Skole "Geography as a Great Intellectual Melting Pot and the Preeminent Interdisciplinary Environmental Discipline," *Annals of the Association of American Geographers*, 94 (2004): 739–743.

11. Many disciplines must contend with concerns over fragmentation via specialization; see George W. Stocking, Jr., "Delimiting Anthropology: Historical Reflections on the Boundaries of a Boundless Discipline," *Social Research* 62 (Winter 1995): 933–966; Timothy V. Kaufman-Osborn, "Dividing the Domain of Political Science: On the Fetishism of Subfields," *Polity* 38 (Jan. 2006): 41–71.

12. Of course, sociology is not alone in this; see Charles L. Cappell and Thomas M. Guterbock, "Visible Colleges: The Social and Conceptual Structure of Sociology Specialties," *American Sociological Review* 57 (April 1992): 266–273. Sociology's evolution speaks to continuous specializations; see Charles Camic, "Three De-

partments in Search of a Discipline: Localism and Interdisciplinary Interaction in American Sociology, 1890–1940," *Social Research* 62 (Winter 1995): 1003–1033.

13. The inexorable imperative of hyperspecialization continues to animate the examination of newly emerging constellations of subjects, so much so that inevitable divergence among various subfields occurs. Further, some specializations actually lead to highly honed subdisciplines, e.g., sociology of philosophy as opposed to the sociology of knowledge. Specialization alone is not responsible for disciplinary formation—professionalization of approaches, methodologies, acknowledged techniques, and academia's reward system exert pressures, if not powerful influence, upon disciplinary identification as it becomes more hyperspecialized.

14. For further reading, see Moti Nissani, "Ten Cheers for Interdisciplinarity: The Case for Interdisciplinary Knowledge and Research," *Social Science Journal* 34 (1997): 201–216.

15. See Roger C. Schonfeld, *JSTOR: A History* (Princeton, NJ: Princeton University Press, 2003).

16. JSTOR, http://www.jstor.org (accessed November 1, 2010).

17. For a sense, although slightly dated, of academic history's disciplinary reach, see Michael Kammen, ed., *The Past before Us: Contemporary Historical Writing in the United States* (Ithaca, NY: Cornell University Press, 1980); for a recent examination of the historical enterprise, see Anne L. Buchanan and Jean-Pierre V. M. Hérubel, "Taking Clio's Pulse… Or Examining Characteristics of Monographic Publications Reviewed by *American Historical Review*," *Journal of Scholarly Publishing* 42 (January 2011): 160–181.

18. As an illustration, in recent years, historians have enlarged the purview of library history, so much so that historical research in this seemingly arcane field of interest has embraced greater historiographic questions as well as larger questions demanding more sophisticated approaches and methodologies emanating from other disciplinary perspectives. For library historians, library history is not an isolated affair treating only hagiographic biographies, institutional histories, and celebratory versions of historical narrative of the library profession and libraries. Firmly situated within larger societal forces impacting libraries, their services, and the profession at large, practitioners of library history have had to move beyond the discrete library perspective and incorporate a wider range of approaches stemming from sociology, readings studies, American and cultural studies, while entertaining and using methodologies from various disciplines not formally associated with previous library historical interest or practice.

19. Historical Abstracts, EBSCOhost, www.ebsohotst.com/ (accessed November 1, 2010); America: History and Life, EBSCOhost,; wwwlebscohost.com (accessed November 1, 2010).

20. JSTOR, http://www.jstor.org (accessed November 1, 2010). For additional observations, see Jean-Pierre V. M. Hérubel, "Situating Clio's Influence in Humanities and Social Science Monographs: Disciplinary Affiliations and Historical Scholarship," *Journal of Scholarly Publishing* 41 (October 2009): 56–66.

21. Interdisciplinary interests have been of interest among historians throughout the 20th century, especially in France, with the advent of Annales historiography and its school. Among American historians, interest in interdisciplinarity found concrete expression with the *Journal of Interdisciplinary History,* founded in 1971. According to ProjectMuse, "The *Journal of Interdisciplinary History* employs the

methods and insights of multiple disciplines in the study of past times and to bring a historical perspective to those other disciplines. Each issue features substantive articles, research notes, review essays and book reviews that relate historical study to applied fields such as economics, demographics, politics, sociology and psychology" [Project MUSE, "Journal of Interdisciplinary History," http://muse.jhu.edu/journals/jih (accessed November 1, 2010)]. An additional exploration into its interdisciplinary nature is Anne L. Buchanan and Jean-Pierre V. M. Hérubel, "Interdisciplinarity in Historical Studies: Citation Analysis of the Journal of Interdisciplinary History," *LIBRES: Library and Information Science Research Electronic Journal* 4 (1994): 1–13; for a recent discussion of interdisciplinarity and literary studies, see Bjorn Hammarfelt, "Interdisciplinarity and the Intellectual Base of Literature Studies: Citation Analysis of Highly Cited Monographs," *Scientometrics* 86, no. 3 (March 2011): 705–725, doi:10.1007/s11192-010-0314-5.

22. JSTOR, http://www.jstor.org (accessed November 1, 2010).

23. An interesting manifestation is ethnohistory, which borrows from ethnology, ethnography, and history to form a new synthesis; see Michael Harkin, "Ethnohistory's Ethnohistory: Creating a Discipline from the Ground Up," *Social Science History* 34 (2010): 113–128.

24. See Jean-Pierre V. M. Hérubel and Anne L. Buchanan, "Disciplinary, Interdisciplinary, and Subdisciplinary Linkages in Historical Studies Journals," *Science and Science of Science* 3 (1994): 15–24.

25. Among possible responses is to consider historical geography as a historical subdiscipline; see Anne L. Buchanan and Jean-Pierre V. M. Hérubel, "Interdisciplinarity: The Case of Historical Geography through Citation Analysis," *Collection Building* 14 (1994): 15–21.

26. For instructive illustrations of various disciplinary morphologies vis-à-vis medieval studies, see Jean-Pierre V. M. Hérubel, "Disciplinary Affiliations and Subject Dispersion in Medieval Studies: A Bibliometric Exploration," *Behavioral & Social Sciences Librarian* 23 (2005): 67–83.

27. A further articulation of disciplinary morphology as it concerns the examination of ideas within historical context is to examine the history of ideas or intellectual history as subdisciplines. Unlike philosophy, where ideas are privileged and separate from historical contextualization, ideas as products of their temporal and special context can be pursued as a discrete field; see Jean-Pierre V. M. Hérubel and Edward A. Goedeken, "Identifying the Intellectual Contours of a Historical Specialty: Geographical, Temporal, and Subject Emphases of the Journal of the History of Ideas," *Serials Librarian* 55 (2008): 276–295.

28. For a general discussion including the multidisciplinary and interdisciplinary constitution of the history of science as subdiscipline, see Jean-Pierre V. M. Hérubel, "Clio's View of the History of Science: A Preliminary Bibliometric Appreciation," *Behavioral & Social Sciences Librarian* 24 (2006): 69–91. Perusal of *Isis*, the official organ of the History of Science Society, will provide greater interdisciplinary and multidisciplinary appreciation.

29. Current Bibliography of the History of Science and Its Cultural Influences, 2009, *Isis* 100, no. S1 (2009) 274–275, http://www.journals.uchicago.edu/doi/pdf/10.1086/652112, (accessed November 1, 2010).

30. A fine example of the history of photography's embrace of diverse disciplinary morphologies is the journal *History of Photography*, which is "an international

quarterly devoted to the history, practice and theory of photography," and its goal "is to be inclusive and interdisciplinary in nature, welcoming all scholarly approaches, whether archival, historical, art historical, anthropological, sociological or theoretical. It is intended also to embrace world photography, ranging from Europe and the Americas to the Far East" (Taylor & Francis, "Journal Details: *History of Photography*," http://www.tandf.co.uk/journals/titles/03087298.asp, accessed November 1, 2010).

31. For incisive observations and discussion, see Julie Thompson Klein, "Interdisciplinary Needs: The Current Context," in "Navigating among the Disciplines: The Library and Interdisciplinary Inquiry," ed. Carole L. Palmer, special issue, *Library Trends* 45 (Fall 1996): 134–154.

32. For a recent treatment of the interdisciplinary nature of LIS education and professionalization concerns, see Cassidy R. Sugimoto, "Mentoring, Collaboration, and Interdisciplinarity: An Evaluation of the Scholarly Development of Information and Library Science Doctoral Students" (PhD thesis, University of North Carolina at Chapel Hill, 2010).

33. See Mattei Dogan, and Robert Pahre, *Creative Marginality: Innovation at the Intersections of Social Sciences* (Boulder, CO: Westview Press, 1990); Mattei Dogan, "The Hybridization of Social Science Knowledge," in "Navigating among the Disciplines: The Library and Interdisciplinary Inquiry," ed. Carole L. Palmer, special issue, *Library Trends* 45 (Fall 1996): 296–314.

34. For a recent discussion and of newly emerging roles, see Marianne Stowell Bracke, Jean-Pierre V. M. Hérubel, and Suzanne M. Ward, "Some Thoughts on Opportunities for Collection Development Librarians," *Collection Management* 35 (July 2010): 255–259.

35. For a sound introduction to the visual studies and art history per se, see Michael Ann Holly and Keith Moxey, eds., *Art History, Aesthetics, Visual Studies* (Williamstown, MA: Sterling and Francine Clark Art Institute, 2002) and James Elkins, *Visual Studies: A Skeptical Introduction* (New York: Routledge, 2003); for the evolution of visual studies vis-à-vis art history proper, see Margaret Dikovitskaya, *Visual Culture: The Study of the Visual after the Cultural Turn* (Cambridge, MA: MIT Press, 2005).

36. For visual studies' interdisciplinary nature, see the *Journal of Visual Culture*. It "offers astute, informative and dynamic thought on the visual. The journal publishes work from a range of methodological positions, on various historical moments and across diverse geographical locations. It is the leading interdisciplinary forum for visual culture studies scholars in film, media and television studies; art, design, fashion and architecture history; cultural studies and critical theory; philosophy and aesthetics; and across the social sciences" (SAGE Journals, "*Journal of Visual Culture*," http://vcu.sagepub.com, accessed November 1, 2010).

37. For interdisciplinary and multidisciplinary aspects in art historical approaches, see E. Dowell, "Interdisciplinarity and New Methodologies in Art History: A Citation Analysis," *Art Documentation* 18 (1999): 14–19; Jean-Pierre V. M. Hérubel, "Art History Dissertation Trends as a Selection Approach for Art History Collections." *Indiana Libraries* 26 (2007): 40–43.

38. For an introduction to magazine research, consult David Abrahamson, ed., *The American Magazine: Research Perspectives and Prospects* (Ames: Iowa State University Press, 1995). For further research, consult Marcia R. Prior-Miller, Bibliography of Magazine Research, 6th ed., 2008, http://mpm.jlmc.iastate.edu/

magazine-bibliography.php, (accessed November 1, 2010); this masterful bibliography compiled selectively by Prior-Miller reflects the multidisciplinary, if not interdisciplinary, nature of magazine studies.

39. Another intriguing multidisciplinary and interdisciplinary orientation to print and media culture is the history of the book; for discussion of various interdisciplinary activities in book history and print culture studies in the main, see Jonathan Rose, "The Horizon of a New Discipline: Inventing Book Studies," *Publishing Research Quarterly* 19 (March 2003): 11–19.

Chapter 3 • • • • • • • •

Scholarly Practices in a Globally Linked, Technology-Enhanced Academy

Jill Woolums

Introduction

This chapter concerns the relationship between interdisciplinary study and the issues of scholarly communication currently under critical debate. Both introduce new issues and challenges in the academy. Decisions made by universities with respect to each have the potential to make positive changes in the scholarly landscape. Not all parties involved with these issues, however, envision a bright future.

Defining the Landscape

Scholarly communication is the process through which scholars, educators, and researchers share their research findings with others. It involves the process of knowledge creation and discovery, reflects the interpretation and transformation of ideas, and involves publication and dissemination of knowledge as well as preservation of a record for posterity. Most significantly, scholarly communication entails a process of critical evaluation—a process through which ideas build upon ideas and knowledge grows.

Scholarly communication has a long history. It is not so much the quantity of information available, as the connectedness of that information through time and the achievement of knowledge that is of interest to scholars. Knowledge is more than information.

The substance of communication within the academy is scholarship. The *Oxford English Dictionary* defines *scholarship* as "The attainments of a scholar; learning, erudition; esp. proficiency... The status or emoluments of a scholar at a... university."[1] Scholarship determines scholarly status, which is achieved through evaluation among peers. To achieve advancement and promotion at colleges and universities, faculty are held to high standards of achievement, generally in four areas: teaching, research, professional leadership, and public service. At large universities in particular, research is of paramount importance. The requirement to do research and publish the results, commonly known as "publish or perish," is the primary criterion for higher status and higher pay. The need to be published by reputable scholarly societies, commercial publishers, and university presses in an era of expansion of higher education has created a highly competitive environment. This competition impacts the crisis in scholarly communication. Publishers must meet the need to publish more. Scholarly societies, nonprofit organizations, and university presses must be highly selective and frequently face budgetary shortfalls that prevent them from meeting the volume of need. This overflowing volume has handed overmuch of the work of publishing to large-scale commercial publishers, which can and do meet the need, but at a significantly higher cost. The escalation in cost is at the root of the scholarly communication crisis.

Scholarly communication is in flux. Traditionally, researchers conduct their investigations according to methods acceptable to their disciplines. The results of research appear in published writings, conference presentations, lectures, and teaching. The delivery of research enriches disciplinary groups and spurs further publication. Historically, the primary formats of published scholarly works have been printed books, articles, dissertations, and conference proceedings. Authors seek prestigious publications, and publishers seek well-respected, well-known scholars.

With the Internet have come a glut of information and the challenge of finding, sorting and sifting through it. The Internet has introduced new formats: blogs, wikis, learning management systems, online discovery tools, electronic repositories, e-books, and e-journals. The Internet has made information, including scholarship, appear to be freely available "on demand." Scholarship, however, comes with a high price, primarily paid by libraries, whose funds are shrinking.

Academic communities are defined by the boundaries of disciplines, many of which date far back to the earliest days of human study and investigation. The evolution of scholarship follows formal methods of accepted practices imposed by academic disciplines. The scientific method may differ from poetic critique, but both are accepted as established protocols pertaining to their respective fields. All disciplines produce scholarship pertaining to their unique interests. A critique comparing the poetry of William Carlos Williams with that of T. S. Eliot is as important to the literary scholar as the scientific surveys developed by William Herschel in his discovery of Uranus is to an astronomer. Interdisciplinarity has been an influence as far back as the earliest days of scholarship. Undergraduate general studies curricula of many liberal arts colleges reflect this influence. Interdisciplinary work investigates a problem or issue from several perspectives. A group of scholars may study cancer in terms of its medical and psychological effects on an individual as well as its economic impact on a person, family, and society. The late twentieth and early twenty-first centuries have witnessed a significant increase in interdisciplinarity by faculty, graduate students, and other advanced researchers. Environmental studies, for example, combines the study of ecology, policy, law, sociology, public health, and natural resources. To solve the problem of pollution, scholars in all these fields come together bringing their expertise.

Barbara Leigh Smith, a proponent of interdisciplinarity, considers its role today in stating, "Interdisciplinary programs are different. They propose that there are priorities, relationships among the fields of knowledge. And they suggest that there are specific things that… [an educated person] should know and know how to do."[2]

The American Association of Universities studied successful interdisciplinary programs. Its study found that such programs (1) engage more than one discipline; (2) produce results that cannot be accomplished by a single discipline alone; (3) are situated at the boundaries among fields (for example, biophysics); (4) focus on large-scope issues related to several disciplines; (5) employ a common tool; and (6) provide opportunities for multi-institutional collaboration.[3]

Michael Moran raises the political aspect of interdisciplinary studies:

> The disciplines have been greatly strengthened in recent decades, and the interdisciplinarity can partly be understood as a response by interests threatened by disciplinarity. It is also a strategy used by disciplines in crisis, and by dissidents from disciplinary hierarchies…. Disciplines therefore are about power, hierarchy and control in the organization of knowledge…. Academics have ensured

that evaluation is dominated by peer review.... Dominant disciplinary paradigms shape the most highly regarded scholarly work. The outcomes, and the consequences of the outcomes, have in turn reinforced hierarchy, by awarding the highest grades to the elite institutions that entered the process with the largest endowments of cultural and material capital.[4]

Moran indicates that interdisciplinarity's goal of problem solving is viewed as less "scholarly." Academics pursuing interdisciplinary research may be seen as outsiders, while such academics may see themselves as innovative, visionary, or representing a newer generation of thinking. Holley indicates that the "challenge of interdisciplinarity engagement is related to the need for organizational transformation... [and must be] cultivated through well-organized efforts to draw scholars outside their disciplinary domains and reward endeavors that do not always align with the traditional norms of higher education."[5]

The increasing emergence of interdisciplinarity places additional demands on the already stressed scholarly communication system. Interdisciplinary projects seek recognition and outlets for publication. The Center for Studies in Higher Education concluded that

there is a need for a more nuanced academic reward system that is less dependent on citation metrics, slavish adherence to marquee journals and university presses, and the growing tendency of institutions to outsource assessment of scholarship to such proxies. Such a need is made more urgent given the challenges to institutional review of assessing interdisciplinary scholarship, new hybrid disciplines, the rise of heavily computational sub-branches of disciplines, the development of new online forms of edition-making and collaborative curation for community resource use, large-scale collaboration, and multiple authorship.[6]

As current models of peer review are being challenged because of their impact on escalating cost, the academy also needs to develop models for assessing interdisciplinary scholarship so as not to unduly increase the amount of publishing and not to disadvantage scholars.

Lee indicates that peer review of interdisciplinary publications requires the acknowledgment that reviewers cannot adequately review for impact and validity outside their own areas of expertise. He suggests that new editorial policies be developed and that

> reviewers should be instructed to confine their comments to their area of expertise, to raise questions before making a judgment, and should be asked explicitly whether they have performed the specific type of analysis used in the manuscript, on the specific type of data it presents. Editors should pay close attention to classic signs of field bias, such as reviews that avoid discussing the paper's actual data; largely speculative criticisms not supported by specific data or literature; or lack of evidence that the criticisms are actually relevant to the specific data in the paper.[7]

This additional work requires more time, money, and expertise, adding more stress to scholarly publishing.

Administrators of large institutions have their own agenda in their support of interdisciplinarity, often in conflict with established faculty. While status is of paramount importance to administrators, their need to meet certain bottom-line goals stems largely from political obligations to government agencies and boards of trustees and from economic ties to corporate and influential private donors. Their perspective, more fully examined below, is generally more favorable toward interdisciplinary programs.

The Players

The key players on the scholarly communication landscape frequently see the issue through narrowly focused eyes. Solving today's crisis in scholarly communication requires an understanding not only of each stakeholder, but also of the interdependency among them. Understanding this interdependency and how individual players' needs often collide is necessary.

Faculty

Faculty are the creators of scholarship. Their research and productivity provide the content transmitted through scholarly communication and publishing. Creation of scholarly content is mandatory for faculty to rise up the ladder of tenure and promotion. Savage indicates: "Whereas insufficiently productive junior faculty may be denied tenure and promotion, senior faculty may be threatened with loss of sabbatical leave or with a heavier teaching load to compensate the school for their failure to publish enough."[8]

Some disciplines, particularly the humanities and social sciences, require book publishing. The urgency for book publishing derives from the department's and university's need for prestige. Savage indicates that "the important thing, the thing from which the prestige of department and university derives, is publication."[9] Sales, cost, and readership are important factors to scholarly publishers that seek economic viability or profit and to libraries dealing with shrinking budgets and shelf space restrictions. These needs place significant pressures on the flow of scholarly communication in the academy.

Journal article publishing is especially important in the physical sciences. The Ithaka *Faculty Survey 2009* found that traditional channels of communication, not new forms such as blogs, Twitter, digital content repositories, "remain the most important ways in which faculty communicate both formally and informally."[10] The study found that from 2003 to 2009 and across disciplines, over 80 percent of faculty studied indicated that "the single most important factor in selecting where [i.e., in which journal] to publish is consistent readership within one's own discipline."[11] It also found that tenure and promotion are faculty's highest priorities, not other activities such as new online forms of communication, open access publications, or free availability of resources. Journals with longstanding reputations of high quality and widespread readership within a discipline remain all important, even in science fields where there is significant depositing of articles into repositories.[12] Traditional publications will dominate scholarship dissemination because "career incentives based on traditional practices are likely to continue, unless there is an overall cultural shift and structural change driven from the highest level of academic administrators."[13] The assessment and status needs of interdisciplinarity could influence a shift. Schonfeld and Housewright also suggest: "Further exploration of the possible ways in which information services organizations can help faculty to maximize the value and impact of their research is certainly called for."[14] How libraries might "maximize" needs further exploration.

Publishers

The Ithaka study ends with questions, including some for publishers. "How can publishers enable faculty members to maximize the visibility of their research outputs in an environment where almost limitless information competes for our attention? Will faculty members continue to value traditional services from their societies as the digital revolution continues, and what new services [from publishers] might evolve?... And, will faculty be able to move beyond publishing practices that are 'unnecessarily constrained' by tenure and promotion processes?" The study concludes that "support of trailblazing faculty disciplines may help these institutions develop the roles and services that will serve a growing range of faculty needs into the future.... Institutions [must] ensure that the 21st century information needs of faculty are met and to secure their own relevance for the future."[15] Can interdisciplinarity provide these "trailblazing faculty disciplines"?

Miller and Harris note that most scholars are rarely concerned with the price of a journal subscription, despite the fact that they are the ultimate consumers. There is therefore a "disconnect between those who pay for information and those who consume it, along with the disconnect between those creating the information and those generating monetary profit from it."[16] To make a profit, publishers increase the number of sales or increase prices. To justify prices, publishers increase number of pages or provide enhanced technology. They also bundle subscriptions into packages, forcing libraries to purchase more than they need. However, escalating prices, coupled with severe cutbacks in budgets, are forcing libraries to cancel subscriptions and forego packages altogether. Commercial publishers eagerly publish high-quality research, but are not inclined to improve the publication process, nor are they "inclined to be innovative unless innovation leads to increased revenues."[17] Corporate publishers serve shareholders and monitor success through "surveys of authors and readers, citation statistics, and trends in rates of submission, publication, and efficiency of the review process."[18]

In the era following World War II, research funding expanded, and with it came an explosion in the volume of published material. Because of the need to publish, scholars turned to commercial publishers when society publishers were unable to handle the volume.

> Commercial firms found there was money to be made publishing the overflow of articles that couldn't be accommodated in society journals…. And since they were incentivised to maximize profit… they raised institutional prices dramatically and relentlessly…. With this foot in the door, commercial publishers built substantial portfolios of journals, aided by a trend of society "outsourcing" of their journal publishing to commercial firms. The high corporate profits from these journals have funded aggressive programs of internal development and wave upon wave of acquisitions and consolidation among publishers.[19]

While internal development provides technological platforms that facilitate the delivery and discovery of knowledge, libraries must weigh these services against the strangling price structures that come with them.

Conley and Wooders conclude that commercial publishers are no longer necessary, and that "in the electronic era, commercial publishers only impede distribution and add insult to injury by charging huge fees for their trouble."[20] After creating an open access scholarly journal in economics, they concluded that all of the traditional services expected of publishers, including printing and binding; typesetting; advertising; secretarial; postage; editorial salaries; referee stipends; and author publication fees are no longer necessary in the electronic environment. The only services for which they see a need are the Internet-based workflow/content-management systems and the software technicians to run them. Their article fails to acknowledge the sophisticated search engines publishers have developed and lacks perspective on the enormous scale of academic publishing and the challenges of accessibility. They also lack a wider view of the complexity of interests involving multiple stakeholders. They do recognize the favorable impact of open access: "Open-access is consistent with our mission as scholars to increase and spread knowledge and also feeds our personal and professional interests much more directly. However, we are still largely living the system of scholarly communication we inherited from the papyrocentric era. This system will not go quietly into the night. Commercial publishers will do their best to hang on to and exploit this inherited capital as long as they can."[21] They acknowledge the tenure-promotion impediment, noting that scholars seek the "most reputable journal... whether this location is an open access journal, a cheaper society journal, or an expensive commercial journal."[22] Although the authors fail to see beyond the paper versus digital debate, they do recognize the crippling economic posture of commercial publishers and propose new entrepreneurial ventures. How these entrepreneurships will function, what services will they provide, how will they be paid and how much, what will prevent them from escalating up to the scale of large commercial publishers when they see the potential of deep pockets to pay them, and what deep pockets will remain solvent enough to employ their services remain unknown. In a broader sense, the success of small ventures is part of the larger economic debate focused on the need for the survival of small, local business in a world dominated by large, global, multinational corporations. The authors fail to discuss the role of libraries, but do hint at the role interdisciplinary programs may play in saving scholarly communication. They indicate that the stability of the status quo will be maintained until "new fields arise and old ones fall out of favor [and] there is opportunity to overturn this historical fact.... Patience is required."[23]

Withey et al., representing the view of university presses and book publishing, addresses the issues differently. They state that the scholarly publishing "system" must "confront the high cost of the front-end of the process: acquiring, peer-reviewing, and editing manuscripts. Second, we must stop being obsessed with output, because format—print, electronic, article length, book length—is rapidly becoming a non-issue.... And finally, since scholarly publishing is a system involving many players, it must be analyzed as a system. No one player can resolve this crisis alone."[24] University presses, as book publishers, must focus increasingly on the bottom line, as institutional funding decreases and demand for publishing manuscripts increases. They recommend a realignment of journal-

and book-publishing efforts to better integrate new technologies and institutional repositories into the system as a whole and teamwork among the players. The recommendations of Withey et al. deserve further study and planning.

Academic Institutions and Administrators

In their book, *Engines of Innovation,* Thorp and Goldstein, both university presidents, examine institutions of higher education in the current fiscally challenged economy.[25] Like Conley and Wooders, they favor entrepreneurial ventures to solve the problems of society and the academy. Thorp and Goldstein see through the eyes of high-level administrators who are accountable to interested parties outside the academy; namely, government, the corporate sector, private philanthropists, and the public. There is little mention of the full scope of services their constituents such as faculty and libraries provide or the issues they face. Taking their cues from Google's Eric Schmidt and Harvard's Michael Porter, they believe that innovation with the nation's great universities leading the way and a comprehensive economic strategy should create the path to a better future.

Thorp and Goldstein see positive implications for interdisciplinary research: "Problem-based innovation in research universities can focus resources from a variety of disciplines on the challenges we face and, in so doing, create new knowledge and economic growth."[26] They also recognize that interdisciplinary research may attract new money for their institutions. Funding sources (i.e., private philanthropists, government grantors) want solutions to BIG problems and are "looking for a measurable return on their investment. It is no longer merely desirable for universities to be the source of innovations. It is now a national priority."[27] Universities are already organized to do the job because they contain "scientists, artists, poets, designers, computer programmers, venture capitalists and entrepreneurs" with the skill sets to address the problems. Thorp and Goldstein want their institutions to find answers and solutions and not cede this role to the private sector and government. They want the academy to embrace "high-impact innovation [that] requires an entrepreneurial mindset that views big problems as big opportunities."[28] By nature, interdisciplinarity has this problem-based focus and brings together the talent and perspective of several disciplines to tackle big problems.

Thorp and Goldstein do not explicitly address the crisis in scholarly communication. However, they see Google as providing an answer:

> Google is spending billions on efforts to put the world's great libraries online, and hundreds of other efforts are aiming to include not only text but audio and video in the new electronic canon—and all of this will be updated in real time. At the most basic level, access to the world's knowledge is being democratized. Although the economics have yet to be worked out (fertile ground for entrepreneurial thinking), what only a few years ago seemed to be a futurist's musing is now happening, and anyone who doubts the new reality should have a look at Google Scholar, the forerunner of the promise of universal knowledge access.... Physical and economic barriers to the free flow of knowledge are going away.[29]

Have they even heard of Elsevier? Thorp and Goldstein fail to see the bigger picture. They demonstrate how stakeholders lack understanding of each other when they state that "the economics have yet to be worked out," that Google Scholar promises universal knowledge access, and that economic barriers to the free flow of knowledge are going away. They lack awareness of the economics of, demand for, organization of, and access to recorded scholarly knowledge. They fail to understand their libraries. They appear unaware of the many entrepreneurial collaborative ventures evolving and already entered into by libraries. Libraries have done such an excellent job at providing "feels like free" resources that they escape notice by primary users.

The authors herald interdisciplinarity as representing entrepreneurial thinking, but fail to see how "entrepreneurial thinking" of their institutional constituents offers hope for positive change. Library entrepreneurial thinking has created repositories, led to archival collaborations such as Western Regional Storage Trust, and resulted in cooperatively developed discovery tools (e.g., OCLC's WorldCat).

Commercial publishers have demonstrated little entrepreneurial thinking regarding economic sustainability in scholarly publishing.

They, along with Google, have incentive only to profit from content digitization. For sustainable scholarly publishing to occur, entrepreneurial thinking must address the conflict between profit-motivated providers and its primarily nonprofit marketplace.

Libraries

Libraries are inclusive with respect to interdisciplinary programs.

The mission of libraries is inherently interdisciplinary. Libraries do not discriminate adversely against any particular field of scholarship. Instead, libraries seek to preserve the whole scholarly record, including all disciplines, regardless of format, be it digital, print, or another medium. Although academic libraries must evaluate quality and live within budgetary constraints, it is their purpose to create collections that match the depth and breadth of academic programs. Libraries' efforts, therefore, benefit the long-term success of interdisciplinary scholarship by preserving its record. When a university deems a research discipline or project important enough to fund, libraries will similarly allocate or reallocate funds to assure access to the published results of such research. Although librarian-selectors align with disciplines, they will add interdisciplinary materials to their collections if faculty demand and supporting funds exist. Budgetary restrictions, however, can create competition for available funds.

As faculty become aware of the economic challenges of scholarly publishing, they recognize libraries' role in purchasing information. Libraries have budgets for buying books and licensing subscriptions, whereas faculty do not. The role of libraries' discovery tools has diminished in the Google era. While there has been an explosion of new discovery tools created by commercial enterprises and sold to libraries for their users, Google, through its name brand, has claimed market dominance in search with its common search engine and Google Scholar. Commercial products sold to libraries, such as EBSCO's Discovery Service and Serial Solutions' Summon, attempt to compete by providing added search functions and deeper indexing. Google, as essentially a marketing tool, markets library catalogs and collections much as it advertises other commercial products. Administrators such as Thorp and Goldstein fail to recognize that libraries pay, Google does not. This gap in awareness persists in the academy.

Google Scholar pales in comparison to the sophisticated search engines developed by commercial publishers. While gaining in breadth as more publishers permit Google to market their articles, Google's search engine does not provide the depth or refinement of search engines developed by large publishers such as Elsevier, ISI, CSA, and EBSCO. Fortunately, library budgets still buy these higher quality search engines for their users, although budget shortfalls in the current recession have led some to cut back on the number of available search engines. How budgetary shortfalls and publishers' economic conditions will impact the future of quality discovery tools remains unknown.

Libraries make informed decisions about their acquisitions based on usage statistics, circulation records, faculty input, citation reports, cost data, and other metrics. In dealing with commercial publishers, Miller and Harris note that the "complexity of negotiations with publishers over electronic content in an industry devoid of any standards is a mounting concern."[30] To compound matters further, published knowledge is increasing in volume faster than ever before, making it difficult for library budgets to catch up. "Since the beginning of the twentieth century the trend has been a rough doubling of knowledge every fifteen years."[31] Shared purchasing among libraries holds some hope for the future. Libraries have struck back at impossible price demands by forming consortia to increase their bargaining power and gain economies of scale.

Libraries have certainly embraced entrepreneurial thinking in the areas of archiving and preservation. Some have procured perpetual rights to preserve digital archives as they have preserved print for generations. Although Google is recognized by the general public for digitizing books (taken freely from major libraries), research libraries have made huge strides toward digital preservation of both printed resources and born-digital materials.

Organizations like LOCKSS, Portico, and JSTOR are engaged in collective problem solving to preserve digital records, and academic libraries have cooperatively made these efforts possible. WEST, initiated by the University of California, strives to ensure adequate preservation of print materials, in sustainable numbers, for several Western universities.

The entrepreneurial efforts of libraries in the past two decades have been considerable. In addition to innovative digital and print archiving and preservation strategies, cooperative purchasing endeavors and collaborative discovery tools continue to evolve. As partners in creating institutional repositories, libraries stand at the forefront of the scholarly publishing debate as leaders in addressing the scholarly communication crisis.

Impediments and Opportunities

Interdisciplinarity presents scholarly communication with both obstacles and opportunities. The way to removing barriers to the creation and preservation of interdisciplinary collections requires the involvement of multiple interested parties. Interdisciplinarity adds more to a rapidly increasing volume of research that must be vetted, published, and purchased. This means new faculty attitudes and skills and sustainable publishing models that include cost -effective production and market-supported pricing. Faculty must value interdisciplinary research, administrators must recognize the prestige interdisciplinary programs can bring to their institutions, and funding sources must see the positive impact of these programs. Successful academic and economic models of scholarly communication mean addressing the scholarly communication/scholarly publishing system as a whole. Publishers, corporate aggregators, researcher-authors, libraries, and technical infrastructure developers must be aware of the needs of each other. Stakeholders both in interdisciplinary studies and in scholarly communication must not only reach their own goals, but also understand the impact of their actions on others. This need for communication suggests the need for more forums, panels, meetings, summits, and cross-attendance at conferences among the parties. Beyond discussions, action plans, guidelines, and commitments need to be established.

Faculty Tenure and Promotion

It would be easy to blame the crisis on the traditional faulty approach to tenure and promotion. Tenure and promotion will not disappear. New solutions require a new approach. At present, there are more questions than answers. Can faculty find other ways to evaluate their peers without creating excessive numbers of books and articles? If so, will this alleviate the economic stranglehold of commercial publishers? Will faculty become willing to publish in open access journals and e-books? Will the open access model succeed as a viable economic model? Will disciplinary faculty become more open to interdisciplinary programs? What will motivate this openness? Will universities receive more money for institutionally based scholarship that crosses disciplinary lines? Will this funding elevate the status of interdisciplinarity?

Interdisciplinary faculty gain institutional support by attracting money from corporate, governmental, and philanthropic sources wanting BIG problems solved. Will such strong support make them less dependent on traditional protocols and motivate them to introduce new models of peer evaluation, less financially burdensome to the scholarly communication system? Will disciplinary faculty become less threatened if new programs are financially self-sufficient and distribute extra funding to participating disciplinary faculty? Will departments accept new peer-evaluation models necessitated by interdisciplinarity? Will interdisciplinary researchers adopt more cost-effective models of publishing, using new technologies and perhaps grassroots venues, and be less in need of commercial publishers?

A recent CSHE study found that conservative values prevail. Most faculty still conservatively cling to the traditional peer-review system to achieve stature and recognition. "Although there is a universal embrace of the rapidly expanding body of digital 'primary' sources and data, there is an equally strong aversion to a 'glut' of unvetted secondary publications and ephemera. The degree to which peer review, despite its perceived shortcomings, is considered to be an important filter of academic quality cannot be overstated."[32] The report acknowledges new platforms, including Web 2.0. "It is also possible, based on our scan of a variety of 'open peer-review' websites, that scholars in less competitive institutions (including internationally), who may experience more difficulty finding a high-stature publisher for their work, will embrace these publication outlets. Time will tell."[33] In addition, "Experiments in new genres of scholarship and dissemination... are taking place within the context of relatively conservative value and reward systems that have the practice of peer review at their core....

We have found that young scholars can be particularly conservative in their research dissemination behavior."[34] Interdisciplinary researchers, even more than their established peers, need to compete for academic status. Although the appeal of less prestigious open access publishers may be attractive to them to make their work accessible, they must also be cautious to not be seen as part of the glut of low-quality information inundating the Web. They also will not want to be seen as aligned with less respected institutions as they compete for placement in higher-ranked academies. Peer review of interdisciplinary research usually requires disciplinary faculty to parse out and evaluate material according to the protocols of their own disciplines. Interdisciplinary researchers, therefore, are dependent on a very traditional system to establish themselves as nontraditional scholars. As interdisciplinary faculty become more established, however, they have an opportunity to once again think outside the box, that is, to invent new protocols for peer review much as they have created new cross-fields of study.

Publishing Business Models

Publishing business models consist of strategic silos and bundles, price escalation, and rigid pricing. Again, questions abound. Will commercial publishers ever lower their profit margins in order to keep buyers? How strapped will libraries need to become and how many cancellations will they need to undertake to trigger the weakening of these corporate giants? Without library purchases, will commercial publishers devise new models directed toward individual scholar consumers? Will they be forced to unbundle for individuals what they refuse to unbundle for institutions? Will the needs of the interdisciplinary community require significant repackaging of products and services? Although no answers are yet apparent, it is clear that continued economic pressure, on all sides, will be a primary driving force toward new, perhaps unforeseen outcomes. Those visionaries who create innovative business models may be in the best position to endure.

Digital technology has also brought turbulence, created new user expectations, and introduced new players into the system. The 2010 report by Bain & Company indicates that the stakeholders in the publishing ecosystem are facing "the redistribution of value among players, a redesign of their roles and, potentially, an evolution in the way content is created—all of which could produce significant new value for the industry in the long term."[35] In addition, "Regardless of device, consumers today expect ubiquitous, instantaneous and free information."[36] Interdisciplinary scholars have an opportunity to embrace new technologies to spread access to their research.

The Bain report recognizes the emergence of powerful digital distribution platforms and Amazon and Google stepping into the role of reader advisors. It predicts an acceleration of the "consolidation of distribution networks around the players with the greatest economies of scale.… Even more fundamentally, new technologies could loosen the control that publishers have over the entire value chain. To maintain their leading role, publishers must not only redeploy resources to digital channels, but also create new services for authors and readers alike.… Emerging authors may value publishers that can provide online and physical marketing and distribution services."[37] These predictions shed light on opportunities in the scholarly communication "ecosystem" as well. Will commercial publishers lose their competitive edge if newer publishing models evolve that satisfy vetting requirements, ease of dissemination, and cost-efficiencies and that financially reward authors? Perhaps the real question is how will such new publishing models evolve? With what institutional or venture capital will their start-ups be funded? Who will lead these efforts—societies, faculty, interdisciplinary programs, libraries, university presses, Amazon, others?

Emerging interdisciplinary authors need new publishing venues. They are positioned for innovation, if not leadership. They straddle and unite disciplines. They connect institutions. They are in a position to influence disciplinary peers by demonstrating successful alternatives. For example, a project that brings together leading thinkers from environmental science, medicine, and social work who represent institutions such as Stanford, Harvard, NIH, Oxford, and the University of California and that has done groundbreaking problem solving stands in a position of power. What it says has credibility and will get noticed. As groundbreakers, they more urgently need to create their scholarly record. This need creates the kind of motivation that could successfully develop new publishing models.

Despite conservative tenure and promotion attitudes, interdisciplinary researchers may be more willing to publish outside corporate boundaries and therefore be more willing to pursue open access and newer publications and publishers if traditional vetting is maintained and high-level credibility exists. They could take the lead in creating less costly, more accessible dissemination models. Assuming their research to be in high demand—since their work spans disciplines and satisfies outside interest groups—they may have leverage in initiating change. If they are successful in achieving prestige, their efforts could lead to new directions in scholarly communication as a whole.

Cooperative publishing is an alternative model. Instead of egregious price setting and out-of-line profit motives, cooperatives offer a more democratic method for the producers and consumers of scholarship to serve themselves. Schroeder and Siegel indicate democratic control and limited return on investment "would assure that prices rise only enough to cover expenses… [and] return on investment will primarily come in continued lower prices for our quality scholarly product."[38] Schroeder proposes that cooperatives could be formed by groups of related scholarly societies willing to "take back" their journals from commercial venues. Cooperative publishers look favorably on open access—something that would considerably ease strained library budgets. Co-ops could provide valuable assistance to start-up publishers.

> Historically, the society model of publishing came very close to the cooperative model, in that profit was not generally a motive and the academic producer/consumer engaged in all five of the major facets of production and distribution, especially if the society publication was based at an academic institution. When production and distribution became too burdensome, however, many societies turned these aspects over to commercial entities, and the model became less cooperative. Now that all these processes can be carried out electronically, however, the time is ripe for a more radical paradigm shift than what is offered by many of the "open access" models we are now seeing.[39]

One such co-op on its way to success is the German Academic Publishers Project. What needs to happen to encourage more such co-ops? What will persuade societies to take back control? Can university presses achieve advantages by adopting a co-op model as institutional support wanes? Perhaps large-scale interdisciplinary, multi-institutional projects could publish their own work much in the way societies have done or develop their own sustainable, cooperative models of publishing and dissemination.

New Roles for Libraries and Librarians

Libraries face budgetary impediments. Budgets have been cut severely while the volume of scholarship is escalating. They must buy more with less, demonstrate relevancy as their services are usurped by search engines and new reader advisors, advocate for change, adapt to technologies that make their services obsolete, and remain committed to quality selection, stewardship, and preservation. In addition, they must also persuade their institutions and faculty of their continuing value and remain as resilient and focused through this turbulent period as in the past.

The Challenge of Continued Relevancy

Faculty, institutions, and publishers recognize libraries' role in purchasing scholarship. This role will likely be more significant in the decade ahead. Universities must buy, and libraries perform this duty. They will, however, need new skills and alliances to succeed in navigating the unknown road ahead.

Embracing Interdisciplinary Studies

Libraries must address issues similar to their institutions to support interdisciplinary programs. The 2005 Association of American Universities study of interdisciplinary programs found key questions to be addressed in creating successful interdisciplinary programs.[40] These questions have corollaries for libraries.

Should the selection of interdisciplinary material be assigned to a bibliographer who is aligned with a discipline, or are there funds to support a new hire? To promote cooperation and minimize competition, bibliographers from different disciplines may need to agree upon shared and separate responsibilities with respect to supporting such programs. A clear structure should be established. Should a lead bibliographer be appointed? What will be the reporting lines? Library administration will need to provide support, via promotion and advancement, for affected bibliographers.

Clear delineation of funding is needed. What funding model best suits the budgets of impacted bibliographer groups? How might cost sharing be implemented? Is there a need for soliciting donor or grant money? Evaluation procedures need to be established, especially if an interdisciplinary program has a sunset provision. Bibliographers should decide on criteria to be used to evaluate the usage of these interdisciplinary collections.

As librarians develop relationships with interdisciplinary researchers, they may encounter fertile ground for advocating cost-effective models of scholarly publishing. Libraries may receive new institutional funds to support interdisciplinary studies and discover they need to spend comparatively less on interdisciplinary materials because of their availability via cost-efficient models. Libraries may find new partners willing to step forward to create vetted repositories assured of longevity by preservationists. These models may serve as exemplary innovations that can be replicated in other disciplines.

Librarians and interdisciplinary faculty could become strong partners in achieving cost-effectiveness, institutional prestige, and entrepreneurial success.

New Skills to Master

Librarians need new skills to achieve their goals in the current economically and politically challenged academic climate. As non-profits, libraries must negotiate with for-profit information providers. They must enter into new partnerships and alliances to find strength and bargaining power and solve the big problems of scholarly publishing. Large state consortia have already formed in states like Ohio and California, and other research libraries have formed regional consortia, such as Lyrasis and the Association of Southeastern Research Libraries. Librarians must maintain strong relationships with faculty for the achievement of common goals. They need to support cost-effective publishing by collaborating with university presses, building institutional repositories, and pursuing new publication models. They need to be effective advocates, not only for the value-added services they provide, but also for change in protocols that will assure an excellent scholarly record for generations to come.

Librarians as Negotiators

Librarians need persuasive negotiation skills now more than ever. Historically, libraries collaborate and cooperate. The vast interlibrary loan network demonstrates this. Now, however, they must negotiate with large corporations whose staffs possess skillful strategic marketing and sales expertise and whose bottom line is their corporate mission. Library schools have not taught classes in business skills like negotiation and marketing. In the future, however, development of these skills will impact libraries' fiscal capacity and operational strength. On-the-job training is needed to develop the business acumen for sustainable strategic planning.

Libraries as Publishers

Libraries have entered into significant partnerships and collaborations in recent years. They collaborate with university presses. They cooperate in building institutional repositories and in creating common tools to facilitate research discovery. For example, WorldCat has now integrated OAIster, formerly a repository of repositories from institutions worldwide. They can partner in new cooperative models and urge faculty, scholarly societies, and interdisciplinary centers to innovate with open access or other cost-efficient methods of publishing.

Librarians as Liaison

Librarian-faculty relationships remain critical. These relationships may need to become more strategic as financial pressures impact all segments of the academy. As librarians embed themselves into curricula, they have opportunities to inform faculty about the crisis in scholarly publishing. Exerting influence in a collaborative atmosphere can serve them well when advocating for alternative models of scholarly publishing.

Librarians as Advocates

Navigating the issues of scholarly communication is becoming a core responsibility of librarians. This is likely to increase as economic challenges persist. It demands excellent business, leadership, and entrepreneurial skills. While they advocate for their own survival, they must advocate for change. Libraries need marketing and public relations programs to better promote their value and services. They must be ready to respond to the questions of their institutional administrators, faculty, students, and the general public. When institutions are funded by tax dollars, libraries are also accountable to government. Libraries need to be ready with facts, data, stories, and evidence-based research to succeed in accomplishing their operational agendas.

Through cooperative ventures, libraries demonstrate alternatives to commercial models. Preservation beyond the borders of local institutions is increasing. Collaborative organizations, such as JSTOR, Portico, LOCKSS, and WEST, strengthen the position of libraries and remove these functions from commercial enterprises less inclined to serve a common good for posterity.

Persuasive advocacy requires a skillful Web presence within the academy and on the greater information landscape. Libraries need up-to-date infrastructures using advanced information technology to remain both relevant and competitive. OCLC has led the way in creating new tools and systems, but more is needed to compete with the research and development teams of corporate enterprises. Additional funding must be found to create these infrastructures. This compels libraries to become better fundraisers.

Libraries possess opportunities for leadership. While panels and conferences have been undertaken, new problem-solving roundtables need to strategize the path ahead. Libraries need strong allies. Partnerships with faculty, professional associations, university presses, scholarly societies, other libraries and consortia, and even commercial publishers would assure libraries' prominent role as a scholarly publishing stakeholder. Libraries need to seize the moment for leadership during this turbulent time. While contracting budgets are formidable, they also stimulate and motivate action toward a more sustainable future.

Notes

1.   *Oxford English Dictionary*, 2nd ed., 1989, s.v. "scholarship," http://www.oed.com/view/Entry/172495 (accessed January 29, 2011).

2. Barbara Leigh Smith, *Reinventing Ourselves: Interdisciplinary Education, Collaborative Learning, and Experimentation in Higher Education* (Bolton, MA: Anker Publishing 2001), 45.

3. Association of American Universities, *Report of the Interdisciplinarity Task Force* (Washington, DC: Association of American Universities, 2005), 2.

4. Michael Moran, "Interdisciplinarity and Political Science," *Politics* 26, no. 2 (2006): 73–76.

5. Karri A. Holley, *Understanding Interdisciplinary Challenges and Opportunities in Higher Education: ASHE Higher Education Report, Volume 35, Number 2* (Hoboken, NJ: Jossey-Bass, 2009), viii–ix.

6. Diane Harley, Sophia Krzys Acord, and Sarah Earl-Novell, *Peer Review in Academic Promotion and Publishing: Its Meaning, Locus and Future* (Berkeley, CA: Center for Studies in Higher Education, 2010), 2.

7. Christopher Lee, "Perspective: Peer Review of Interdisciplinary Scientific Papers," *Nature* Web Debate, 2006, doi:10.1038/nature05034 (accessed January 30, 2011).

8. William W. Savage, "Scribble, Scribble, Toil and Trouble: Forced Productivity in the Modern University," *Journal of Scholarly Publishing* 35, no. 1 (October 2003): 44.

9. Ibid., 42.

10. Roger C. Schonfeld and Ross Housewright, *Faculty Survey 2009: Key Strategic Insights for Libraries, Publishers, and Societies* (New York: Ithaka S+R, 2010), 25.

11. Ibid.

12. Ibid., 26.

13. Ibid., 32.

14. Ibid., 33.

15. Ibid., 34.

16. Cass Miller and Juliana C. Harris, "Scholarly Journal Publication: Conflicting Agendas for Scholars, Publishers, and Institutions," *Journal of Scholarly Publishing* 35, no. 2 (2004): 79.

17. Ibid., 81.

18. Ibid.

19. Richard K. Johnson, "A Question of Access: SPARC, BioOne, and Society-Driven Electronic Publishing," *D-Lib Magazine* 6, no. 5 (May 2000), http://www.dlib.org/dlib/may00/johnson/05johnson.html.

20. John P. Conley and Myrna Wooders, "But What Have You Done for Me Lately? Commercial Publishing, Scholarly Communication, and Open-Access," *Economic Analysis and Policy* 39, no. 1 (March 2009): 76.

21. Ibid., 86.

22. Ibid.

23. Ibid., 81.

24. Lynne Withey, Carlos J. Alonso, Cathy N. Davidson, and John M. Unsworth, *Crisis and Opportunities: The Futures of Scholarly Publishing*, ACLS Occasional Paper No. 57 (New York: American Council of Learned Societies, 2003): 48.

25. Holden Thorp and Buck Goldstein, *Engines of Innovation* (Chapel Hill: University of North Carolina Press, 2010).

26. Ibid., 2–3.

27. Ibid.

28. Ibid., 6.

29. Ibid., 13.
30. Miller and Harris, "Scholarly Journal Publication," 82.
31. Ibid.
32. Diane Harley, Sophia Krzys Acord, Sarah Earl-Novell, Shannon Lawrence, and C. Judson King, *Final Report: Assessing the Future Landscapes of Scholarly Communication: an Exploration of Faculty Values and Needs in Seven Disciplines* (Berkeley, CA: Center for Studies in Higher Education, 2010): iii.
33. Ibid.
34. Ibid., v.
35. Patrick Behar, Laurent Colombani, Sophie Krishhnan, and Bain & Company, *Publishing in the Digital Era* (Boston: Bain & Company, 2010): 2.
36. Ibid., 8.
37. Ibid., 11.
38. Robert Schroeder and Gretta E. Siegel, "A Cooperative Publishing Model for Sustainable Scholarship," *Journal of Scholarly Publishing* 37, no. 2 (January 2006): 90.
39. Ibid., 95.
40. Association of American Universities, *Report of the Interdisciplinarity Task Force.*

Managing the Interdisciplinary Information Universe: Artisan Activities in a Machine Environment

Ann Copeland

Introduction

The language of interdisciplinary studies is vital and active, involving collaboration, problem solving, interactions, creativity, integration, diversity, reform, emerging fields. All these terms reference a dynamic landscape of academic alliances in pursuit of new areas of knowledge across disciplinary divides. Researchers currently engaged in interdisciplinary studies also have extensive digital resources to draw on—datasets, digitized heritage (memory) collections, e-books—and increasingly can take advantage of new modes of scholarly communication in which to "publish" their research in innovative ways—hypertext, digital exhibitions, metasites, blogs, and born-digital texts within institutional repositories. Against this dynamic background, academic librarians are engaged in an old and enduring problem: how to manage, control, and organize knowledge so that it is accessible and available to those who are looking for it. The challenges wrought by newly created interdisciplinary studies are part of a very long continuum, but one with new stripes.

The interdisciplinary landscape for technical services staff, in particular, is creating new challenges. Newly emerging cutting edge areas are often difficult to classify within a discipline-based system. Charged with locating, acquiring, cataloging, and preserving resources, these librarians must now be concerned with the next tier of research materials to be mined. Traditionally considered to be marginal, ephemera, grey literature, uncataloged "hidden collections," artifacts, and media are now very important. Collecting, preserving, and promoting such resources for untold future areas of interdisciplinary research will not be easy, especially with ephemeral Web documents like blogs and tweets. These challenges, and the extent to which librarians are at work to expose our collections to the wider interdisciplinary research community, are the subjects of this chapter.

Bibliographic Control

Bibliographic control has come a long way since the Library of Congress began producing cataloging cards in 1902 for others to purchase. While cataloging has become an increasingly shared activity by libraries throughout the world, which share records through a single bibliographic database (OCLC WorldCat), the "dramatic transformation of the field of librarianship brought about by digital technologies," caused the Library of Congress to commission a report in 2007, which forecast even greater changes to come: "The future of bibliographic control will be collaborative, decentralized, international in scope and Web-based…. Data will be gathered from multiple sources; change will happen quickly; and bibliographic control will be dynamic, not static."[1]

The report hit the cataloging community very hard, particularly its declaration that cataloging can no longer be an "artisan activity." Our current "information universe" consists of data of all kinds relating to a resource from within or without—citation links, publisher's metadata, user-contributed data, rankings and reviews, circulation and sales figures. For the Library of Congress, these valuable bits of information are all relevant in the universe of bibliographic control.[2]

While systems are currently being made to generate and gather these valuable bits of information, in cataloging shops today the artisan activities of creating authorized headings for names and entities and classifying and assigning subject headings still hold strong. When it comes to interdisciplinary works, even artisans are challenged. While the problem could stem from understanding on the part of the cataloger in the face of an emerging trans-, multi-, or interdisciplinary topic, more likely it is the fact of our current cataloging rules and apparatus. The notion that bibliographic control will be dynamic and come from many sources is good news for exposing the literature of interdisciplinarity.

Classification

The limitations of our current tools are well known. The Library of Congress Classification System, the de facto classification used by most academic libraries in this country, originated in 1897 when the library decided to develop a classification based on the one million books in its collections. Having laid out its schema in the early part of the twentieth century, it has a disciplinary grounding that is not versatile enough for today's increasingly interdisciplinary environment: "Since interdisciplinary topics were difficult to accommodate in this system, many arbitrary choices have been made over the years. Each schedule was developed separately, following its own internal logic … and it is difficult to generalize about the schedules as a whole."[3]

Some schedules, but not all, have a particular number for interdisciplinary aspects of a subject. Additions are made to the classification through an application process by members of the library community, who propose headings based on published literature in the field—what we call literary warrant. However, timeliness is an issue. For example, "Interdisciplinary Research—General and Science" is classified in Q180.55.I48. The heading was created in 1988 and updated in 1990, but it is clear from documentation that the term was being used internally by the Library of Congress as early as 1970. The lag in establishing the term unfortunately means that titles written *about* interdisciplinary research prior to 1988 most likely are not located in this number, nor would these records have this subject heading. "Interdisciplinary approach to knowledge," classified in BD255, is found under "Speculative philosophy—Methodology—Formalization of knowledge"; the subject heading and the classification number were established in 1986. In other parts of the schedule, "Interdisciplinary approach" is a "special aspect" of a discipline; for example, "Interdisciplinary approach in education" correlates to curriculum studies.

Timeliness is improving in large measure because of the online world in which we catalog now. Rather than requiring paper forms and photocopied evidence from publications to justify new terms, submission is much more facile; the growth of cooperative cataloging programs in the past decade has resulted in many more catalogers actively submitting proposals to authorize new subject headings and classification numbers. New terms and classifications can be posted in our online cataloging tools much more rapidly than waiting for the new printed editions of schedules to be published. And some retrospective machine corrections seem to be running.

Classifying interdisciplinary, multidisciplinary, or transdisciplinary works within their most obvious disciplinary homes echoes the arrangement of our physical library spaces where "subject libraries" force one to choose a "location" when that topic could very well be found in several places. Those seeking information on women's studies, area studies, cultural studies, visual studies, environmental studies, or American studies, for example, may be forced to go to many different areas to gather information on these topics. One historian acknowledged that she uses all Penn State's branch libraries (engineering, mathematics, geography, art, and architecture) in addition to the subject libraries, maps library, and special collections library for her work on the history of agriculture, landscape architecture, and gender as they develop in rural contexts.[4] A scholar speaking at a panel on "Area Studies, Globalization, and Research Libraries" noted, "Libraries have to be mindful of how a book is cataloged or classified; where the work resides very much influences how it gets found (or not) and used (or not). And scholars do browse … seriously."[5]

However, the notion that an interdisciplinary work is chiefly "about" something at all is problematic for some interdisciplinarians: "Some information scientists worry that language is too ambiguous to allow a universal classification: they argue that only within narrow groups of scholars can the words used to classify carry an agreed meaning."[6] Further, some researchers in the United Kingdom and Italy are chiefly interested in the theories and methods of investigation employed to consider phenomena across disciplinary lines. The lack of a notation to signify methods and theories and the problem of the disciplinary classification in itself are a particular burden for them. They argue "that information science can best serve the needs of interdisciplinary scholarship (which is of increasing importance) by developing universal classifications of the phenomena studied by scholars and the theories and methods applied by scholars. Present systems of document classification are grounded in disciplinary terminology and thus serve interdisciplinary scholarship poorly."[7]

Their "manifesto" does speak to the variety of methods and orientations in an interdisciplinary field like science and technology studies, where various and differing perspectives and methods have been noted:

Much as independent nation states have trouble marrying their divergent interests and political cultures into agreements on common problems, so the traditional disciplines encounter frictions in their efforts to focus on phenomena—from climate change to the roiling of global financial markets—that seems to demand investigation from multiple perspectives. How should number-crunchers speak to qualitative analysts, or critical theorists engage with advocates of game theory and rational choice? How should inductive, evidence-based, and practice-oriented scholarship find common ground with principled approaches that draw authority from historical texts and frameworks that seem to have little bearing on the issues of the present?[8]

Subject Headings

Criticisms relating to currency have also been leveled at our standard list of subject headings in academic libraries, the *Library of Congress Subject Headings* (LCSH). The Library of Congress itself has said that LCSH are "often out of synch with common terminology," and that the terms and their associated related (narrower, broader) terms are often not intuitive. While the Library of Congress does update terms to more current language, change requests are not always acted on because of the impact that would have on previously cataloged materials.[9]

For interdisciplinary works, this becomes very problematic. In addition to terms not being intuitive or current, catalogers have rules about the number of headings (ideally one, and generally no more than three) and are discouraged from adding a heading for a topic that occupies less than 20 percent of a book. This means that single chapters within works may not be well represented by the subject headings assigned to a book and that relationships between disciplines may not adequately be brought out.

By example, a recent book, *Poultry Science, Chicken Culture: A Partial Alphabet* by women's studies and English literature professor Susan Merrill Squier, is "A manifesto for agricultural studies … in conversation with the fields of science studies, environmental studies, and animal studies."[10] In the introduction, Squier comments on the transdiciplinarity nature of the work:

With this study of chickens, and agriculture more broadly, I return to two themes from my earlier work on biomedicine: my interest in the ways that human biomedicine has used other species as what I call research reservoirs and my commitment to a transdisciplinary mode of inquiry.... Once again I explore the social and scientific effects of the mining of female life—now both human and avian, in the agricultural as well as the medical sciences—for intellectual lore and economic ore. And I work at and between the boundaries of the disciplines because I am convinced that the resulting strategic marginality affords me perspectives unavailable to those wearing strictly disciplinary lenses.[11]

For the many chapters within Squier's "abcedarium," "an alphabetical series of ten case studies ... from augury, biology, and culture through disability, epidemic, and fellow-feeling to gender, hybridity and inauguration,"[12] the Library of Congress provides the appropriate, if general, subject headings:

Chickens.
Chickens—Social aspects.
Animal culture—Moral and ethical aspects.

While we could not expect subject headings to adequately represent the nuanced subjects Squier explores, there should be more of an attempt to reflect the relationships between humanities and social sciences, literature and science, that obviously informs and even drives her work: "I imagined this book as a primer about poultry, but I soon came to think of it as a primer in interdisciplinarity as well."[13]

In this age of interdisciplinarity, catalogers will need to be much more alert to the published literature and to actively petition for new subject headings. LC is not unresponsive, as can be seen, for example, with the subject heading "Visual analytics." The term was established in 2007 and based on warrant from the same year. The justification in the authority record includes this statement:

Visual analytics is the science of analytical reasoning supported by interactive visual interfaces. Visual analytics ... requires interdisciplinary science beyond traditional scientific and information visualization. The field embraces statistics, mathematics, knowledge representation, management and discovery technologies, cognitive and perceptual sciences, decision sciences, and more.[14]

For years, catalogers have been creating subject strings that combine multiple facets or aspects of a subject into searches of the type:

England—Civilization—17th century—Sources

Woolf, Virginia, 1882-1941—Homes and haunts—England—London.

Topical subjects are further divided by subtopics, places, chronological periods, and form or genre terms (what an item *IS*). These strings are "pre-coordinated" headings that have been constructed by the cataloger according to rules within the four-volume *(SHM) Subject Headings Manual*.[15] As there are no general rules for combining terms, but rather a dense enumeration of rules, they have been variously applied over the years. Over the past decade, there has been a strong move to uncouple these strings to allow our systems to support "post-coordinated searching" in which disconnected facets of a subject are combined together in a search by the user, rather than predetermined by catalogers.

With the growth of electronic resources, there is great need for an automated subject access method for Web resources. A research project called FAST (Faceted Application of Subject Terminology) is splitting out LCSH vocabulary into Dublin Core metadata elements for simplicity and interoperability.[16] The breakthrough here is the recognition that LCSH terms may be combined with facets from other standards and lists. Such combining may be of great assistance with interdisciplinary topics. In one case study, for the interdisciplinary field of women's studies, Kayo Denda used an "ontology," or broad subject domain, constructed from terms in course descriptions and syllabi and relevant LCSH searches and appropriate keywords, for retrieval of relevant resources.[17]

Specialized subject vocabularies provide authoritative terms uniquely related to a particular field. They facilitate indexing, catego-

rization, and retrieval of information. Having these vocabularies on
the Web has allowed the exchange of information between specific
communities across the globe. Vocabularies need to be available for
reuse by systems in order to facilitate exchange and sharing. LC predicts that in the future, "vocabularies will be managed in registries
or other structures to facilitate more rapid updates than are possible
with centrally managed lists. Knowledge organization systems will
facilitate multilingual versions of vocabularies and cross-walking between them."[18] All of this relies on standards and authorized headings, which is thankfully acknowledged by all parties; OCLC and the
Library of Congress are embracing many new international authority
files in support of a Virtual International Authority File (VIAF).[19]

Knowledge Organization Systems

How this will all happen is the work of knowledge organization, itself a highly interdisciplinary field concerned with the structure of
knowledge and how it is organized for retrieval. In this pursuit, in-
dexers, philosophers, catalogers, and artificial intelligence specialists
have looked to classification, particularly faceted classification, and
retrieval theory. The knowledge organization system (KOS), considered a supplementary tool that helps the reader to find his way around
the text, has evolved:

> What is now grandly known as "knowledge organisation" has a
> long history. The simplest forms of a knowledge organisation system
> (KOS) are, after all, the contents list and the index of a textbook.
> The knowledge is in the text; the KOS is a supplementary tool that
> helps the reader to find his way around the text. But as such finding
> aids have become more complex, and taken on wider functions, they
> have acquired grander names, such as retrieval languages, taxono-
> mies, categorisations, lexicons, thesauri, or ontologies. They are now
> seen as schemes that organize, manage, and retrieve information.[20]

Indeed, much of the KOS literature is concerned with conceptual
content mapping to facilitate search and display. While interoperability
at the encoding level exists through XML, the complex semantic relationships between "concept schemes" (thesauri and controlled vocabu-

laries) are still being worked out. The Simple Knowledge Organization System (SKOS) provides a model for expressing the structure of "concept schemes" and allowing them to be merged with other data and published on the Web. On one level these systems are about identifying, labeling, and documenting concepts, and on another level these systems are concerned with mapping conceptual resources to conceptual resources in other schemes. For those who work between communities or between or across disciplines, these conceptual maps will be essential:

> Discipline based indexing vocabularies and classification schemes tend to be inadequate for subject access to interdisciplinary intellectual content, and mapping semantic relationships remains a major research challenge. These problems greatly complicate ... how information is cataloged or encoded with metadata for retrieval, and the organization of information services for interdisciplinary research communities.[21]

Fundamental changes are being implemented to bring cataloging into a new linked data environment, which may ultimately help with these some of these problems. The new cataloging standard, *Resource Description & Access* (RDA), has been written to update the *Anglo-American Cataloging Code* (AACR2). RDA addresses all resources, digital and analog, and provides for records that will be suitable for many environments, such as the Internet and Web OPACs. In addition, catalogers will be moving away from thinking of bibliographic records in a closed structure, one that for the last forty years has been delivered through an encoded machine readable communication standard (MARC 21). The Library of Congress announced the Bibliographic Framework Transition Initiative in May 2011 to explore new means of delivering records in the digital environment.[22] A desire to integrate metadata provided by nonlibrarians—such as vendors—with traditional bibliographic information is driving the need for a new "carrier" for the records created using RDA.

Communities and Tags

In a recent article, "Progressing toward Bibliography; or: Organic Growth in the Bibliographic Record," Ascher suggests that we might add information to cataloging records over time, highlighting various features of a resource as new areas of study arise.[23] In creating fuller descriptions, Ascher also suggests using Web 2.0 tools such as tagging, user reviews, comments, and so on, but cautions that there is a great deal of work that needs to be done before these tools can be integrated into library workflows. While user contributions would need to be reviewed before being posted in library's online catalog, changes in the next generation of library catalogs are already being driven by Web 2.0 technologies. Tables of contents, reviews, and citations are being supplied by vendors to display within the bibliographic record. These greatly expand our access to information though keyword searching and evaluation. While it may be too early to tell if these additions add value for interdisciplinary research, stretching the boundaries of the traditional record surely is moving in the right direction.

Websites that employ crowdsourcing—inviting the community to contribute information through an open call—are growing in number. The Library of Congress, among others, has posted images and invited others to fill in missing genealogical and historical information.[24] Visual arts collections have invited viewers to contribute "tags" to describe design features, or aspects of what a picture is "about," supplementing what we already know about the medium, artist, and date of a given work.[25] Similarly, interdisciplinary communities can contribute reviews, bibliography, syllabi, and so forth to wikis such as the one for science and technology studies (STS); with over forty institutions in the United States alone offering degrees in STS, there is no doubt a plethora of content to be shared.[26]

Hidden Collections, Ephemera, and Primary Sources

The challenge of providing access to uncataloged or unprocessed rare materials in libraries throughout the country has been a primary focus of the Association of Research Libraries (ARL) for the better part of the last decade.[27] The Library of Congress acknowledged the problem in its 2007 report as well, emphasizing backlogs of nontextual formats such as photographs, films, videos, and sound recordings; a key recommendation was to make the discovery of special collections materials a priority.[28]

Many interdisciplinary researchers are utilizing primary sources, and libraries can truly make a difference by bringing these materials to light. For example, Penn State geography professor Deryck Holdsworth, a historical geographer, routinely uses archival and field evidence, combined with mapping, to trace long-term transformations of regions and places. A recent article that he co-authored in the interdisciplinary journal *Social Science Computer Review* (*SSCR*), "Historical GIS and Visualization: Insights From Three Hotel Guest Registers in Central Pennsylvania, 1888–1897," describes using information from historic hotel guest registers from three small places in Central Pennsylvania in the nineteenth century to map and analyze visitation patterns, using GIS and Hotelviz, an integrated software for visual data analysis.[29] In the area of women's studies, photographs, television series, and art objects are being collected by Harvard's Schlesinger Library to document popular culture and the feminist response; film is a "vast resource of interdisciplinary richness that can serve as cultural artifact, social representation, and industry history" for African American women's history.[30]

There is a growing interest in ephemera—everyday items produced for a limited use and not expected to last—for the tremendous research value they provide in many areas. Symposia, conferences, and digital projects have focused attention on these items for the information that can be gleaned from what has miraculously survived. For example, ephemera such as advertising trade cards from the eighteenth and nineteenth centuries reveal much about consumerism, prices, industries, and the values of a particular culture. The crime broadsides called "Last Dying Speeches" or "Bloody Murders" that were sold to the crowds gathering to watch public executions in eighteenth- and nineteenth-century Britain include accounts of executions for crimes such as counterfeiting, murder, treason, and horse stealing.[31] Theatre bills trace the provincial stage and provide evidence of popular taste.[32]

A recent conference at the Cotsen Children's Library, Princeton University, featured many interdisciplinary topics, all drawn from the study of ephemera. All described what historical juvenile ephemera can tell us about children's experiences from the eighteenth century to today. Speakers discussed aspects of childhood in Great Britain and the United States

> from the perspectives of book history, gender studies, and the histories of science, religion, political movements, education, and literature. Subjects of presentations will include paper dolls, writing sheets, cook books for Jewish children, ephemera produced by the Puffin Club and Girl Guides, paperback covers, poetry and manuscripts by children, the figure of Moses, grammar games, and Peter Parley's scientific miscellanies.[33]

One of the most interesting talks concerned a collection of 1,200 baby record books dating back to 1872 collected by the UCLA Library Special Collections' History & Special Collections for the Sciences division, located in the Biomedical Library:

> These are memory books in which parents record a child's activities and developmental milestones, and which provide a place to gather photographs, locks of hair, greeting cards, quarantine certificates, postcards, school records, and other ephemeral mementos. Many books track individualized medical information—from height and weight to experiences with various childhood diseases; some also provide infant health care advice for raising a healthy, well-nourished child. Although the collection development strategy focuses on infant development, health and illness, the books and their handwritten and pasted-in contents have been used for both cross-sectional and longitudinal research in sociology, material culture, linguistics, architecture, advertising, and other topics and disciplines.[34]

Digitizing these primary resource materials and thematic collections is greatly facilitating research for scholars who can obtain access to materials without having to travel to collections. Whether in thematic sites like "Reading: Harvard Views of Readers, Readership, and Reading History," which describes itself as "an online exploration of the intellectual, cultural, and political history of reading as reflected in the historical holdings of the Harvard Libraries,"[35] or contextualized exhibitions, or in unmediated presentations, these digital collections offer an eclecticism that invites interdisciplinary connections.

Grey Literature

Also problematic are government documents, conference proceedings, and source materials that are not controlled by commercial publishers and not obtained in usual ways. One interdisciplinary researcher at Penn State who searches for reports on architectural and landscape survey work done either by government employees (National Park Service, etc.) or cultural resource management firms refers to these resources as "under the radar."[36] Commonly known as grey literature, its importance for research has been well documented in the literature.[37] Compounding the problem of obtaining, acquiring, and preserving this kind of material is the predominance of born-digital material and the ease with which content may be posted to and published on the Web. Grey literature now also includes electronic theses and dissertations, blogs, surveys, and electronic reports by research institutes, and governmental and nongovernmental bodies.

While the problem of acquiring and integrating grey literature into our collections has been discussed for decades, the fact that these materials are in digital forms now as well as print presents even greater obstacles to collecting, processing, preserving, and making them accessible.[38] Sustainability issues are very real. In addition to URL loss, as more informal ways of posting information replace more formal methods of communicating, archiving will have to be a programmatic effort. For instance, one place that curators and librarians announce new acquisitions or exhibitions is through blogs.[39] Will these postings be preserved, or will the record of such events be lost?

Further, university publications may be closed to discovery if they are submitted exclusively to institutional repositories. The growth of institutional programs, bodies, centers, and conferences in interdisciplinary studies promises plentiful reports and working papers in the future. There are over 500 authorized headings in the Library of Congress Authority file with *Interdisciplinary* in their names, such as Conference on Non-Traditional and Interdisciplinary Programs; Yale University's Interdisciplinary Center for Bioethics; Dickinson College, Clarke Center for the Interdisciplinary Study of Contemporary

Issues, to name just a few. While not all these bodies will publish literature, many will; librarians will be challenged to keep up with cataloging and supplying metadata to allow those in institutional repositories to be discoverable.

Conclusion

Librarians for some time to come will need to continue to perform the artisan activities of cataloging, classifying, and creating authorized headings to expose resources supporting interdisciplinary work. We will need to work with LCSH in combination with thesauri from other communities and rely on knowledge organization systems of the future to cross-walk between them. While acknowledging the value of Web-based search engines and keyword searching, we need to be ardent defenders of controlled vocabularies, both to ensure access to works in languages other than English, and because "machine-searching techniques rely on the existence of authoritative headings even if they do not explicitly display them."[40]

Librarians will also need to be cognizant of new modes of scholarly communication on campus, the potential for born-digital resources to be hidden within our institutional repositories, and the threat of URL loss. Catalogers who petition the Library of Congress for new subject headings could actively play a part in improving access to new interdisciplinary areas; communication with faculty who are publishing in these areas will help this effort. Librarians should continue to monitor Web 2.0 technologies to see how they might be employed to bring out interdisciplinary topics, as "Ultimately, interdisciplinarity requires collaboration among individuals, artifacts, and cultures that have traditionally been separated by institutional structure."[41]

Notes

1.   Library of Congress Working Group on the Future of Bibliographic Control, *Report on the Future of Bibliographic Control: Draft for Public Comment* (Washington, DC: Library of Congress, Nov. 30, 2007), 1, http://www.loc.gov/bibliographic-future/news/lcwg-report-draft-11-30-07-final.pdf.
2.   Ibid., 7.
3.   "Historical Notes: The Library of Congress Classification," in *CSM: Classification and Shelflisting Manual*, (Washington, DC: Cataloging Distribution Service, Library of Congress, 2008), viewed in Cataloger's Desktop, Library of Congress website, http://www.loc.gov/cds/desktop.
4.   "Department Faculty: Sally McMurry, Professor of American History," Penn

State Department of History and Religious Studies Program website, http://history.psu.edu/faculty/mcmurrySally.php (accessed March 11, 2011).

5. Christopher Bush, "The Lost Samurai: Researching Across and Between" (panel presentation, ALA Annual Conference, Chicago, July 9–15, 2009), as quoted in "ACRL in Chicago: ACRL Programs at the ALA Annual Conference," *College and Research Libraries News* 70, no. 8 (Sept. 2009): 449.

6. Richard Szostak, "Transcending Discipline-Based Library Classifications," in *The Oxford Handbook of Interdisciplinarity*, ed. Robert Frodeman, Julie Thompson Klein, and Carl Mitcham (New York: Oxford University Press, 2010), 180.

7. Rick Szostak, "Interdisciplinarity and the Classification of Scholarly Documents by Phenomena, Theories, and Methods," in *La interdisciplinariedad y la transdisciplinariedad en la organización del conocimiento científico* [Interdisciplinarity and transdisciplinarity in the organization of scientific knowledge], proceedings of the VIII Congreso ISKO-España, León, Spain, April 18–20, 2007, ed. Rodríguez Bravo Blanca and Alvite Díez M.a Luisa (León, Spain: Universidad de León, Secretariado de Publicaciones, 2007), 471, as quoted in "The León Manifesto," International Society for Knowledge Organization website, http://www.iskoi.org/ilc/leon.htm (accessed March 11, 2011—page now discontinued). The work discussed on the webpage includes the faceted notation proposed to trace the methods and theories used to study phenomena across the disciplines, such as observational method or statistical analysis (expressed as theories X, Y or of the type Z). http://www.iskoi.org/ilc/leon.php#proceedings. Viewed Feb. 28, 2012

8. Shiela Jasanoff, "A Field of Its Own: The Emergence of Science and Technology Studies," in *The Oxford Handbook of Interdisciplinarity*, ed. Robert Frodeman, Julie Thompson Klein, and Carl Mitcham (New York: Oxford University Press, 2010), p. 204.

9. Library of Congress Working Group, *Report on the Future of Bibliographic Control*, 30.

10. Susan Merrill Squier, *Poultry Science, Chicken Culture: A Partial Alphabet* (Piscataway, NJ: Rutgers University Press, 2011), 6.

11. Squier, *Poultry Science*, 6–7.

12. Squier, *Poultry Science*, 6.

13. Squier, *Poultry Science*, 13–14.

14. Library of Congress Authorities, s. v. "Visual analytics," OCLC, http://authorities.loc.gov/cgi-bin/Pwebrecon.cgi?AuthRecID=7208211&v1=1&HC=2&SEQ=20120228091551&PID=IX7FlzGt2SFluG3RgcP8jOT-Sn4oY (accessed March 8, 2011).

15. Library of Congress Cataloging Directorate, *Subject Headings Manual*, 4 vols. (Washington, DC: Cataloging Distribution Service, Library of Congress, 2008).

16. See, for example, Rebecca J. Dean, "FAST: Development of Simplified Headings for Metadata," *Journal of Internet Cataloging* 4, no. 1/2 (2001): 35–47.

17. Kayo Denda, "Beyond Subject Headings: A Structured Information Retrieval Tool for Interdisciplinary Fields," *Library Resources & Technical Services* 49, no. 4 (October 2005): 266–275.

18. Library of Congress Working Group, *Report on the Future of Bibliographic Control*, 22.

19. "VIAF, implemented and hosted by OCLC, is joint project of several national libraries plus selected regional and trans-national library agencies. The project's goal is to lower the cost and increase the utility of library authority files by

matching and linking widely-used authority files and making that information available on the Web" (from "VIAF: The Virtual International Authority File," VIAF website, http://viaf.org, accessed March 8, 2011).

20. Brian Vickery, "A Note on Knowledge Organisation," Informations-viden-skabelige Akademi website, http://www.iva.dk/bh/lifeboat_ko/concepts/Vickery_a_note_on_knowledge_organisation.htm (accessed March 11, 2011).

21. Carole Palmer, "Information Research on Interdisciplinarity," in *The Oxford Handbook of Interdisciplinarity*, ed. Robert Frodeman, Julie Thompson Klein, and Carl Mitcham (New York: Oxford University Press, 2010), 175.

22. Library of Congress, "Bibliographic Framework Transition Initiative," http://www.loc.gov/marc/transition (accessed July 8, 2011).

23. James P. Ascher, "Progressing toward Bibliography; or: Organic Growth in the Bibliographic Record," *RBM* 10, no. 2 (Fall 2009): 95–110.

24. See, for instance, the Library of Congress's Flickr site: "We invite your tags and comments! Also, more identification information. (The current titles come from the agency's original documentation, which was sometimes incomplete)" (from "1930s–40s in Color," Historic Photos (Library of Congress Flickr Pilot Project," http://www.flickr.com/photos/library_of_congress/sets/72157603671370361, accessed July 11, 2011); another example is "Memorial Services for John F. Kennedy," Seeds of Change: The Daily Reflector Image Collection, East Carolina University Digital Collections, http://digital.lib.ecu.edu/reflector/3708 (accessed July 11, 2011).

25. "VADS: the online resource for visual arts," http://vads.bath.ac.uk/ has invited the public to tag their images. For instance, a Walter Crane wallpaper image of two swans looking at each other has the subjects "wall coverings, wallpapers, designs"in the catalog record; viewers added the tags: "wings, flap, craft, symmetry, reflection, bird" for cross-collection searching by those terms (Walter Crane, "Swan, Rush and Iris," http://www.vads.ucreative.ac.uk/flarge.php?uid=53720, accessed Mar. 8, 2011—tags no longer viewable). Another project, Steve: The Museum Social Tagging Project, "grew out of a desire to solve the problem of the 'semantic gap' that separated museums' formal descriptions of works—usually created by art historians or other specialists—and the vernacular language used by the general public for searching," (IMLS Final Report for "Researching Social Tagging and Folksonomy in the Art Museum." Submitted by the Indianapolis Museum of Art and Robert Stein in fulfillment of requirements for the steve Project's National Leadership Grant, March, 2009, linked from http://www.steve.museum/?page_id=24#Research-Proposals-Reports-and-Documentation, accessed February 28, 2012).

26. STS Wiki, accessed July 8, 2011, www.stswiki.org.

27. Association of Research Libraries, "Exposing Hidden Collections: 2003 Conference Summary," http://www.arl.org/rtl/speccoll/EHC_conference_summary.shtml (accessed March 11, 2011).

28. Library of Congress Working Group, *Report on the Future of Bibliographic Control*, 19.

29. David A. Fyfe, Deryck W. Holdsworth, and Chris Weaver, "Historical GIS and Visualization: Insights from Three Hotel Guest Registers in Central Pennsylvania, 1888–1897," *Social Science Computer Review* 27, no. 3 (August 2009): 348–62.

30. "ACRL in Chicago: ACRL Programs at the ALA Annual Conference," *College and Research Libraries News* 70, no. 8 (Sept. 2009): 450.

31. Harvard Law School Library, "Dying Speeches and Bloody Murders: Crime Broadsides Collected by the Harvard Law School Library," Harvard Digital Collection, http://broadsides.law.harvard.edu (accessed March 11, 2011).

32. University of Oxford Bodleian Library, "John Johnson Collection of Printed Ephemera," http://www.bodley.ox.ac.uk/johnson (accessed March 11, 2011).

33. Russell Johnson, "Durable Trifles," website for Enduring Trifles: Writing the History of Childhood with Ephemera, a conference at the Cotsen Children's Library, Princeton University, February 17–19, 2011, http://www.princeton.edu/cotsen/research-collection/academic-conferences/ephemera/johnson/index.xml (accessed March 11, 2011).

34. Ibid.

35. Harvard University Library Open Collections Program, "Reading: Harvard Views of Reading, Readership, and Reading History," http://ocp.hul.harvard.edu/reading (accessed March 11, 2011).

36. Sally McMurray (professor of American History at Penn State), e-mail message to the author, March 11, 2011.

37. Todd A. Chavez, "Grey Literature in Karst Research: The Evolution of the Karst Information Portal," in *Grey Literature in Library and Information Studies,* ed. Dominic J. Farace Joachim Schopfel (Berlin: DeGruyter, 2010): 181–197.

38. Gretta E. Siegel, "Institutional Grey Literature in the University Environment," in *Grey Literature in Library and Information Studies,* ed. Dominic J. Farace Joachim Schopfel (Berlin: DeGruyter, 2010): 69–84.

39. See, for example, the *Houghton Library Blog,* http://blogs.law.harvard.edu/houghton.

40. Library of Congress Working Group, *Report on the Future of Bibliographic Control,* 16.

41. Karri A. Holley, *Understanding Interdisciplinary Challenges and Opportunities in Higher Education* (San Francisco: Wiley, 2009), 29.

Collection Development: Acquiring Content Across and Beyond Disciplines

Gretchen E. Reynolds, Cynthia Holt, and John C. Walsh

Introduction

In considering the question of interdisciplinarity in the academy and its effect on university libraries' collection development approaches, practices, and policies, the authors began with a thorough review of the existing literature. During this process it became clear that current perspective from throughout the academic library community would necessarily be a vital component of our examination. This resulted in preparation and broad distribution of a survey. Similarly, the authors felt that for a case study, it would be invaluable to gather in-depth feedback from a cohesive group of liaison librarian selectors with experience in addressing interdisciplinarity in the academy at their home institution's library.

Development of Interdisciplinarity in the Academy

The first major work in the field of interdisciplinary research and education was published in 1972 by the OECD, based on the first international seminar in interdisciplinarity in 1970 and the first international survey of interdisciplinary research and education.[1] *Interdisciplinarity: Problems of Teaching and Research in Universities* defined *interdisciplinarity* as "the interaction between two or more different disciplines" which may reveal itself in a range of interactions from "simple communication of ideas to the mutual integration of organising concepts, methodology, procedures, epistemology, terminology, data."[2] The concept of interdisciplinarity is not a new one, as the ideas of integration and synthesis of knowledge have roots in ancient Greece; however, the interdisciplinary movement in United States academe has its roots around the time of World War I.[3]

Dogan and Pahre refer to the concept of hybridization when discussing interdisciplinarity, considering it a more appropriate term to describe the state where the knowledge of two or more disciplines has been crossed.[4] They define two types of hybrids: (1) the formal, institutionalized manifestations of disciplines crossing boundaries, such as cross-departmental programs, research centers, and area studies programs and (2) the informal hybrids that develop through interpersonal contact and discussion across the disciplines. In terms of academic library support, formal hybrids tend to be more adequately supported and represented in the collection development funding structure than informal hybrid areas.

In the library literature, the analysis of citations in a journal article or research paper has long been a tool used to illustrate the interdisciplinary nature of research.[5] Citation analysis has been shown to have some limitations for interdisciplinary analysis; therefore, interdisciplinarity has recently been illustrated through "clickstream" analysis, which is the analysis of detailed log data from a scholarly web portal (publishers, aggregators, and institutional consortia) that tracks the sequences of user requests that are issued by a variety of users across many different domains.[6]

Traditional Collection Development Models

In addition to understanding the available literature on collection development and interdisciplinary scholarship, it is also necessary to look at traditional collection development models through the lens of interdisciplinarity. The predominant model for dividing the collections budget in academic libraries is mirroring the institutional academic structure. Usually funding is by subject, with well-established disciplines historically receiving more consistent support from academic libraries than newer subjects and interdisciplinary fields of study.[7] This is traditionally accomplished either through allocation formulas[8] or is based on historical allocations,[9] the basis of which is often lost in the mists of time. Within departmental/subject allocations, budgets in academic libraries are frequently divided by format, such as serials, monographs, online resources, newspapers, and microforms. Generally, e-resources are either funded from a single central fund line, as a format within a subject allocation, or a hybrid model where the central fund line is used for resources of systemwide interest and the subject line is used for more narrowly focused resources. The subject funding structure can be rigid and often provides little flexibility for funding of new research areas as they arise. This can be especially true in economic downturns when library collection development budgets are static or decreasing. Unfortunately, this can result in gaps in interdisciplinary areas that the librarians have not identified as in scope for the department for which they collect.

There is limited published research on university library support for new programs. At the University of Illinois at Chicago, Lanier and Carpenter discuss dealing with new academic programs.[10] Sinha and Tucker focused on the library's response to rapid increase in new program and degree introduction at the University of Nevada, Las Vegas.[11] Recently, Austenfeld investigated the same concept at smaller academic libraries.[12] Both Sinha and Tucker and Austenfeld agree that involvement in the process of institutional new program development is essential for building a collection that supports the curricular and research needs of the institution.[13] Involvement in new program development can be helpful in addressing formal, institutionalized hybridization but does not address the informal hybridization.

According to Austenfeld, "The fundamental reason for the library to participate in the [new program] review process is that the budgeting practices of academic institutions tend to limit future expenditures in any particular area. If library funding for a dedicated collection expansion is not allotted as part of the original course or program approval process, it can be nearly impossible to obtain later."[14]

The Current State

Collection development models need to consciously incorporate methods for identifying and supporting areas of disciplinary intersection. Recently, the literature shows an emerging trend toward allocation of collection development budgets more holistically, with central funding for multidisciplinary electronic resources and serials, and broader discipline-based allocation for monograph selection, such as a shared fund for science and technology, for arts and humanities, and for social sciences.[15]

An interesting development in collection development is patron-driven acquisitions (PDA). In the PDA model, bibliographic records for a preselected pool of monographic content are loaded into the library catalog, reflecting either print or electronic monographs or both. As patrons encounter these items in the catalog and request a print monograph or access an electronic monograph via a predetermined trigger point, the item is acquired for the library's collection. Another example of patron-driven collection development is through monitoring of interlibrary loan requests. Requests meeting predetermined criteria are purchased automatically and added to the collection. In 2000, Purdue University Libraries implemented a "Books on Demand" service based on interlibrary loan requests submitted by patrons for recently published English-language scholarly books. Two years later, in analyzing the usage of the service, bibliographers were surprised to note that there were a "high number of books requested by scholars outside their subject fields. The librarians concluded that these cross-disciplinary requests were a significant enhancement to their collection development efforts."[16] In 2009, they revisited the service, and the data analysis corroborated the initial findings. The bibliographers also concluded that this model should not be the only approach, but rather one valuable tool among many in collection development. PDA can be a useful means of addressing the collections needs of informal hybridization at institutions.

The concept of "embedded librarianship" is discussed in the literature tangentially to collection development. The literature focuses almost exclusively on integrating librarians into the departments, classrooms, and research teams in the area of instruction, with the premise being that embedded librarianship will move the relationship of librarians with faculty beyond "just collection development."[17] This focus on instruction overshadows the opportunity to investigate whether embedding librarians into departments and research teams can actually enhance the ability of librarians to more fully understand the collection development needs of their customers, especially in addressing the interdisciplinary needs of informal hybrids. As subject-specific academic libraries are forced by economics to close and librarians are moved further from the faculty with whom they work, the concept of embedding takes on greater importance. Working closely with faculty as a full member of the research enterprise, whether that be in the department or as a member of a research center team, would allow librarians to become intimately aware of faculty research and the resources that they are using in support of their research, especially if librarians embed themselves as part of the grant-writing process. In addition, embedding through involvement in the administrative (e.g., department meetings, hiring process, and tenure review) and social (e.g., parties, departmental lectures, and departmental sports teams) aspects of the department or research team cannot be underestimated in enabling the development of the collegiate relationship between faculty and librarians. Greater connectivity with faculty leads to a more in-depth understanding of faculty, their relationships with other researchers (potentially outside of their defined subject area), and their specific research needs, especially any interdisciplinarity in their research. Greater understanding of the customer is the cornerstone of effective collection building.

Research on Two Fronts

After finding mixed results in their literature review, the authors gathered direct feedback from the academic library community on interdisciplinarity in research and its intersection with collection development. In addition to better understanding this topic as it pertains to the library community, the authors also wanted to understand how this occurs in their own university, George Mason University (Mason) and how the team-based liaison model currently in place at Mason is responding to interdisciplinary activity in the Mason research community. To accomplish these goals, the authors conducted a brief survey of the library community. Simultaneously, they also conducted a case study of liaison librarians at Mason. These liaisons are both the primary point of contact between the libraries and the research community and the primary selectors in Mason's collection development process.

External Community: The Survey

To gather information on how the greater library community is experiencing interdisciplinarity, the authors developed a brief survey to distribute to the greater academic library community. This survey was envisaged not as one with a statistically determined, valid sample population to gather comprehensive quantitative data. Rather, it was a qualitative call for feedback about the perceptions of the collection development–focused academic library community regarding interdisciplinarity at their institutions and how they are addressing it within their own collection development activities.

After a simple list of five questions was developed and human subjects review board approval was secured, the survey was posted on twenty library-related listservs, all of which had some genuine interest in collection development activities within academic libraries. The authors described the research project and survey questions and included a link to the online survey form. Within three weeks the team received responses from 158 individuals, with each of the individual questions garnering replies from between 74 and 92 respondents. The survey included the following questions:

1. Have you observed increasing interdisciplinarity in your university community or in your University Library? If so, how?
2. How is your library or institution responding to increased interdisciplinarity in academia?
3. What effect has interdisciplinarity had on your collection development practices and activities?
4. Is your library using a particular approach to respond to interdisciplinarity in general or in collection development? If so, please describe.
5. What is working well and what challenges do you still face in your collection development approach to increasing interdisciplinarity?

The overwhelming answer received from 92 respondents to question 1 was *Yes:* interdisciplinarity was either on the rise, had by now long been the case, or was in fact entrenched at their institutions. Though one or two respondents were of the mind that even asking this question was just a bit moot at this time in that this entrenchment has been de facto for at least a decade, most were of the opinion that it has been within the past several years that notions of interdisciplinarity have gained great prominence on their campuses. Although there was some discussion of interdisciplinarity as little more than the intersections between and among disciplines, with words such as *hybridization* being used more than once, most saw interdisciplinarity as staking out new territory. The manner in which campus and curricular interdisciplinarity manifests can range from the very structure of general education and "core" curricula as well as a focus on collaborative and interdisciplinarity student projects as seen at smaller institutions, to the ever-increasing establishment of research centers and institutes. Often cited are the facts that such institutes and centers are more favorably perceived and are at a competitive advantage for grants when interdisciplinarity plays a major role. In fact, one respondent described what may be perhaps one inevitable result of an overwhelming interest in interdisciplinarity: namely, creating a research center comprised of the most "expert" (it was not clear from the response what was meant by this term, e.g., best, most experienced, most collaborative, most successful at bringing in grants) faculty across essentially all (related?) disciplines within a very broad area (such as "Science"). Although the highest number of, as well as the more detailed, replies from respondents regarding interdisciplinarity focused on sciences and engineering, there was also quite a significant focus on the social sciences as well as the arts and humanities. It appears that academic librarians, particularly those involved with collection development, are acutely aware of the interdisciplinary "turn" within the academy that has firmly taken hold during the first decade of the twenty-first century.

Many of the 169 total respondents answering questions 2 and 3 interpreted these questions similarly or with overlap, resulting in an interesting and very significant grouping of answers centered around the larger notions of people, processes, and funding. In terms of staffing, a significant portion of respondents, over 10 percent, cited establishment of liaison/selecting librarian teams or other similar team-based staff adjustments, as Mason did. More than twice that number discussed the need for greater collaboration within the libraries among subject specialists as well as between subject specialists and academic faculty. Furthermore, while several respondents called for the enhancement of both librarian expertise and responsibility, nearly all of these were of the opinion that this was already being self-directed by our liaison/selecting librarians. In fact, two respondents believed that librarians are already the fulcrum for getting disparate faculty together in collaboration. Another key observation made by several respondents is the idea that collection development is becoming ever more collaborative and that no one can afford to do this work in isolation anymore. Lastly, in this broad area of response, there was significant discussion of the need for librarians to be at the table for discussions of curriculum planning and new program development as well as the concomitant resources to support such development. Many of the new directions in this domain are interdisciplinary. This last finding concurs with what the literature states.

In terms of processes, respondents were in general and strong agreement about the need to rework two tried-and-true "warhorses," namely methods of research materials budget allocation (read: formulas) and collection development policies. In terms of the latter, a few replies advocated for, or at least discussed, the reality of essentially ignoring collection development policies that have become outdated in many ways, but particularly so in their overriding focus upon disciplines. Many others focused, perhaps more positively, on the need for a complete overhaul of collection development policies recognizing the greatly increased interdisciplinarity within the academy today. It should be noted that in the case study, Mason liaison librarians reported that a recent project requiring liaisons to create subject-specific collection development policies and new collection development approval and notification plans helped liaisons to identify new programs in the university and allowed liaisons an opportunity to revisit the curriculum and requirements of existing programs. Through this process, liaisons identified an increase in collaboration across academic departments, as well as new courses, programs, and research activities in existing academic departments.

When discussing resource allocation, many respondents mentioned their own institution's practice of allocating our increasingly scarce collections dollars into fewer and much larger "pots." Alternatively, many respondents expressed a desire for their institution to move towards such a practice and also stated that the collaboration demanded of such an approach was a positive. An alternative approach, mentioned by many fewer respondents, is to create and allocate resources to an increasing array of very specialized funds, focusing on the loci of each individual disciplinary intersection. If academic libraries are to incorporate interdisciplinarity into collection development, they must start with restructuring library collection development budgets so that the structure of the budgets encourage collection development collaboration between librarians in areas where interdisciplinarity exists and is flexible enough to adjust when new areas of inquiry arise in the institution.

Interestingly, "big deal" journal packages fared surprisingly well in survey responses, in that they discourage the meticulous legacy practice of assigning every journal to a particular disciplinary fund. However, at least one respondent did discuss that proposition that it is often more difficult to get funding for expensive digital resources when the argument is essentially that they help out "everybody." (Perhaps there is a limit to how much interdisciplinarity is a good thing!) There was mention of institutional repositories as contributors to increasing interdisciplinarity awareness on campuses, as well as the notion that PDA often helps to increase librarians' and the library's awareness of the high level of interdisciplinarity among our users' work. This observation on PDA echoes the findings of the literature review.

In terms of any particular approaches libraries may be employing to solve the interdisciplinarity conundrum (question 4), the 74 respondents overwhelming mentioned collaboration along with communication as being the most important, and many in fact called again for formal collaboration through the formation of librarian teams or selection committees for costly digital resources and electronic journal packages. There was also further discussion on the need to reapproach our collection development policies, including the use of them as tools for understanding burgeoning interdisciplinarity within academia. One institution has gone so far as to establish a campuswide committee to examine the best way to seamlessly integrate interdisciplinarity into the curriculum across that institution's academic departments.

Finally, question 5 asked about successes and challenges in accommodating interdisciplinarity as librarians develop our college and university library collections. From the 75 respondents to this question, the following may be gleaned. Academic libraries are still relatively near the start of this interdisciplinary enterprise, although it has already become something of an established paradigm, for want of a better word. What is working very well already is the move to increased collaboration, enhanced communication, and implementation of team structures among our professional cadre of selectors and liaison librarians. During the past decade or more, the rise of library consortia and their prominent role in securing costly digital collections for their members has certainly enhanced the collaborative model at every turn. Most of the major challenges have to do with funding. Especially in these times of dwindling support, convincing the powers that be to fund interdisciplinary areas in addition to the long-standing disciplinary academic units is difficult. Furthermore, academic librarians are having just as much trouble in moving away from our legacy allocation (formula) legacy funding models in many cases. Metrics, particularly to measure, quantify, and "assign" use of interdisciplinary materials, are also new and difficult in this interdisciplinary environment. Lastly, it seems that many digital resource providers have taken the interdisciplinarity approach of providing ever more specialized niche products, rather than working with library and user communities to develop truly interdisciplinary resources of significance.

Internal Community: George Mason University Libraries—A Case Study

While the survey was underway within the greater library community, a case study was conducted among liaison librarians at George Mason University Libraries to ascertain how Mason librarians are experiencing interdisciplinarity and how well Mason's current team-based liaison model is working in an interdisciplinary research environment. George Mason University, located in the heart of Northern Virginia's technology corridor near Washington, DC, is an innovative, entrepreneurial institution with national distinction in a range of academic fields. Founded in 1972, the university has grown into a major educational force as a state institution. Mason is a distributed university with campuses in Fairfax, Arlington, and Prince William counties. Enrollment is 32,562, with 199 degree programs at the bachelor's (75), master's (87), doctoral (36), and professional (1) levels.

George Mason University is one of many with a liaison librarian program. At Mason, liaison librarians serve as the primary contact between the library and academic departments, interacting with both faculty and students, and are in a unique position to have knowledge of the research activities and information needs of the university community. Liaisons are responsible for specialized reference, instruction, and outreach in assigned academic departments and programs. Liaison librarians also serve as the primary selectors of research resources and are responsible for most aspects of collection development in their respective liaison areas.

As Mason's liaison librarian program expanded and the number of research programs increased, Mason Libraries recognized a need to restructure and realign its liaison librarian program to meet growing interdisciplinary research needs. In July of 2008, Mason Libraries restructured its liaison librarian program into broad discipline-oriented teams, now referred to as the team-based liaison model. Currently, twenty-one liaisons are grouped into teams for sciences and technology, arts and humanities, and social sciences. This team-based liaison model was implemented to help facilitate interdisciplinary efforts within the libraries, to better utilize liaison librarian expertise, and to facilitate collaboration, cooperation, and knowledge sharing among liaison librarians in related fields. This model is currently used primarily for collection development collaboration, but is intended to include other areas of the libraries' services.

The case study used a focus group as its primary instrument, which was entirely voluntary and facilitated by one of the authors, a fellow liaison librarian. Nine liaison librarians participated in the focus group, which included liaisons from all three liaison librarian teams and two of the three campuses. The first five questions in the focus group were essentially identical to those posed in the survey. The final questions concentrated on the team-based liaison model used at Mason and how well this model works for matters related to interdisciplinarity. The questions unique to the focus group are

- University Libraries restructured its liaison program into teams to help address the interdisciplinary trends in academia. In your opinion, how is this model working?
- Is the liaison team model an effective response to increasing interdisciplinarity?
- How does this approach work, specifically with collection development?
- What challenges do you still face in terms of collection development and interdisciplinarity?
- How would you like to see interdisciplinarity addressed at University Libraries, specifically related to collection development?

Mason liaison librarians reported that they were observing increasing interdisciplinarity within the university and within their subject liaison areas. As seen in the survey data, the university is developing new academic programs and courses that share faculty and are cross-listed between two or more academic departments. Liaison librarians also reported an increase in interdisciplinarity in subject areas that are not traditionally interdisciplinary. An example of this would be computer game design, which links computer science, engineering, and art.

Liaison librarians reported that the use of approval plans and notification plans helped to facilitate knowledge of a wider range of relevant resources, including new publications outside of their traditional collection development areas. The approval vendor's database helps liaisons to search for publications that did not, and would not, show up on their selection profiles and see what resources fall into the subject profile of other selectors. The liaison can see if another selector will be purchasing a book that may be of interest to faculty but is traditionally outside the subject area profile, in addition to recommending books to other liaisons that might fall outside their identified scope of collecting. In effect, the approval vendor's database facilitates both knowledge of new resources and collaboration among selectors.

Liaison librarians reported that, in general, it is challenging to keep up with changes in their assigned subject areas and departments, especially as those changes and developments involve a wider range of subject areas. Liaisons report that even with frequent communication with faculty and students in their fields, it can still be difficult to keep abreast of emerging trends and emerging research activities, especially changes in the curriculum of their programs which are increasingly interdisciplinary. As Mason's librarians do not sit on curriculum committees or faculty committees, they are generally not part of curriculum-related dialogue. Involvement in new program development at the earliest stages is crucial in addressing formal hybrids, or institutionalized interdisciplinarity.

Liaison librarians also reported that, even in the face of increasing interdisciplinarity and growing collaboration between academic departments, they continue to rely on professional communication to respond to interdisciplinary needs. On the academic department side, librarians depend on basic liaison librarian outreach skills, such as communication with faculty and students, knowledge of faculty and graduate student research interests, and participation in assigned department activities and events. Within the library, this means that liaison librarians rely on communication and collaboration with each other.

In an environment of scarce time and ever increasing responsibilities, liaison librarians make use of the team-based liaison model for discussions about changes in their subject areas, developments in the library, new publications, changes in databases and e-resources, and questions related to outreach and instruction. When discussing the team-based liaison model, each of the focus group participants reported that this model has been instrumental in increasing communication, collaboration, and mutual support among librarians, particularly in the area of collection development for e-resources, which are selected, prioritized, and recommended by the liaison teams. In this area, the team-based liaison model works quite well, with few exceptions.

The team-based liaison model also faces challenges in communication across teams. Currently, Mason liaison librarians are assigned to one liaison team. This means that liaison librarians who have programs that fall into different liaison team areas will work almost exclusively with one team and not be part of the collaborative efforts of another team. The individual teams feature very effective communication and collaboration benefits within the team. This is excellent for programs, projects, and ventures that feature interdisciplinarity within each team. However, the teams themselves tend to remain in distinct silos. One of the lessons learned at Mason is that several liaisons felt a need to "float" between two of the teams. When a project that requires significant collaboration across the teams arises, such as purchasing a collection of books for a new program, like real estate management, that combines the librarians from the sciences and technology and social sciences teams, the team-based liaison model presents a less viable method for accomplishing this work. Siloing of the teams also impedes the individual liaison's ability to utilize the collaborative strengths of the team-based liaison model to increase or enhance service to all of his or her academic programs.

Food for Thought

Both the survey and the case study yielded similar feedback. According to participants in both the case study and the survey, both universities and libraries are experiencing increasing interdisciplinarity. The results of both the survey and case study also tell us there is a sense that the traditional services and strengths of librarians are allowing academic libraries to successfully respond to the interdisciplinary research needs of faculty and university research centers.

First, communication between the university library and collegiate faculty and research communities is critical to effective and responsive interdisciplinary collection development. Many libraries excel in creating and building relationships that invite and advance this type of communication, whether through a team-based liaison model or an alternative model. The survey and the case study confirmed that a librarian's relationship and communication with faculty allows him or her better to anticipate research needs and select relevant materials for the library collection.

Second, the authors heard that technology facilitates interdisciplinarity for both librarians and for faculty. With access to a wider variety of materials through databases and other e-resources, faculty are able locate, use, and request materials beyond the traditional boundaries of their established disciplines. Conversely, librarians are able to monitor, review, and select from a wider range of materials through approval plans, notification plans, and searchable tools such as approval vendor databases. While tools such as these certainly enhance and facilitate responsive collection development, the process continues to rely upon the library's knowledge of faculty research interests and communication between the library and the research community.

While these traditional services and strengths of academic libraries are certainly the foundation of building and maintaining a collection that is effective in an environment of increasing interdisciplinarity, there is certainly ample space for growth and further refinement of library services to better meet the research needs of interdisciplinary scholarship. Perhaps it is worthy of consideration that academic libraries can expand upon patron-driven acquisitions, embedded librarianship, more holistic and flexible allocations of the collections budget, and efforts to strengthen the presence of the library within the academy, particularly in the budgeting enterprise.

The literature and experience show that PDA has promise as a valuable collection development tool. While not intended as a predominant selection method, PDA could aid academic libraries in better understanding the information needs of faculty engaged in interdisciplinary research, and especially the needs of disciplines that are moving in an increasingly interdisciplinary direction. By capturing knowledge of gaps in the collection illuminated by patron requests, mitigating those gaps through PDA, and then funneling that information back into the hands of liaison librarians and selectors, academic libraries could strengthen library collections while also developing an understanding of interdisciplinary information needs in research communities.

Currently, embedded librarianship is focused primarily on instruction and outreach. Academic libraries must raise the question of whether the successful practice of embedded librarianship can be further developed to apply to collection development. Since embedded librarianship offers a rich and multidimensional relationship between the libraries and academic communities, perhaps it is possible to take advantage of this relationship and expand upon it to include collection development activities. This might mean giving faculty a more direct opportunity to influence the purchasing decisions of selectors. Perhaps it would mean developing new models of greater participation in collection development and selection activities.

The structure of the library collections budget is one area that libraries can consider in their mission to develop collections reflective of our interdisciplinary research communities. The survey revealed that within the academic library community there is an interest in moving away from narrowly defined spending allocations towards broad discipline-oriented funds. Instead of managing a fund for each program, research center, and scholarly community on campus, the library would instead have an option within the budget structure to purchase some materials through a general fund for the social sciences, for example. The authors also advocate for movement towards this approach of a more flexible allocation structure.

In the area of structural enhancements, it is crucial that academic libraries have representation in the formal discussions and communication structure regarding the creation of new programs and departments, new research centers, and new research and curricular initiatives. Even if budget allocations move towards a more general fund structure as outlined above, library representation in campus dialogue on the creation of new courses and research endeavors is critical for libraries to provide services and collections that anticipate the needs of researchers engaged in interdisciplinary scholarship. Without such representation, the library's work can only be reactive. Formal representation in the structure of these committees allows the library to be proactive, knowing in advance of new programs and research centers, and anticipating the library's ability to serve the research needs of those programs and centers.

In conclusion, it is evident that our academic libraries, and particularly our academic liaison librarians, have successfully brought to bear a host of our profession's traditional strengths in response to recent and ever-widening developments along the interdisciplinary front now sweeping across our academic institutions. Furthermore, academic library administrators and librarians believe that ever-increasing efforts, as well as wholly new approaches, will be demanded of us as interdisciplinarity continues to spread throughout the academy throughout the twenty-first century.

Notes

1. Liora Salter and Alison Hearn, *Outside the Lines: Issues in Interdisciplinary Research* (Montreal: McGill-Queen's University Press, 1996), 28, ebrary Academic Complete, http://site.ebrary.com/lib/georgemason/docDetail.action?docID=10141732 (accessed March 6, 2011).
2. Léo Apostel, Guy Berger, Asa Briggs, and Guy Michaud, eds., *Interdisciplinarity: Problems of Teaching and Research in Universities* (Washington, DC: Organisation for Economic Co-operation and Development [OECD] Center for Educational Research and Innovation [CERI] 1972), 25.
3. Julie Thompson Klein, "Interdisciplinary Needs: The Current Context," *Library Trends* 45, no. 2 (1996): 136.
4. Mattei Dogan and Robert Pahre, *Creative Marginality: Innovation at the Intersections of Social Sciences* (Boulder, CO: Westview, 1990).
5. Kristen B. LaBonte, "Citation Analysis: A Method for Collection Development for a Rapidly Developing Field," *Issues in Science & Technology Librarianship* no. 43 (Summer 2005), http://www.istl.org/05-summer/refereed.html (accessed December 1, 2010).
6. Johan Bollen, Herbert Van de Sompel, Aric Hagberg, Luis Bettencourt, Ryan Chute, Marko A. Rodriguez, and Lyudmila Balakireva, "Clickstream Data Yields High-Resolution Maps of Science," *PLoS ONE* 4, no. 3 (2009): 1, doi:10.1371/

journal.pone.0004803 (accessed March 28, 2011).

7.   Hur-Li Lee, "Toward a Reconceptualization of Collection Development: A Study of the Collecting of Women's Studies Materials by a University Library System" (PhD diss., Rutgers–New Brunswick, 1997), 43, ProQuest (AAT 9814095)(accessed December 1, 2010).

8.   John M. Budd and Kay Adams, "Allocations Formulas in Practice," *Library Acquisitions: Practice and Theory* 13, no. 4 (1989): 381–390, doi:10.1016/0364-6408(89)90049-5 (accessed March 7, 2011).

9.   Peggy Johnson, *Fundamentals of Collection Development and Management, Second Edition* (Chicago, IL: American Library Association, 2009), 85.

10. Don Lanier and Kathryn Carpenter, "Enhanced Services and Resource Sharing in Support of New Academic Programs," *The Journal of Academic Librarianship* 20, no. 1 (1994): 15–18, doi:10.1016/0099-1333(94)90129-5 (accessed March 21, 2011).

11. Reeta Sinha and Cory Tucker, "New Program Growth and Its Impact on Collection Assessment at the UNLV Libraries," *Library Hi Tech* 23, no. 3 (2005): 362–371, doi:10.1108/07378830510621775 (accessed March 21, 2011).

12. Anne Marie Austenfeld, "Building the College Library Collection to Support Curriculum Growth," *Collection Management* 34, no. 3 (2009): 209–227, doi:10.1080/01462670902975027 (accessed March 21, 2011).

13. Sinha and Tucker, "New Program Growth"; Austenfeld, "Building the College Library Collection."

14. Austenfeld, "Building the College Library Collection," 212.

15. Sonia Bodi and Katie Maier-O'Shea, "The Library of Babel: Making Sense of Collection Management in a Postmodern World," *The Journal of Academic Librarianship* 31, no. 2 (March 2005): 148, doi:10.1016/j.acalib.2004.12.009 (accessed March 29, 2011).

16. Kristine J. Anderson, Robert S. Freeman, Jean-Pierre V. M. Hérubel, Lawrence J. Mykytiuk, Judith M. Nixon, and Suzanne M. Ward, "Liberal Arts Books on Demand: A Decade of Patron-Driven Collection Development, Part 1," *Collection Management* 35, no. 3 (2010): 126, doi:10.1080/01462679.2010.486959 (accessed December 1, 2010).

17. Barbara I. Dewey, "The Embedded Librarian: Strategic Campus Collaborations," *Resource Sharing & Information Networks* 17, no. 1/2 (2004): 11, EBSCOhost (17141222) (accessed March 28, 2011).

Area Studies Librarianship and Interdisciplinarity: Globalization, the Long Tail, and the Cloud

Dan Hazen

Introduction

Area studies, driven by national security concerns and Cold War geo-politics, took shape as a distinct scholarly domain shortly after the Second World War. Region-specific, university-based programs of interdisciplinary teaching and research would promote long-term stability and prosperity by deepening the country's capacity for international engagement. Since its inception, the enterprise has thus sought to balance instrumental priorities with a broad academic agenda. The tensions have at times been acute, for example during the social and political tumult surrounding the Vietnam War. The varied streams of knowledge and analysis that comprise area studies have also led some to challenge its underlying intellectual validity. On the other hand, post-Soviet proclamations of a "flat" world and the end of history have been trumped by ongoing national assertiveness and enduring essentialisms. The field still has a place.

Academic libraries have supported area studies with distinctive programs and services. Non-Western collections work, for example, focuses on esoteric materials in unfamiliar languages that can be difficult to acquire. These "long tail" acquisitions, and the staff to support them, draw upon structures that reflect both the interdisciplinarity of area studies and the high-overhead, low-use resources upon which it depends. At its inception, area studies librarianship stood at the forefront of adaptive innovation.

Scholarly needs, the nature and availability of international information, and technological change have shaped area studies librarianship. This essay examines each in turn, beginning with a review of the area studies boom of the mid- and late-twentieth century. This interdisciplinary endeavor, while beholden to external agendas, also took shape in a setting of well-established approaches to knowledge. Scholarship drew upon exclusively analog resources that were often hard to obtain. Area studies librarianship's more recent development still reflects these original features, as further shaped by economic pressures, the ongoing shift toward digital information and technologies, and new service perspectives. Continuing globalization, and some of the general models now being proposed for research libraries, poses additional challenges.

Area Studies in Historical Perspective: Knowledge and Geopolitics

1. Antecedents: Higher Education and Knowledge

Area studies combine impulses from both the academy and the public sector. America's earliest colleges, dating from the seventeenth century, were founded to train clergymen. Practical needs eventually mandated a broader approach, fully apparent by the mid-nineteenth century when the Morrill Act (1862) promoted new "land grant" institutions. These public universities, funded by sales of federal lands, continue to focus on the formation of educated citizens, plus vocational training in "agriculture and the mechanical arts."

The nation's most prominent universities, drawing heavily on the German academic tradition, were by the late nineteenth century also supporting original research. Scholarship intensified in traditional fields, and the emerging disciplines of the social sciences explored new approaches as well. Economics, for example, increasingly emphasized quantitative analysis. Sociology, anthropology, and psychology sought to discover the laws of human behavior. Many scientific fields moved toward experimentation and model-making, along with classification and taxonomy. Expanding research, with the associated outlays for infrastructure and new graduate programs, fueled self-propelled growth.

Scholars held tight to their fields through this time of disciplinary consolidation. Professional organizations delimited their disciplines, which they then reinforced with specialized journals. These societies, as well as individual scholars, also patrolled each field's methodologies, foundational theories, and canonical texts with a zeal that extended even to details like formats for footnotes. Disciplinary orthodoxy was the norm.

By the early twentieth century, American universities supported research and teaching in both practical and academic fields. Discipline-specific departments carried out their agendas in conformance with carefully delineated practices and goals. Cross-disciplinary concerns did not easily find a place.

2. The Area Studies Project

Europe's early modern expansion provoked curiosity and speculation as unfamiliar people, creatures, objects, and places came into view. The imperial surge of the nineteenth century reinforced the need for organized knowledge to support administration, indoctrination, and trade. More sophisticated efforts at general understanding also arose.

The United States had emerged as an imperial power by the late nineteenth century, a status foreshadowed by the Monroe Doctrine's early (1823) assertion of hemispheric hegemony and then ratified by the country's occupations of Cuba, the Philippines, and Puerto Rico. America's participation in twentieth century conflicts befitted its strength and policy-making position. Pivotal roles in the Second World War, postwar reconstruction, and the Cold War pushed national security and international relations further to the fore. Sputnik, launched in 1957, was a singularly jolting event. Support for area studies was part of the response.

Scholarship on many foreign topics was well established by the early twentieth century. The American Oriental Society, for example, had been founded in 1842; its *Journal* followed in 1843. Classical languages and literatures—Hebrew, Sanskrit, Chinese—, non-Western religions, and national and regional histories were familiar as well. More specialized journals and associations followed later, among them the *Hispanic American Historical Review,* founded in 1919; and the Conference on Latin American History, established in 1926. As these examples suggest, regional scholarship built from disciplinary perspectives. The annual *Handbook of Latin American Studies,* launched in 1935, likewise evaluated significant scholarship through separate sections for each field. Most scholars of foreign areas, finally, were based in discipline-oriented academic departments.

External mandates and support have been crucial in establishing the footings for area studies. The Institute of International Education, for example, was established in 1919 in order to foster world peace through education and understanding. The Ford and Rockefeller Foundations, in alliance with the Carnegie Corporation, complemented their separate international efforts with a major joint initiative in the mid-1940s. Some foundations, with Ford among the leaders, have supported programs and offices throughout the world. Others focus more narrowly. The Henry Luce Foundation, created in 1936, thus emphasizes East and Southeast Asia; the Edward Larocque Tinker Foundation, established in 1959, is concerned with Latin America and the Iberian peninsula. More recently still, the Bill and Melinda Gates Foundation has pursued its own and also joint programs to combat infectious disease in Africa.

Federal programs have reinforced these efforts by providing direct support for academic activities and also through initiatives that rely upon area studies expertise. The Fulbright-Hays Act of 1946 seeks to reinforce international understanding through academic exchanges. The National Defense Education Act of 1958, part of the country's post-Sputnik mobilization, funded university-centered programs of language instruction, research, and training. Institution-based fellowships for graduate students in language and area studies complement support for interdisciplinary, region-specific National Resource Centers that draw upon specialists based in traditional departments, but seek a broader focus as well. Outreach to the general public is another central concern.

External support for academic area studies has provoked controversy as well as organizational change. Area studies scholarship has always included language instruction, literary studies, and descriptive accounts of different peoples and places. Academics committed to abstract analysis and methodological rigor can be skeptical of these broad-brush approaches. A second source of dissent, which has arisen within and also around the field, pits those who focus on culture and society against scholars committed to more encompassing propositions. Modernization theory was an early foil. Similar debates have regularly resurfaced, for example when rational choice theory came into vogue. Tensions have again arisen with regard to the most useful organizing principle for cross-national research in a globalized world: universal issues like water, the environment, or human rights may transcend regional bounds. Finally, the practical goals of many area studies funding agencies and practitioners have sparked enduring debates around academic neutrality and the appropriate limits of scholarly engagement in real-world affairs.

Area studies scholarship builds upon interdisciplinary underpinnings that go well beyond the disciplinary divisions that framed, and constrained, America's universities of the early twentieth century. These always-broad interdisciplinary categories continue to expand. Scientists, legal scholars, architects, and public health experts are among those who are pushing area studies beyond its traditional roots in the humanities and social sciences. Scholars who hail from the regions that area studies address are defining priorities that are distinct from America's policy concerns. Researchers imbued with the assumptions and methodologies of more than one discipline are increasing the theoretical density of area studies work. New forms of knowledge and expression have been embraced as well.

The geographic scale and focus of area studies also continue to shift. Geopolitics helps account for the growing prominence of Central and Inner Asia, and declining interest in Eastern Europe. "Global studies" encourages scholarship on cross-cutting issues like infectious disease, energy, and the environment. Mobile and merged populations, massive movements of goods and ideas—both legal and illicit—, and the interdependencies associated with instant communications require broad analytical frameworks.

While the area studies centers that were established in the 1950s were disruptive to discipline-based academic structures, non-departmental units are by now quite common. Some interdisciplinary programs, for instance in ethnic or women's studies, have also achieved departmental status of their own. Trans-disciplinary approaches are broadly embedded in cultural studies and postmodern scholarship, and more radical interdisciplinarity is emerging at the frontiers of biology, chemistry, and engineering, or in the mind-brain-behavior vortex. Area studies no longer lead the interdisciplinary charge.

Research Libraries and Global Information

Area studies programs have been shaped by both academic impulses and practical concerns. Research libraries have in turn made special arrangements to support area studies collections and services. The challenges of acquisitions include evaluating what has been produced across many disciplines and fields, discovering how these materials have been disseminated, and making sure that they are accessible to users. Foreign materials have stretched traditional approaches.

1. Understanding global information

Mid-twentieth century scholarship focused on discipline-based studies that relied upon, and produced, library collections that emphasized the scholarly record of academic journals, research reports, and specialized monographs. Primary sources, particularly those reflecting popular culture, were typically pursued by only a few large libraries and special collections. The rise of area studies helped to broaden this panorama.

The many cultural preoccupations and intellectual traditions subsumed within area studies may not always match the West's academic concerns. The meaning, value, and research significance of some local materials are therefore not always clear. In the realm of museums, similarly, artifacts acquired for their aesthetic or scientific appeal can carry unrecognized cultural or religious weight for the originating groups. Libraries' collection decisions are further complicated by the many modes through which culturally relevant knowledge may be conveyed. Epic poems, ritualized dialog, and other oral performances, for example, are difficult to capture and intrinsically diminished when frozen into other formats. Even written words can be created for purposes distinct from those familiar to academics. Area studies draws upon expressions of local knowledge that can be difficult to discern.

The challenges posed by knowledge that outsiders do not perceive, and also by knowledge whose purposes are unexpected, are easy to miss. Area studies scholarship, paradoxically, has itself sometimes complicated the picture by opening the way for new research centers in other parts of the world. These organizations have typically recruited experts who were trained in developed-world institutions and who focus on familiar questions and methodologies. Academic globalization can promote intellectual homogenization.

2. Area Studies Librarianship: Structures and Mechanics

Research libraries face practical as well as epistemological issues in managing area studies materials. Historical precedents have shaped some of these approaches, just as they have affected broader academic structures. Local practice defined most research library operations in the early twentieth century. Homegrown classification systems, each of which reflected its author's understanding of knowledge and collections, were common. Over time, the Dewey Decimal system and, increasingly, the Library of Congress classification became the norm. Their success reflected their inherent appeal, but also the efficiencies afforded by the standardized catalog cards (including call numbers) that were produced by the Library of Congress. Some of the side effects were profound, for example insofar as both systems are based upon topics rather than geography. Materials about any given region are therefore dispersed across a subject conspectus that, in turn, reflects and reinforces a universe defined by disciplines.

The splintering of area studies holdings across subject-based classification systems was somewhat mitigated as libraries created separate card catalogs for different scripts. While efficient operations were the primary goal, these script-based catalogs facilitated geographically focused scholarship by co-locating bibliographic records for vernacular publications. Separate stack areas and service points were likewise common, again for efficiency as well as service. Script-specific operations, on the other hand, could split holdings on a particular region between publications in Western languages and indigenous tongues. Libraries' measures to accommodate area studies materials neither addressed interdisciplinarity as a conceptual goal nor integrated these resources within a geographically aware bibliographic or physical arrangement.

Computerized catalogs, first through transliteration schemes and now through Unicode, allow more profound bibliographic integration. Sophisticated search capabilities likewise simplify region-specific discovery. Geo-referenced information carries even greater potential. But various library tools, for example some of the catalog front ends now in vogue, still cannot manage non-Roman scripts. Non-print materials also complicate access with their overlapping requirements for special equipment, staff with format expertise, and language and subject skills.

The foreign materials that are essential for area studies scholarship are produced in all parts of the globe, in hundreds of languages.

Libraries strive to identify, acquire, catalog, house, service, and preserve these resources through processes that require language expertise; cultural knowledge to correctly interpret subjects and themes; and familiarity with unusual materials, for example to maintain different kinds of text blocks and bindings, or to master regional formatting protocols for media materials. User services rely upon individuals with similarly broad knowledge and skills. Few libraries can sustain staffs with comprehensive expertise in all of these realms, such that available area studies specialists often perform many different functions. Traditional staffing models that focus on single-function library jobs have been challenged by area studies.

Libraries' support for area studies entails an interplay between generalized procedures and systems, and the requirements of materials and services that fall outside the norm. Acquisitions, in particular, require tailored approaches. Libraries build their collections on the basis of policies that delineate program-based priorities and needs. These policies in turn inform selection decisions to choose specific items from the overall universe of potentially relevant materials. Publishers and booksellers in some parts of the world have created the exhaustive bibliographies and lists that give structure to their information marketplace. Many areas, however, lack these tools. Area studies collections therefore rely upon a variety of acquisitions models, each with its own strengths and weaknesses.

Some libraries have built area studies holdings by acquiring private collections that may include hard-to-get pamphlets, broadsides, and non-print materials as well as mainstream publications. However, while bulk acquisitions can instantly create strong retrospective collections, they do not address current receipts. Until fairly recently, ongoing international acquisitions were complicated by cumbersome export regulations, bureaucratic complexity, slow bank transactions, and difficult communications. Problematic commercial mechanics were often compounded by the limitations of local market structures, for instance in their generally weak coverage of provincial publications. The emergence of area studies scholarship nonetheless created a demand that some local booksellers rose to address. Exchange programs were also essential for materials that could not be purchased, for example non-commercial publications and most resources from the Soviet bloc.

Non-library initiatives provided additional channels for foreign acquisitions. Public Law 480, passed in 1954, supplied surplus agricultural products to selected countries, whose local-currency payments were placed in special accounts. These funds were earmarked for specific uses, including library acquisitions. By the early 1960s, PL480 was a mainstay for collections from India, in particular. These free shipments of duplicative materials quickly narrowed after cost-recovery fees were instituted in the late 1980s. Other external programs have also encouraged international acquisitions. Institutions seeking National Resource Center fellowships and funds, for instance, are judged on their library holdings as well as their academic programs. Extra support for collections often follows.

The wide-ranging needs of area studies scholars focus on low-use materials in unfamiliar languages. Cooperative acquisitions offer an alternative to potentially redundant local purchases, and area studies resources have been in the vanguard. Libraries located close to one another often exploit their complementarities, as in the longstanding collaborations between Duke and the University of North Carolina, or Stanford and Berkeley. New technologies, shared catalogs, and expedited delivery services have enlarged the geographic scale for bilateral cooperation, for instance in the emerging partnership between Columbia and Cornell. Regional consortia like the BorrowDirect group in the Northeast, the Council on Institutional Cooperation in the Midwest, and the University of California system, are also moving toward explicitly complementary collections. Area-focused groupings of specialist librarians are likewise pursuing cooperative ventures of their own.

Librarians have long aspired to comprehensive collections cooperation. The Farmington Plan, launched in 1942, was a structured effort to sustain national-level coverage of foreign publications during a time of war. Its country-based collecting assignments and careful reporting mechanisms underlay a program that continued until the early 1970s, when relatively ample funds and easy acquisitions allowed a less prescriptive approach. The RLG Conspectus, a decade later, again sought to ensure comprehensive coverage on the basis of closely documented local collecting strengths and gaps. High overhead and uncertain budgets undermined its appeal. By the mid 1990s, yet another round of alarming reports galvanized the Association of American Universities and the Association of Research Libraries, with support from the Andrew W. Mellon Foundation, to launch the "Global Resources Program." This continuing initiative, since relocated to the Center for Research Libraries as the "Global Resources Network," includes an expanding array of specific cooperative programs and projects.

The Global Resources Network is one of several programs that have created new, membership-based entities to act on their participants' behalf. The Cooperative Africana Microform Project, founded in 1963, was the first of the six area studies microform projects that are associated with the Center for Research Libraries. CAMP pioneered the general model through which member dues (and occasional external support) are deployed to reformat rare or endangered materials, with the microfilm or digital surrogates then serviced through CRL. The logic of the marketplace can more spontaneously allow independent purchasers to collectively fund programs with community-wide benefits that no single participant could provide on its own. Some Library of Congress Field Offices, for example, have repurposed their PL480 operations as self-sustaining cooperative programs whose fixed costs are shared among the participants. Without these programs, some foreign materials might simply drop out of sight. Similarly, some research libraries fund their own specialized acquisitions efforts through external sales, occasionally relying on commercial partners for marketing and fulfillment. The lines blur even more when vendors deploy their own area studies experts to capture content and develop products whose fate then depends on the market's response.

Library support for area studies has raised several kinds of questions. Interdisciplinarity has challenged discipline-based structures for operations and service. International acquisitions entail overlapping requirements for special procedures and staffing arrangements. Nonetheless, the rise of more intensively interdisciplinary fields, in combination with new technologies, has moved area studies away from the cutting edge.

Global Resources, the Information Marketplace, and the Digital Turn

The specialized library collections that support area studies fall into a "long tail" of low-use resources that are expensive to acquire, process, and maintain. Changing modes of access, the evolving economics of cooperation, and the impact of the cloud now allow different approaches to acquisitions. These may nonetheless fall short in offsetting research libraries' generally weakened support for foreign materials.

Area studies librarians have come to rely heavily upon the in-country book dealers who emerged during the boom years of the 1950s and 1960s. But book budgets are tight, and more and more libraries now emphasize digital resources and patron-driven purchases. High usage is regarded as a primary indicator of collections success, and non-English materials rarely make the grade. For their part, many international booksellers are exploring new business models as their sales dwindle. Some focus on bestsellers and core titles, at times also reducing their coverage of less prominent materials. Many booksellers are moving toward vertical integration as they offer value-added services like cataloging and binding. Their library clients perceive outsourcing as a means to control costs, and also to compensate for local gaps in particular language skills. These activities, however, may again divert vendors from providing comprehensive coverage. Some suppliers are also moving into the digital realm, for example by packaging e-journals into new aggregations or through their own digitizing projects.

The research library community's shrinking demand for foreign materials has compounded the challenges of an already uncertain information marketplace. Area studies librarians, themselves an endangered species, are to some degree compensating through travel to book fairs and on acquisitions trips. More robust solutions will require specialized acquisitions that are also aggressively cooperative, better tools for discovery, and fluid mechanisms for access.

Today's narrowing marketplace has also generated more ambiguous measures. Area studies librarians have heretofore pursued broad representations of popular culture and primary sources, as well as the scholarly record, from all parts of the world. Contemporary pedagogy calls for direct student engagement with primary sources, further strengthening this demand. However, limited local library capacities, in conjunction with the expanding need for instructional materials, have encouraged vendors to assemble their own, necessarily partial, digital selections of primary sources. These ready-made packages may further diminish direct acquisitions from the regions of origin, reducing our collective coverage still more. Cooperation among libraries, and also new library/vendor partnerships, may allow better results.

Area studies initially challenged both the traditional categories of discipline-based scholarship and established approaches to library operations. Area studies librarianship, then, has always focused on difficult materials and labor-intensive routines. Digital technologies and automation, by contrast, allow ever more efficient operations whose transformative impacts have redefined the possibilities and the economics of library service. As automation has become a first order of business, intractable cost centers—like area studies collections—have lost some of their luster.

Electronic technologies, of course, allow much more than processing efficiencies. Automated bibliographic data can be ordered and displayed in ways that explode the limitations of card catalogs or library shelves. Evolving search algorithms have transformed possibilities for discovery, with the semantic web and other capabilities promising even more. Digital objects, then, are protean resources that can be combined and mined at will. Research library collections, historically, have consisted of carefully constructed selections of materials that together represent some topic or field. Area studies scholarship continues to reflect geographical and disciplinary/interdisciplinary categories, such that traditional understandings of collections still have a place. Nonetheless, the centrality of collections has shifted as digital content can be mined to create ad hoc topical gatherings— a.k.a. "results lists," or perhaps "collections"—on the fly. Key word and phrase searching need not be limited to pre-established categories, and discovery no longer presumes disciplinary underpinnings. The implications extend to selection and curation as well as operations and service.

Hardcopy publications and analog media remain common throughout the world. But digital technologies have enlarged our panorama, as they also pose new challenges of capture, organization, and analysis. The solutions to these needs are most likely to emerge from realms whose policy mandates and digital infrastructures are already strong. Scientific research, for instance, is increasingly funded on the condition that both research findings and supporting data become broadly accessible. The scientific enterprise enjoys ample support, and scholarship is overwhelmingly digital. Future innovations are likely here, not in area studies.

Area Studies in a Network World

Area studies scholarship has required broad-based global collections that transcend disciplinary boundaries. Research libraries' imaginative responses ranged from specialized staff to customized acquisitions routines and new approaches to card catalogs and other long-standard arrangements. For libraries, as for the academy as a whole, area studies stretched traditional concepts and structures.

But today's environment for area studies scholarship and information is fundamentally different from that of the 1950s and 1960s. Within area studies, interdisciplinarity has become more pronounced, and geographical interests are at once more diverse and more inclusive. Cross- and trans-disciplinary research and teaching, while continuing staples of area studies work, nonetheless pervade all fields. Contemporary pedagogical models encourage broad engagement with primary sources, whatever the topic. Overseas campuses, offices, and partnerships, along with distance learning, are globalizing the academy—albeit in ways that often privilege the formation of an internationalized technocratic elite over regionally nuanced understanding.

Collections expectations have changed as well. The rise of area studies programs required research libraries to pursue far-flung materials that were often difficult to acquire. The world's output of print publications continues to grow, and the international marketplace remains uneven. But America's research libraries, individually and collectively, are acquiring less and less of these materials: comprehensive collections seem a dream of the past. Moreover, locally held hardcopy holdings no longer drive library operations as before, further diminishing the role of programs that depend heavily on specialized analog collections.

The momentum of information has shifted decisively toward digital resources and cloud-based data. Organizing access to vast quantities of electronic information, much of it beyond libraries' direct control, promises clear benefits in facilitating new forms of learning and new kinds of scholarship. The cloud, moreover, is equally amenable to discipline-based scholarship and to activities that ignore these boundaries. Digital information forms a post-disciplinary realm.

Conclusion

Area studies shook the academic world and research libraries by injecting multiplicity and flexibility into structures that were organized around longstanding disciplinary divisions and library routines. These monochromatic endeavors gradually adapted to a new world of nuance and tonality, in which agency was also shared among scholars, libraries, and external actors. New academic agendas have extended interdisciplinarity into new realms, and the phase change from analog to digital information has radically transformed both the scholarly and the library environments. Area studies, still conditioned by the once-radical models and requirements of the mid-twentieth century, are no longer a primary catalyst for either interdisciplinarity or library innovation.

Note on Sources

Materials concerning area studies and U.S. higher education are abundant. The role and place of international engagement by the United States, and also of American higher education, are matters of sometimes heated contention. Readers seeking additional background information could begin with sources such as the following:

Committee to Review the Title VI and Fulbright-Hays International Education Programs; Mary Ellen O'Connell and Janet L. Norwood, eds., *International education and foreign languages: keys to securing America's future*. Washington, DC: National Academies Press, 2007.

David Szanton, ed., *The Politics of Knowledge: Area Studies and the Disciplines*. Berkeley: University of California Press, 2004.

Neil L. Waters, ed., *Beyond the Area Studies Wars: Toward a New International Studies* [Middlebury, VT]: Middlebury College Press; Hanover, NH: University Press of New England, 2000.

Christopher J. Lucas, *American Higher Education: A History*. New York: Palgrave Macmillan, 2006.

Frederick Rudolph, with introductory essay and supplemental bibliography by John R. Thelin, *The American College and University: A History*. Athens: University of Georgia Press, 1991.

John R. Thelin, *A History of American Higher Education*. Baltimore: Johns
   Hopkins University Press, 2004.

This chapter, which is geared toward interpretation rather than documentation, mentions many organizations and events that are not specifically referenced. Almost all of these groups, programs, and centers
have their own websites that are easily discovered with standard Internet search engines. The *Chronicle of Higher Education* provides strong
coverage of current events and trends, primarily within the United
States though with some international coverage as well.

Digital Collections and Digital Scholarship in the Academic Library: An Interdisciplinary Opportunity

Mark Dahl

Introduction

Scott Walter recently argued that research libraries have taken the "service turn": some of their most distinguishing features are now services rather than collections.[1] Academic libraries of all sizes may find an opportunity to provide services at the intersection of digital collections and digital scholarship, a place where interdisciplinarity often thrives. To realize this opportunity, libraries must develop services that fit their institution and truly provide value in the context of collaborative digital scholarship.

In the last decade, many academic libraries have gotten into the business of creating unique digital collections. A first move in this direction often involves digitizing primary materials of special relevance to the institution or region and making them available online. Research libraries and smaller institutions alike have also developed institutional repositories to house local scholarship and promote new means of scholarly communication. Some institutions have even developed mandatory submissions policies for scholarly work produced at the institution.

As Clifford Lynch observed in 2003 one can draw a distinction between building digital collections of raw materials and creating layers of interpretation on top of those materials.[2] The line between collection and interpretation is a fine one as almost any kind of collection could be considered interpretive at some level. But as libraries cross into projects that are more analytical, thematic, and oriented towards a particular scholarly vision, they move from the realm of digital collections to digital scholarship, a broad concept. According to a report published by the American Council of Learned Societies, digital scholarship in recent practice encompasses collection building, tool creation, and the use of those collections and tools to generate new intellectual products.[3]

Activity around digital scholarship, particularly digital humanities, has grown in recent years. The National Endowment for the Humanities launched its Digital Humanities Initiative in 2006 and two years later established its Office of Digital Humanities, which provides a variety of grant programs in support of the digital humanities. In 2008 the Center for History and New Media at George Mason University held the first The Humanities and Technology (THAT) Camp, and since then scholars and technologists have flocked to regional THAT Camps around the world.

Digital Scholarship and Interdisciplinary Digital Projects

Digital projects, especially those that go beyond the collection of raw objects to incorporate editorial questions, interpretation, and the creation of tools for scholarly inquiry, often offer the opportunity for interdisciplinary collaboration. Within the digital humanities, projects are increasingly large, multidisciplinary endeavors. Often several scholars in related disciplines will work on the editorial process for an online collection of texts or images. Projects that involve intensive use of computing resources can also provide an opportunity for collaboration between humanists and computer scientists.

For example, the Perseus Digital Library, a project in existence since 1985, is a wide-ranging collection of texts and images with a primary focus on the interdisciplinary field of classical studies, which includes subfields such ancient history, art history, archaeology, epigraphy, numismatics, papyrology, and philology. The project provides access to ancient texts and incorporates sophisticated translation, cross-referencing, and dictionary tools that assist in close reading and analysis of the works in the collection. The digital library is built to support the specialist and the generalist in a wide range of fields, and as Editor-In-Chief Gregory Crane notes, its incorporation of sophisticated details and functionality originally intended for specialists in particular disciplines has often proven useful across a range of fields.[4]

More than a set of collections and related tools, the Perseus Project might be described as a laboratory that continually pushes the boundaries of digital libraries and the humanities from an interdisciplinary perspective. The Perseus Project recently collaborated on a grant project to study challenges and opportunities confronting, as Crane et al. put it, "the humanities in general and classical studies in particular as we shift from small, carefully edited and curated digital collections to very large, industrially produced collections." Collaborators on this project included specialists in classical literature, German, English, linguistics computer science, and digital libraries.[5]

The Garibaldi/Risorgimento digital archive produced by the Brown University Library Center for Digital Scholarship "seeks to provide a comprehensive resource for the interdisciplinary study and teaching of the life and deeds of one of the protagonists of the Italian unification process (1807–1882), against the historical backdrop of nineteenth-century Europe, reconstructed with the help of materials from special collections at the Brown University libraries." The centerpiece of the project is an interactive electronic reproduction of the library's Garibaldi panorama, which includes voice-over narration and explanatory notes about characters depicted in the illustration. The project brings together scholars across continents through its editorial board and production team from disciplines that include Italian studies, anthropology, history, comparative literature, and computer science.[6]

The Center for History and New Media at George Mason University produced the September 11th Digital Archive, a collection of photographs and personal accounts of the September 11th tragedy collected through individual submissions over the Web. While the archive and its sponsor are primarily associated with the field of history, the nontraditional composition of the archive and its focus on a contemporary historical event effectively positions it as a resource beyond disciplinary categorization. To mark the archive's acceptance into the Library of Congress's collections, the library hosted a symposium at which historians, librarians and archivists came together to reflect on the use of digital materials in the writing of history.[7]

Digital projects can provide a way for fields that are intrinsically interdisciplinary to integrate a diverse set of resources in uncommon ways. The Our Americas Archive Partnership integrates a heterogeneous collection of primary sources to support research in hemispheric American studies, a transnational scholarly approach to American studies. The collection encompasses sources from three distinct collections: an Early Americas digital archive based at the University of Maryland, the Americas Collection based at Rice University, and a collection documenting the social history of Mexico and Latin America based at Instituto Mora in Mexico.[8] Caroline Levander explains why a digital archive is so crucial for the challenges of this multidisciplinary field:

> First, the amount of data sorting that researchers must do necessitates greater flexibility across knowledge and textual fields. Scholars trained as Mexicanists, U.S. Americanists, or Brazilianists can manipulate national archives to conduct nation-based research, but these research skills and data fields are insufficient for research that endeavors to engage multinational and transnational contexts. The sheer amount of material defies traditional research methods, even as the intellectual focus of the research makes nation-focused archives and nation-organized search engines largely irrelevant.[9]

The project aims to move beyond nation-based ways of organizing knowledge and allow inquiry that explores "political and cultural relationships along and across national borders." The project, which includes Rice University's Fondren Library as a primary collaborator, incorporates traditional library classification and tagging using terminology from the Hemispheric Studies field.[10]

The field of environmental studies is also interdisciplinary by nature. Often it incorporates perspectives from the natural sciences, social sciences, and humanities around a particular environmental challenge. Lewis & Clark College's environmental studies program has initiated a site-based research approach to focus student attention on the many facets of environmental issues around certain geographic sites, some close to the college geographically and others associated with college overseas programs. As successive generations of students research various topics related to these sites, the program is creating a digital library of research resources, including secondary sources like articles, books, and maps, as well as primary sources such as datasets. In consultation with the college's Watzek Library, the program has developed an evolving digital library for organizing these resources incorporating bibliographic software and Web 2.0 tools.[11]

The Organizational Context

Colleges and universities that seek to foster digital scholarship may achieve this aim through various organizational structures and relationships. Digital projects often begin without a formal organizational home and result from collaboration between dispersed parties at an institution: often faculty in various departments work alone or with librarians and technologists whose primary job roles are focused in other areas. In other cases, projects are incubated in a center for digital scholarship or digital humanities that may or may not be located within the library in a physical or administrative sense. Units that focus on digital collections in libraries may play a leading or accompanying role in digital scholarship projects.

There are no established parameters for digital scholarship centers inside or outside of libraries. But each model tends to adhere more closely to certain characteristics. In a 2008 presentation, a group of academic technologists supporting digital humanities drew a distinction between digital humanities projects more closely aligned with faculty and those that are more closely aligned with a library:

> DH (Digital Humanities) projects, at the point where they interact with a faculty member, and try to instantiate their vision in digital form, are mostly focused on flexibility, branding and the best practices that come to them from other DH projects.

> DH projects when they are regarded as library resources are tend to prioritize longevity and standardization. They need to be incorporated into larger sets of collections, and be available for re-use. They are informed by DL standards.[12]

Faculty often leads digital scholarship centers outside of libraries, such as the Perseus Project at Tufts and the Digital Humanities Initiative at Hamilton College.[13] Such centers tend to focus on the scholarly process and provide support for scholarly work itself, often sponsoring fellows and graduate assistants. They are likely to have education programs including events and workshops and, in cases such as the UCLA Center for Digital Humanities, support courses and degree programs.[14]

Within libraries, units that build digital collections are often those that are most closely aligned with digital scholarship. They tend to orient their work around distinct collections or projects, and commonly these collections are connected with the archival or special collections holdings of the institution. Some library digital initiatives focus on collecting raw materials and making them accessible through a uniform digital asset management system like ContentDM. For example, the Claremont Colleges Digital Library offers a variety of digital objects including images, video, and textual documents across a range of subject areas including anthropology, history, political science, and the natural sciences, the contents of which are drawn from faculty and institutional collections.[15]

Some library digital collections programs are more oriented towards interpretive collections and might also be described as digital scholarship centers or programs. The UCLA Digital Library collaborates on a number of interactive digital projects such as the St. Gall Monastery Plan and the Hypercities project. The Center for Digital Scholarship at Brown University Library supports many branded, thematic digital projects such as the Garibaldi/Risorgimento Project, a companion website to the book *Flatland* by Edwin Abbot, and a collection of materials about Paris in the nineteenth century. Many of these projects have been created in collaboration with academic departments or specific faculty and most have websites with interfaces designed to navigate the content. The Oregon State University Libraries created the Oregon Explorer, a natural resources digital library that combines topical overviews on a number of environmental issues as well as various datasets and interactive maps.[16]

In many institutions, work on digital scholarship is distributed across various units, and collaboration and even some degree of competition are the norm. The University of Virginia Library houses a variety of units that support digital scholarship, including the Institute for Advanced Technology and the Humanities (IATH) and the Virginia Center for Digital History, which are both physically housed in the library but administratively separate. Units within library administrative purview include Digital Curation Services, oriented towards digitization of analog collections and long-term curation of digital assets, and the Scholar's Lab, which addresses the "digital research and scholarly analysis needs of faculty and advanced students in the humanities and social sciences."[17] The library also houses a research computing lab with a focus on data management. An EDUCAUSE Center for Applied Research report described Virginia's approach to digital scholarship as dispersed: "The ethos of 'let a thousand flowers bloom' reaped a lush garden of flexibility, creativity, and scholarship. Ideas have been cross-fertilized through networks of bi-lateral and multi-lateral relations," says the report, though not without some sacrifices in centralized coordination.[18]

Smaller institutions also have a range of configurations. The University of Richmond houses a Digital Scholarship Lab in its library that reports to the Vice President for Information Services, which engages in a number of advanced digital humanities projects connected with US history, such as the History Engine and Visualizing Emancipation. The library also has its own digital initiatives unit primarily focused on digitization, collections, and preservation.[19] Willamette University and Lewis & Clark College support a range of digital collections initiatives out of their libraries, many of which could be labeled as digital scholarship. Willamette's Hatfield Library recently developed software to help integrate digital repositories with multimedia authoring tools as part of an NEH Digital Humanities Startup grant.[20] Wheaton College has a digital history project led by a US historian that works closely with the college archives on collaborative student-centered projects.[21]

Defining Services, Attracting and Selecting Projects

Whatever the organizational configuration, libraries have an opportunity to enable interdisciplinary work by developing services that support digital scholarship. One can view digital scholarship services as traditional library information management activities such as cataloging and systems development turned outward. In essence, when the library supports digital scholarship, it performs information management as an external service instead of performing it on its own collections. Getting the right set of skills to meet scholars' needs may require the cultivation of new expertise, however. The mix of services offered by a library digital scholarship program may include physical spaces, technical infrastructure, project management, and technical and creative expertise.

One of the most basic services that a library can offer in support of digital scholarship is a human gathering space. As former director of IATH John Unsworth put it in 1999,

> It might seem that networked humanities research projects such as those sponsored by IATH could easily be distributed across campus, and that no physical facilities should be required—but in fact, I believe the most important part of IATH's success has been the existence of a central place where faculty from across the humanities and technical staff versed in humanities computing can work together. The Institute has become the University's most genuinely interdisciplinary space, and its staff and fellows benefit in a number of ways from cohabitation.[22]

The Power of Pull is a recent influential book on innovation in the early twenty-first-century networked environment. Its authors make the case that even in the digital age, tacit knowledge—that is, knowledge that is best transferred via a direct interpersonal connection—is a key ingredient to advancing cutting-edge work in many fields of endeavor. Moreover, the authors argue that those innovating in any field will "pull" relevant information resources from a flow of information while engaging in rapid feedback loops with peers.[23] Digital scholarship centers in libraries can be places where scholars, students, librarians, and other professionals transfer tacit knowledge and "pull" together critical resources as they collaborate on innovative projects. In this way, the center can foster scholarly innovation and at the same time prepare students for careers in many fields of endeavor in a digitally mediated, interconnected world.

Besides physical spaces, libraries can provide virtual ones in which digital scholarship can reside: servers, repository software, and other virtual containers for digital resources. Many libraries made the provision of software, platforms, and infrastructure their first priority as they began developing digital collections programs. As computing resources move to the cloud and as academic fields create their own repositories for content, however, the role of an academic institution as a host for digital resources may not be as compelling or necessary as it has been. A student or faculty member can now get started with a small collection on the digital collections platform Omeka.net free of charge and expand it from there with a minimal fee. In many cases, it will remain important for libraries to continue to provide virtual resources and spaces, but perhaps libraries' more significant role in the future will be guiding students and scholars as they endeavor to select and integrate the available resources and virtual homes for projects on the Internet. Scholars in a field will likely be familiar with resources in their discipline, but they will rely on information professionals at libraries and elsewhere to connect more general resources and tools that might be needed for tasks such as preservation, curation, transcription, translation, visualization, and mapping.

In part because they are often interdisciplinary in nature, digital scholarship projects are complex endeavors that contrast with the lone-scholar model of research in the humanities. They involve a sophisticated coordination of people, technology, and intellectual objects often highly dispersed in the physical and virtual worlds. A scholar leading a project may pose the research questions and develop a methodology for answering those questions, but experts in a digital scholarship center are often better at developing and managing the work plan for the project. In the accessCeramics project at Lewis & Clark, the library has served as the logistical manager of the endeavor. This has encompassed writing grant proposals, developing and maintaining the project's technical infrastructure, and managing the day-to-day complexities of submissions to the collection. The arrangement allows the faculty leader of the project to work on curation of the collection and outreach to external constituencies.[24]

Libraries that can bring together technical and creative expertise to digital projects will be the ones that are most successful at developing them. Expertise in digitization, digital preservation, metadata management, computer programming, and design are often essential for successful digital projects. Some of these areas, particularly programming and design, may seem like less of a natural fit for libraries than areas such as metadata management or preservation, which tie nicely into traditional library roles. But design and programming are often what separates a mediocre digital project from an outstanding one. As Dan Cohen, director of George Mason's Center for History and New Media, writes:

One of the more uncomfortable truths about digital humanities—indeed, likely one of the reasons for resistance to digital humanities among traditional scholars—is that design matters. Those of us who have chosen the life of the mind like to think that ideas and insights will find an audience and make an impact regardless of such superficial things as the vehicle those ideas and insights are communicated through. Design also smacks of marketing, which most professors consider unseemly.

But good design for a website, service, or tool means, as Roy Rosenzweig and I put it in *Digital History*, that your resource will be *useful* and *used*. *Useful* because your resource will be structured in such a way that a user will be able to fully explore and learn from it; *used* because the user will be drawn into the resource and highlight its existence to others.[25]

Digital projects that are likely to break ground are ones that present, analyze, cross-reference, or otherwise manipulate information in innovative ways. Even with many software platforms and resources available on the Internet, this still requires advanced skills in programming, database management, and systems integration. In the recent past, the code4lib community has demonstrated that programmers in libraries can creatively improve library catalogs, research guides, and repositories. Development of digital scholarly projects is a fertile area for libraries to deploy programming skills as an outward-facing service.

Most digital collections/digital scholarship units in large academic libraries reveal these areas of expertise in their staff directories. For example, the digital library development center at the University of Chicago lists a web project manager, a web and graphic design specialist, and two programmer/analysts among their staff.[26] But even relatively small academic libraries should consider developing in-house expertise in the above areas. As an alternative or supplement to local expertise, contracting out for some services needed for digital project development may also make sense. Contracting out services such as web development can be a daunting endeavor for those that are unfamiliar with it, and libraries that can facilitate this process may provide their scholarly clientele with an extremely valuable service.

Recruiting appropriate projects may be an initial challenge for a digital scholarship program. A library may take advantage of its existing connections with faculty and use strategies such as events and workshops to draw new faculty into the fold. Interdisciplinary academic units or centers are often particularly fertile ground for the cultivation of projects as some of them may be looking for solutions akin to the Our Americas Archive that bring together resources in nontraditional ways. Above all, a digital scholarship program's most powerful recruiting tool is a strong track record of innovative projects and the resources and expertise that make those projects possible.

A successful digital scholarship program will find that it has more potential projects than it can support. Unlike traditional library services, support for digital scholarship is more consultative than transactional and may signify a significant transfer of resources to a relatively small group of scholarly clientele. Selection of projects that have the greatest impact possible is crucial. Program leaders must look to the program's mission to identify priorities, and this will naturally vary by institution. Depending upon the setting, priorities could include student engagement, community connections, scholarly innovation, or interdisciplinarity. Columbia University's Digital Bridges program, which brings students and faculty into active engagement with library digital collections, cites "interdisciplinary discovery" as a beneficial aspect of its projects.[27] In any case, an interdisciplinary emphasis may be one way to assure that the benefits of a digital project are enjoyed more widely within an institution and beyond.

Conclusion

By cultivating scholarly digital projects, libraries can support collaborative and, in many cases, interdisciplinary scholarly work. There are many models for supporting such projects, but to develop a thriving program in this area, libraries need to provide services that make them an essential part of the project. These services may include a mix of physical spaces, technical infrastructure, project management, and technical and creative expertise. A successful digital project is one that brings together experts across an array of fields to work at the cutting edge of knowledge or practice. Being able to play a role in such an endeavor is an exciting prospect for libraries. More importantly, it is one potential way that academic libraries can evolve to support scholarship in the complex and evolving information environment of the early twenty-first century.

Notes

1. Scott Walter, "'Distinctive Signifiers of Excellence': Library Services and the Future of the Academic Library," *College and Research Libraries* 72, no. 1 (January 2011): 6–8, http://crl.acrl.org/content/72/1/6.full.pdf (accessed March 7, 2011).
2. Clifford A. Lynch, "Institutional Repositories: Essential Infrastructure for Scholarship in the Digital Age," *portal: Libraries and the Academy* 3, no. 2 (April 2003): 327–336, http://muse.jhu.edu/journals/portal_libraries_and_the_academy/v003/3.2lynch.html (accessed March 3, 2011).
3. American Council of Learned Soceities, *Our Cultural Commonwealth* (Washington DC: ACLS, 2006), 7, http://www.acls.org/uploadedFiles/Publications/Programs/Our_Cultural_Commonwealth.pdf (accessed March 7, 2011).
4. Gregory Crane, "The Perseus Project and Beyond: How Building a Digital Library Challenges the Humanities and Technology." *D-Lib Magazine* 4, no. 1 (January 1998), http://www.dlib.org/dlib/january98/01crane.html (accessed March 7, 2011).
5. Gregory Crane et al., "Classics in the Million Book Library," *Digital Humanities Quarterly* 3, no. 1 (Winter 2009), http://digitalhumanities.org/dhq/vol/3/1/000034/000034.html (accessed March 7, 2011).
6. Brown University Library Center for Digital Scholarship, "The Garibaldi Panorama: Visualizing the Risorgimento," http://dl.lib.brown.edu/garibaldi/about.html (accessed March 7, 2011).
7. "September 11 as History: Collecting Today for Tomorrow" (Library of Congress symposium, Washington, DC, September 10, 2003), http://www.loc.gov/rr/program/911symposium (accessed March 7, 2011).
8. Lisa Spiro, "Our Americas Archive Partnership: Charting New Cultural Geographies" (presentation, Digital Humanities 2009, College Park, MD, June 2009), http://scholarship.rice.edu/handle/1911/26635 (accessed March 7, 2011).
9. Caroline Levander, "The Changing Landscape of American Studies in a Global Era," in *Working Together or Apart: Promoting the Next Generation of Digital Scholarship* (Washington, DC: Council on Library and Information Resources, 2009), 28–20, http://www.clir.org/pubs/reports/pub145/pub145.pdf (accessed March 7 2011).
10. Ibid., 27–33.
11. "Situated Research Sites—Environmental Studies," Lewis & Clark College, http://www.lclark.edu/college/programs/environmental_studies/student_resources/situated_research_sites/, page now discontinued (accessed March 7, 2011).
12. Hope Greenberg, Scott Hamlin, Elli Mylonas, and Patrick Yott, "Supporting Digital Humanities Research: The Collaborative Approach," (presentation, NERCOMP, Providence, RI, March 12, 2008), http://net.educause.edu/ir/library/pdf/NCP08094.pdf (accessed March 7,2011).
13. "DHi: Digital Humanities Initiative," Hamilton College, http://dhinitiative.org (accessed March 7, 2011).

14. "Center for Digital Humanities," University of California Los Angeles, http://www.cdh.ucla.edu (accessed March 7, 2011).

15. "Claremont Colleges Digital Library," Claremont Colleges Libraries, http://ccdl.libraries.claremont.edu/ (accessed March 7, 2011).

16. "Oregon Explorer," Oregon State University Libraries, http://oregonexplorer.info (accessed March 7, 2011).

17. "Digital Curation Services," University of Virginia Library, http://www2.lib.virginia.edu/digitalcuration/; "Scholars' Lab," University of Virginia Library, accessed March 7, 2011, http://www2.lib.virginia.edu/scholarslab/ (accessed March 7, 2011).

18. Harvey Blustain and Donald Spicer, *Digital Humanities at the Crossroads: The University of Virginia*, ECAR Case Study 6 (Boulder, CO: EDUCAUSE Center for Applied Research, 2005), 10, http://net.educause.edu/ir/library/pdf/ers0605/cs/ecs0506.pdf (accessed March 7, 2011).

19. "Digital Scholarship Lab," University of Richmond, http://dsl.richmond.edu/ (accessed March 1, 2012); "Digital Initiatives," Boatwright Memorial Library, University of Richmond, http://library.richmond.edu/digital/index.html (accessed March 1, 2012).

20. "Digital Humanities Start Up Grant," Willamette University, http://libmedia.willamette.edu/acom/neh/ (accessed March 7, 2011—page now discontinued).

21. "Wheaton College Digital History Project," http://wheatoncollege.edu/digital-history-project/ (accessed March 7, 2011).

22. John Unsworth, "The Library as Laboratory" (presentation, American Library Association Annual Meeting, New Orleans, LA, June 27, 1999), http://www3.isrl.illinois.edu/~unsworth/ala99.htm (accessed March 8, 2011).

23. John Hagel, John Seely Brown, and Lang Davison, *The Power of Pull: How Small Moves, Smartly Made, Can Set Big Things in Motion* (New York: Basic Books, 2010).

24. Mark Dahl and Jeremy McWilliams, "Accessceramics.org: A Digital Image Database Collaboratively Sourced Using Flickr," (presentation, EDUCAUSE 2009, Denver, CO, November 2009), https://docs.google.com/present/view?id=dc7wb8dq_7364v4kz4cc (accessed March 7, 2011).

25. Daniel Cohen, "Design Matters," *Dan Cohen's Digital Humanities Blog*, November 12, 2008, http://www.dancohen.org/2008/11/12/design-matters/ (accessed March 7, 2011).

26. "Who We Are," Digital Library Development Center, University of Chicago, http://dldc.lib.uchicago.edu/who.php (accessed March 8, 2011).

27. "About Digital Bridges at CCNMTL," Columbia CNMTL, http://ccnmtl.columbia.edu/digitalbridges/about/ (accessed March 8, 2011).

The Changing Role of the Subject Specialist Librarian

Evelyn Ehrlich and Angela Carreño

The authors distinguish two distinct phases in their treatment of the effects of interdisciplinary scholarship on the academic library, especially as it affects the subject librarian roles. Significant qualitative differences, particularly pertaining to its reach in new knowledge creation, characterize each phase. As interdisciplinary scholarship evolves in phase one, its research strands seem to be ever more pervasive throughout the academic fabric, but it is only as we enter the second decade of the twenty-first century, with phase two emerging, that we see the multidisciplinary discourse becoming foundational to new knowledge creation.

In the academic library, meeting the responsibilities of faculty liaison has long been understood as key to the subject librarian's success. Being in regular contact with one's department is seen as providing an anchor and bringing purpose to the subject librarian's work. From the perspective of library administration, having a formally structured and effective liaison program in place guarantees that the library's collections match faculty research interests and that the spectrum of services offered meet the teaching and learning needs of faculty and students, thereby ensuring that the library fulfills its obligations toward supporting the research and educational mission of the university. It is through outreach that subject librarians stay informed about any changes in "their" faculty's research agendas with topics, methodologies, or processes. As early as in the 1970s, liaison activities made their appearance in academic libraries, covering the spectrum from ad hoc to very structured. In terms of associated tasks, liaison relationships progressed from collection- to user-focused, with the appropriate attendant expansion of subject librarian involvement.[1] When over the last three decades of the twentieth and the first decade of the twenty-first century, integrative—including interdisciplinary, cross-disciplinary, transdisciplinary, and multidisciplinary—research evolved from "hot trend" into the "new reality" on campus, academic libraries were challenged to develop corresponding services. Acknowledging the fact that there is no sound interdisciplinary research without disciplinary departments continuing to teach their methodologies, a hybrid campus environment emerged whereby boundary-crossing research happens in centers and institutes. To give a sense of proportion, according to data from the Gale research group, the top twenty-five research universities average close to one hundred centers per institution.[2] The library, therefore, was faced with no small task in trying to meet the expectations of a campus continuing to value a dominant disciplinary culture, while simultaneously entertaining the proliferation of a strong interdisciplinary subculture.

While there is little in the library literature before 1996 on the change, in that year *Library Trends* devoted an entire issue to capturing its magnitude; through in-depth studies covering a broad range of the academic library and "interdisciplinary research needs," it laid the foundation on which later studies could build. Julie Thompson Klein, who played a major role in codifying what interdisciplinary research entailed for the academy, in the lead article in that issue specified "heterogeneity, hybridity, complexity, and interdisciplinarity" as "characterizing traits of knowledge in the latter half of the twentieth century."[3] If one juxtaposes that characterization with the library's preoccupation with standards and its nineteenth-century-based schemes of organizing knowledge, one can appreciate Klein's assessment that essentially "the problem of interdisciplinarity is the problem of fit."[4] What that specifically means, Susan Searing exemplified; by using women's studies as test case, she showed in great detail how poorly it fares in the library's organizational systems, ranging from the Library of Congress classification scheme to subject analysis to shelving arrangements. She concluded that interdisciplinary subjects "must be squeezed into pre-existing outlines of knowledge that no longer fit the shape of current scholarly output."[5]

Other studies concentrate on gaining a better understanding of the interdisciplinary scholar's information-seeking behavior and discuss the fit of library services from that vantage point.[6] Interdisciplinary information needs are best understood using the concept of scatter as framework. According to Marcia Bates, who draws on L.

J. B. Mote's 1962 study, *scatter* denotes a specific field's measure of resources, structure, and organization, whereby low scatter fields are built on well-developed principles, have a well-organized body of literature, and have well-delineated subject areas.[7] Accordingly, interdisciplinary work is defined by high scatter, which makes searching for, finding, and keeping up with relevant information sources challenging undertakings. As one scholar explained to Don Spanner: "if you know Isaiah Berlin's *Essay on the Hedgehog and the Fox*... a fox knows many things, and a hedgehog knows one big thing... so I would describe myself as a fox or a kind of rhisomatic thinker—a kind of root system that extends out. I'm more about being concerned with drawing connections."[8] What additional challenges set interdisciplinary research apart from its disciplinary counterpart? The above studies point to scholars having to compensate for inadequate resources and collections; overcome insecurities in terms of language, expectations, and overall culture of the disparate disciplines traversed; and carefully manage the time available to keep up with a wide-ranging body of materials and maintain a far-reaching network of colleagues.

At best, the response of the academic library to campus interdisciplinary information needs can be described as a patchwork attempt to bring to bear the combined forces of some organizational changes, such as more flexible fund structures; to broaden collections building, particularly of grey literatures; and to carve out—by way of restructuring—new positions with dedicated interdisciplinary responsibilities or distribute them across a number of subject librarians. Accordingly, Susan Searing gives examples of librarian positions created in support of diversity studies, women's studies, and ethnic studies, and an innovative approach of a South Asian studies librarian position being shared between two institutions.[9] Yet it is the subject librarian who is assigned center stage in this ad hoc combining of library services for interdisciplinary scholarship. The subject librarian is expected to insert herself or himself into the appropriate stages of the interdisciplinary research process and ultimately has the unenviable task of attempting the impossible: reconciling the fluid contours of interdisciplinary scholarship to "square" library systems.

Lynn Westbrook's study shows that scholars in women's studies find subject librarian assistance most helpful in the explorative stages of research, particularly in searching for grey literature across disciplinary databases. Librarian assistance is also appreciated when it comes to tracking down specific resources, ensuring correct citations, searching comprehensively and avoiding information gaps, and applying evaluative filters that help with broad versus deep reading decisions.[10] Additionally, subject librarians developed an array of almost routine services that tackled the particular challenges of interdisciplinary scholarship. For example, they compiled custom-tailored new-book lists to address the currency issue. They took advantage of tables of contents and search strategy alerts offered by databases and journals. They gathered together in research guides authoritative reference works that provided an entrance to the fundamental concepts and to the assumptions and intellectual frameworks of nonaffiliate disciplinary fields. They taught effective database search strategies, particularly how to translate the research question into the search terminology native to the particular database. They focused in collection development on more specialized materials to offset the broad brushstroke collecting of approval plans. Finally, they used their network of professional relationships with colleagues inside and outside of the library to further the "drawing connections" work of the interdisciplinary scholar. On the more innovative end of the services spectrum, some librarians exploited Web 2.0 technologies, such as tagging, to add more nuance to the traditional subject headings, or used social networks, such as Facebook, to identify students and scholars engaged in interdisciplinary work. Some, taking their cue from innovative embedded virtual reference services, embedded themselves on research teams to contribute their unique strengths of subject expertise combined with information retrieval and information management knowledge. "Librarians' participation in multidisciplinary and interdisciplinary efforts is important when collective expertise in examining problems and solutions utilizing an integrated systems approach is needed."[11]

Yet, in the face of these service offerings, what appears most significant in the literature on interdisciplinary information-seeking behaviors is the absence, for the most part, of using the expertise of subject librarians as a research strategy. Instead, these scholars talk about the importance of having a network of colleagues, particularly from other intellectual communities and domains, as the most valued and effective authoritative resource.[12] Westbrook's findings go even one step further; they point to an actual avoidance of subject librarian assistance. To give a flavor of the discussion, the proffered rationales include the librarian lacking sufficient subject expertise, being too invested in the disciplinary mindset, and being primarily there to assist students. The overarching reason for not seeking out a librarian, however, seems to be the recognition that the research process is intrinsic to the creation of knowledge, and hence is the responsibility of the individual scholar.[13]

In the final analysis, in phase one, the demands of interdisciplinary scholarship did not explode the discipline-focused underpinnings of the academy. Instead, as Jacobs observes, "the present arrangement of discipline-based departments, combined with interdisciplinary research centers, provides an inelegant but practical way to nurture disciplinary skills while allowing the flexibility for scholars to come together around new and topical areas."[14] Likewise, interdisciplinary scholarship did not revolutionize the academic library's practices of knowledge organization and its institutional structures, both of which for the most part progress along hierarchical trajectories. It can be said that interdisciplinary research has succeeded, aided by a confluence of factors that originated to some extent by design and to some extent by serendipity. Success originated partially in the reactive help from subject librarians who guided scholars through unforgiving library systems and steered them toward workarounds, but who also saw opportunities in new technologies to devise effective tools and strategies for interdisciplinary research. More important, though, it was technological and digital library developments, such as full-text searching of large text corpora, federated searching across databases, enriched metadata and the exposure of metadata to external search engines, and the emergence of research portals and virtual communities that contributed to the success of interdisciplinary scholarship.[15]

Moving to phase two of our treatment, several developments within the academy have led to a rapidly changing research and teaching landscape. First, multidisciplinary methods are increasingly prevailing in the search for new knowledge. Researchers are recognizing that the solutions to problems challenging humankind, such as climate change, disease, hunger, poverty, and violence, are not to be found in isolated disciplines but arise instead from broad and integrated approaches.[16] Unlike the interdisciplinary research of phase one, where individual researchers crossed over into another or several other disciplines, in phase two researchers from different disciplines team up and, capitalizing on their multiple perspectives and expertise, create a common understanding and framework for discovery and innovation. Second, profound changes are taking place in scientific research. According to computer scientist Katy Borner, supercomputers capable of analyzing the raw data produced by scientific instruments make it possible for scientists to find order and patterns in raw data that had been "too great, slow or complex for the human eye and mind to notice and comprehend" in the past.[17] That research is highly collaborative, increasingly multidisciplinary, and geographically distributed. Additionally, the use of open source and Web 2.0 software has made it easier to repurpose and combine software-based techniques and to share research findings; the visualization of data has become an increasingly important synthesis tool for both educational and research purposes. Third, in the humanities, humanities computing has evolved into the digital humanities, which seeks to apply the humanistic inquiry to a scholarly landscape greatly changed by digital technologies. Even while its definition varies and is even contested, it seems nonetheless fair to say that the field is methodological by nature, collaborative in practice, and multidisciplinary in scope. Kathleen Fitzpatrick best summarized the yin and yang in digital humanities:

> The state of things in digital humanities today rests in that creative tension, between those who've been in the field for a long time and those who are coming to it today, between disciplinarity and interdisciplinarity, between making and interpreting, between the field's history and its future. Scholarly work across the humanities, as in all academic fields, is increasingly being done digitally. The particular contribution of the digital humanities, however, lies in its exploration of the difference that the digital can make to the kinds of work that we do, as well as to the ways that we communicate with one another. These new modes of scholarship and communication will best flourish if they, like the digital humanities, are allowed to remain plural.[18]

Finally, a new learning culture seems to manifest itself across the disciplines whose tenets include these: information is digital and ubiquitous; play is a strategy to embrace complexity and change; learning proceeds from an active engagement with the world through peer-to-peer interactions and communities of like-minded learners; and questions are more important than answers.

In addition to these internal drivers, the question of how well subject librarians meet the challenges of multidisciplinary research cannot be treated in isolation from the larger external context higher education finds itself in at the beginning of the twenty-first century. The combined challenges of the rapid and transformative changes the digital revolution has brought and continues to bring to every aspect of society; the serious questions leveled at the academy, ranging from content to pedagogy to value; the changes in student demographics; the pressures of an increasingly global and networked world; and lastly, the reality of ever-greater budget constraints: all lead to the question of whether this portends the end of a higher education as we know it. But one might equally ask whether these destabilizing factors, if responded to in the right fashion, might engender a rejuvenated academy. By extension, these same questions have to be put to the academic library; after all, it is inextricably tied to the destiny of its parent institution.

The challenge subject librarians face, then, is to effectively contribute to a university's efforts to produce a new generation of professionals equipped with the knowledge, skills, and vision to work and innovate in this increasingly complex world. How can the subject librarian make meaningful contributions and strike the right balance between supporting innovative, large-scale, collaborative, multidisciplinary projects and the continuing legacy work that is more disciplinary in nature?

The 2009 Ithaka S+R *Faculty Survey* makes it clear that faculty do not consider it essential to use the library to carry out research. Scholars are increasingly finding needed materials directly online without intermediation from the library:

> The availability of new network-level services, such as digital content resources, a variety of new kinds of discovery tools, new services for information organization and use, and scholarly and

pedagogical interaction and collaboration tools, have been the most important factors in motivating these changes. As scholarly resources become available in digital form, users want to use them in that form, and will use whatever tools that are most convenient to get to them.[19]

However, a few observations taken from the survey are relevant to the roles of subject librarians, pointing to areas of needed involvement: (1) libraries should give careful consideration to new ways of service delivery, particularly through collaboration and participation "in the cloud" or at the network level; (2) libraries should leverage geographic and institutional proximity in the development of discovery services such as proactive embedded librarianship and curated local collections used to promote social learning and support collaborative research; (3) participation in faculty's teaching activities could provide an entry toward broader engagement with faculty.

Guided by Ithaka S+R's strategic imperatives, the authors set out to find examples of implementation that illustrate the broad range of opportunities for transformative services, while simultaneously demonstrating that subject librarians can be innovative and enterprising in addressing service needs in multidisciplinary studies (see appendix).

Reading through the cases, what strikes one about these subject librarians is their deep level of engagement coupled with a willingness to leave their comfort zone and venture into uncharted territory. Clearly, they already exemplify the new expectations for the academic library professionals James G. Neal called for at the 2011 ACRL annual meeting: "We must seek individuals who have a clear sense of mission and well-developed self vision, with the requisite base of knowledge, an understanding of strategic positioning, and a commitment to continuous improvement… who can tackle the deep subject expertise and the diversity of assignments required in the future academic research library."[20]

Attributes exemplified by subject librarians in these cases—particularly what mindset qualities are required on the part of the librarian—include moving out of the traditional library into "on-site" settings, thereby enabling collaboration; moving from a supporting role into partnerships; being an integral part of a research team; being "upstream" in the research process (i.e., working with the researchers rather than merely with the research products); having an entrepreneurial mindset (i.e., being proactive in identifying and pursuing opportunities); and being tolerant of risk.[21]

As early as in 2001 and again in 2011, Neal, recognizing the need for the academic library to change radically in order to remain a valued player on campus, laid out an expansive taxonomy of faculty and library relationships, also applicable to relationships between faculty and subject librarians, that moved from servant, to stranger, to friend, to partner, to customer, and finally to the team or knowledge management relationship.[22] While the relationships described are not mutually exclusive, clearly the taxonomy expresses a hierarchy, with the latter descriptions being more desirable. The library literature shows other early examples of calls for qualitative changes in the liaison relationship. For example, dismissing traditional liaison relationships as too passive, the authors of a 2001 article argue instead for "high-impact information consulting that leads to effective partnerships... consulting that is dynamic, proactive, and adds value to the organization."[23] Also, the use of qualifying adjectives such as *hybrid, blended,* and *embedded* when talking about librarians in the more recent literature seems a good indication of changing roles and mindsets.[24] Additionally, there are other indicators that profound changes are either already underway or expected to happen. ARL's recent *Research Library Issues* on the twenty-first-century research library workforce and on liaison librarian roles provide a much needed theoretical framework. The following are relevant to our treatment: Mark A. Puente calls for a research library workforce that is collaborative and can contribute to library, campus, regional, national, and international partnerships and projects. He observes, "the need has never been greater for library and information professionals to embody a collaborative orientation as they engage in dialogue about the information needs of their constituencies and as they think creatively about ways to embed themselves in the research process." In addition to deep subject expertise, Puente lists knowledge of scholarly publishing, intellectual property rights, web development, database building, and other technical competencies as desirable skill sets.[25] At the University of Minnesota, the position description framework has served as a basis to redefine traditional liaison roles. From the ten areas Karen Williams lists, the following are relevant for multidisciplinary library support: campus engagement, e-scholarship and digital tools, outreach to the local community, fund raising, and leadership.[26]

However, even in light of all these activities, the cases the authors describe in the appendix represent exceptions and not the norm in academic libraries. A close look at the barriers seems then an important step toward understanding what challenges need to be overcome before subject librarians more broadly embrace these new roles. The authors identified three interconnected barriers or roadblocks hindering change: (1) subject librarian mindset and knowledge, (2) library administration leadership, and (3) faculty perception of librarian roles. A well-conceived framework of expectations for subject librarian roles, combined with an ongoing training program that provides subject librarians with the requisite knowledge and skills, and an administrative structure that facilitates the execution of these new roles are prerequisites for mindset changes. While thoughts around role expansion seem to have crystallized and some places are testing the waters in implementing new roles, there is a glaring vacuum in educating and training these "new" subject librarians.[27] Not only is there a gap when comparing the covered topics in a 2010 analysis of course syllabi in academic librarianship with some of the more innovative areas listed by Williams, such as e-scholarship and digital tools, but the overall focus is still collections- rather than user-centered.[28] While library school education for the most part appears adequate in preparing subject librarians for the legacy aspects of their positions, it is less satisfactory when it comes to competencies and skills related to these new roles. To prepare subject librarians for their partnership roles with faculty, Daphnée Rentfrow recommends establishing "a separate track designed specifically for academic librarians. What matters is that we will need scholars with PhDs and experience in library-related issues as much as we will need degree-holding librarians with additional research experience. Either degree alone—PhD or MLIS—will not suffice to meet the needs of faculty, scholars, and students in the next decades."[29] Until library school education catches up, the gap is bridged, albeit somewhat tenuously, by variations on the apprenticeship theme.[30]

At least on the academic research library level, there is recognition on the part of library directors of the urgent need for subject librarians to at least explore these uncharted territories. The same cannot be said, however, for the leadership of the academic library in general, based on the recent Ithaka S+R library director survey, which shows that content still commands the resources allocation.[31] How prepared then are library directors, even in research libraries, to implement the mandate of radical systemic change?[32]

Finally, the Ithaka S+R library director survey is merely the latest instrument to uphold that in the eyes of faculty, the library is predominantly a content provider. Changing that perception—really more a misconception—is, according to Rentfrow, the "greatest challenge facing the modern research and academic library. Without faculty support and understanding and without their regular collaboration with librarians, the research library will not survive."[33] There is sufficient library literature that focuses on incremental strategies toward having faculty view librarians as potential research partners. For example, Anthony Fonseca and Robert Tomaszewski recommend librarian involvement in venues outside of librarianship, such as subject-specific organizations, journals, and committees, thereby increasing visibility of librarians in faculty spaces.[34] Yet a higher impact strategy seems to be the Ithaka S+R *Faculty Survey* recommendation of advanced participation in faculty teaching activities as leading to full-fledged faculty-librarian collaborations (see the cases in the teaching collaboration section of the appendix).[35] Finally, like librarians, faculty are trying to find their bearings in this rapidly and radically changing environment; this may provide the impetus to finally see the interdependence of the two parties.

In conclusion, the coalescing of the many internal and external forces that are beginning to shape the research and educational environment in the twenty-first century has created the perfect storm in which multidisciplinary research activities are merely one element of many bumping up against the status quo in the academic library. The haphazard institution-by-institution responses to interdisciplinary research in the last decades of the twentieth century may have been acceptable then, but now the stakes are high, and only a coherent and concerted effort by all stakeholders will ensure the academic library's continued importance to the research and educational mission of higher education. The traditional subject librarian expertise in collection development and management, in reference and instruction, and in describing and interpreting content continues to matter, inasmuch as it provides the foundation. However, that foundation alone is no longer sufficient, as the cases in the attached appendix demonstrate; profound mindset changes are required. Even then, a subject librarian with the necessary strategic understanding of library opportunities and the willingness to venture into the unknown is still beholden to structures—internal and external to the library—to conceptual frameworks, expectations, and assumptions that will have to change before a radical transformation of the academic library can be effected. The examples the authors have chosen showcase a broad range of possibilities for subject librarian involvement, and at the same time convey a sense of excitement suggesting that change when embraced can be inspiring and invigorating.

Appendix

Services at the Network Level
Case 1: Open Education

Subject librarians will need to think carefully in concert with their colleagues about how to take advantage of the open education movement to scale their contribution to teaching and learning on their individual campus. Open education resources offer a sustainable option for subject librarians trying to contribute to digital media literacy and the university's efforts to improve copyright literacy. The multidisciplinary open courseware libraries offer scalable options to subject librarians trying to help students interested in joining peer-to-peer learning communities or in independent study. It is also an intriguing option for faculty trying to engage in self-learning in fields beyond their specialization. Subject librarians are uniquely positioned to help faculty to enhance the learning environment of students by taking advantage of sharable educational material that helps to incorporate Web 2.0 capabilities.[36]

Case 2: Contributing to the Efforts of Professional Organizations (Subject-Based or Library-Based)

On March 30, 2011, SPARC launched a new e-forum for the subject-based digital repository community. In describing the new forum, a SPARC news release said, "The e-forum will enable subject repository managers, both inside and outside libraries, to share procedures and best practices, discuss possible joint projects, and support each other in providing access to an important realm of scholarly literature."[37] Jessica Adamick and Rebecca Reznik-Zellen make a convincing case for broader subject repositories, where the needs of specialized research with its own language and practices are recognized.[38] This is a network-level effort that will potentially meet a glaring need in multidisciplinary knowledge management and would benefit from the involvement of subject librarians.

Case 3: Collaborations with Publishers and Vendors

Cambridge World Shakespeare Online, a transhistorical, international, and interdisciplinary project, received an NEH Digital Humanities start-up grant to support workshops in several locations worldwide between 2009 and 2011, allowing librarians, scholars, performers, teachers, and students to contribute to its conception and design. The intention is to design "a digital workspace and reference resource supporting research and collaboration among scholars, teachers, students and performers worldwide."[39] This could become a standard tool for collaborative research and learning. It is important for subject librarians to take the time to contribute to the development of other such products.

Embeddedness
Case 1
Jake Carlson, a data research scientist at Purdue University Libraries, and Jeremy R. Garritano, the acting head of the Chemistry Library at Purdue University, reported on an organizational effort to embed librarians in project-based e-science research settings. The authors, drawing on their involvement with a project designed to expose undergraduate students to authentic scientific research, offer practical advice and identify skill sets that librarians new to e-science should expect to adapt to or develop. They further argue that library science skills provide a foundation for subject librarians to communicate effectively with researchers and other information professionals to address data curation and management needs. Knowledge of grantmanship, according to the authors, facilitates the transition from a supportive role to a collaborative role.[40]

Case 2
Another model of embeddedness is evolving in instruction, where subject librarians are members of a team contributing to the teaching needs of a multidisciplinary program of study. The Honours B.Sc. Integrated Science (iSci) program at McMaster University is an example of such an embedded model. The iSci program was designed and developed over a period of four years by research and teaching-track faculty representing each of the scientific disciplines, as well as by librarians from the university libraries. The program is administered by a director and is taught by an interdisciplinary team of twelve instructors (the iTeach team), one of whom has expertise in information

science. The focus is on active learning using appropriate technologies. Students are expected to learn fundamental processes and skills needed for effective inquiry-based learning conducted in teams. In an *EDUCAUSE Review* article, Colgoni and Eyles state, "The iSci program is viewed as an incubator for new ideas, teaching and learning strategies, technologies, and partnerships that may be more widely applied in the McMaster and global university environments."[41]

Case 3

Another example of embeddedness involves the subject librarian as participant in a university-funded fellowship program that is designed for faculty to explore interdisciplinary studies. Natasha Cooper is the bibliographer for education, information studies, and public communications in the Bird Library at Syracuse University. She applied for and was awarded one of six faculty fellowships in the College of Visual and Performing Arts' Interdisciplinary Research Group (IRG) during the 2009–2010 academic year. According to a Syracuse University news release, "The IRG is a faculty-driven, cross-college incubator for scholarly development" that spotlights a new theme each year and provides a catalyst and resources for developing creative research and teaching projects. "The goal of the IRG is to establish a peer environment that fosters a longstanding, accumulative and non-competitive… social… network."[42]

Local Collections and Community
Case 1

The Center for Digital Storytelling (CDS) is an international non-profit training, project development, and research organization dedicated to assisting people in using digital media to tell meaningful stories from their lives. Its focus is on partnering with community, educational, and business institutions to develop large-scale initiatives using methods and principles adapted from its original Digital Storytelling Workshop. It also offers workshops for organizations and individuals and serves as a clearinghouse of information and resources about storytelling and new media.

In 2005, two members of the University Library System at Ohio State, Karen Diaz, the e-learning librarian, and Anne Fields, the reference librarian and collection manager for education, attended the CDS's standard workshop in Berkeley, California. They returned and initiated a project to integrate digital storytelling into the library system's information technology and curriculum support services. In 2006, the CDS was invited to Ohio State to lead a workshop for a group of faculty and staff. This session led to the formation of an Ohio State University Digital Storytelling Leadership Team, comprised of members drawn from several parts of the university. The leadership team actively explored and developed approaches to the academic use of digital storytelling methods. The promise of the new pedagogy generated enough faculty engagement and enthusiasm to lead to active use of digital storytelling as a curriculum component for students across multiple disciplines. In 2008, Fields and Diaz authored *Fostering Community through Digital Storytelling: A Guide for Academic Libraries*, the first book on extensive university-level applications of digital storytelling.[43]

Case 2

Rebecca Federman, the culinary arts subject librarian (and the electronic resources librarian) at the New York Public Research Libraries, spent a number of years building a community of food studies enthusiasts through her animated blog *Cooked Books*. She was able to capitalize on this slow and steady outreach effort when the time came to engage the community in her crowdsourced collections initiative undertaken in collaboration with Amy Azzarito, the former NYPL Digital Experience producer, and Ben Vershbow, the NYPL labs manager. Rebecca noticed a strong interest among users of the menu collection in doing research on specific dishes, which was very difficult. Although the 10,000 menus in the collection had been digitized, there was no efficient way to search their content. Rebecca and her colleagues considered and rejected optical character recognition (OCR) software as a tool for transcribing the menus because the menus were often handwritten, used abbreviations, and had extremely inconsistent fonts. The group enthusiastically endorsed Amy Azzarito's recommendation to try to build a searchable database by inviting individual members of the food studies community to help crowdsource the content. On Saturday, April 23, 2011, Rebecca announced the existence of the site via her blog *Cooked Books:* "This past Monday evening, the New York Public Library launched 'What's on the Menu?' a web site which invites the public to transcribe our digitized historical menus."[44] By Wednesday, April 27, 2011, the *New York Times* published an article describing this crowdsourced effort that had already rallied thousands of participants. Ben Vershbow is quoted as being amazed at the great enthusiasm of the response, noting that he and Ms. Federman used only social media to invite participation.[45] The selection of the collection, captivation of interest through social media, and partnership with the user in transforming the content into something new—a searchable database—are compelling and translatable to an academic environment. There should be space and opportunity for subject librarians to pursue such ideas and undertakings.

Case 3
Shannon Bohle (avatar Archivist Llewellyn in Second Life) serves as the volunteer director of the Neil A. Armstrong Library and Archives at NASA CoLab in Second Life, the first library or archives in a synthetic immersive environment. She was selected as a 2010 Linden Prize Top 10 Finalist for her "Library and Archives at NASA CoLab in Second Life" project, an interactive and educational project which could be an interesting template for subject librarian/archival collaboration in support of active learning. The project uses Second Life as a platform for "gaming as learning." This philosophy was implemented using existing NASA educational materials by creating virtual world versions of historical publications, links to NASA websites, current and former astronaut Twitter pages, and NASA TV. The library and archives originated new content for Web 2.0 social networking and communications applications. The site generates excellent participatory responses from a range of users: school groups, professors, researchers, and the general public interested in NASA.[46]

Teaching Collaborations with Faculty
Case 1
On February 18, 2011, Phoebe Acheson, the classics librarian at the University of Georgia, posted the following: "I'm lending myself to a *Reacting to the Past* game in the history department for the next sever-

al weeks—a role-playing game in which students hone their analysis, rhetoric, and writing skills by re-enacting debates around historical crisis points."[47]

Pioneered by historian Mark C. Carnes, *Reacting to the Past* has been implemented at over 300 colleges and universities in the United States and abroad. Mark C. Carnes wrote a commentary on active learning and the value of this game: "When absorbed in intellectual games of this nature, students find the customary diversions of college—beer pong, World of Warcraft, Facebook, fraternity hijinks—less compelling. The ideas, texts, and historical moments on which academic discourse depends become a part of their lives, and the friendships they forge in the heat of prolonged competition can transform their class into a community."[48] It makes perfect sense for a subject librarian to be a full participant in such a community. This is a game that requires a set of skills—speaking, writing, critical thinking, problem solving, leadership, and teamwork—in order to prevail in difficult and complicated situations. Faculty would welcome full engagement with the pedagogy on the part of librarians.

Case 2
Megan A. Norcia has reported on an interesting pedagogical project she worked on in 2004, during her tenure as a postdoctoral CLIR fellow. The purpose of the project was to enhance the educational experience of undergraduates engaged in literary studies by immersing them in the study of a primary text. The project was an outgrowth of her involvement with the development of a digital archive at Lehigh University—*I Remain: A Digital Archive of Letters, Manuscripts, and Ephemera*—and a desire to promote collaboration among humanities faculty on innovative uses of the archive in teaching and learning. She makes the point in her article that a collection needs marketing and advocates who will raise interest in, and awareness of, its possibilities. She finds a logical venue for outreach to faculty and uses it to present her ideas about pedagogical possibilities. A faculty member who is known to be innovative and committed to enhancing the learning experience of his students through the use of technology expresses interest in working with her on a pilot project in American studies. Their jointly designed course, in a nutshell, has five groups of students

work collaboratively in an online environment with an assigned letter written by either John Adams, Benjamin Franklin, Thomas Jefferson, John Jay, or George Washington. Each group works closely with a librarian guide to identify sources to support the contexts they are building to create historical and social frameworks for the letters. The librarians and faculty learn about the letters and the process of contextualizing them right alongside the students. Each student submits a narrative description of his or her experience with "doing history" using the assigned letter, and the narrative, in turn, becomes part of the digital archive. This visceral experience of the archival research process generates an enthusiastic response from student participants.[49]

Notes

1. Laurence Miller, "Liaison Work in the Academic Library," *RQ* 16 (1977): 213–215; Connie Wu et al., "Effective Liaison Relationships in an Academic Library," *College & Research Libraries News* 55 (1994): 254, 303.
2. Jerry A. Jacobs, "Interdisciplinary Hype," *The Chronicle Review*, November 22, 2009, http://chronicle.com/article/Interdisciplinary-Hype/49191.
3. Julie Thompson Klein, "Interdisciplinary Needs: The Current Context," *Library Trends* 44, no. 2 (1996): 136.
4. Ibid., 135.
5. Susan E. Searing, "How Libraries Cope With Interdisciplinarity: The Case of Women's Studies," *Issues in Integrative Studies* 10 (1992): 8.
6. Marcia Bates, "Learning About the Information Seeking of Interdisciplinary Scholars and Students," *Library Trends* 44, no. 2 (1996): 155–165; Don Spanner, "Border Crossings: Understanding the Cultural and Informational Dilemmas of Interdisciplinary Scholars," *Journal of Academic Librarianship* 27, no. 5 (2001): 352–360; Carole L. Palmer and Laura T. Neuman, "The Information Work of Interdisciplinary Humanities Scholars: Exploration and Translation," *Library Quarterly* 72, no. 1 (2002): 85–117; Lynn Westbrook, "Information Needs and Experiences of Scholars in Women's Studies: Problems and Solutions," *College & Research Libraries* 64, no. 3 (2003), 192–209; Allen Foster, "A Nonlinear Model of Information-Seeking Behavior," *Journal of the American Society for Information Science and Technology* 55, no. 3 (2004): 228–237; Xuemei Ge, "Information-Seeking Behavior in the Digital Age: A Multidisciplinary Study of Academic Researchers," *College & Research Libraries* 71, no. 5 (2010): 435–455.
7. Bates, "Learning About the Information Seeking," 156.
8. Anonymous scholar, , quoted in Spanner, "Border Crossings," 355.
9. Susan Searing, "Meeting the Information Needs of Interdisciplinary Scholars: Issues for Administrators of Large University Libraries," *Library Trends* 44, no. 2 (1996): 317.
10. Westbrook, "Information Needs and Experiences," 197, 205.
11. Martin A. Kesselman and Sarah Barbara Watstein, "Creating Opportunities: Embedded Librarians," *Journal of Library Administration* 49, no. 4 (2009): 314, doi:10.1080/01930820902832538.

12. Palmer and Neuman, "The Information Work," 102, 104.
13. Westbrook, "Information Needs and Experiences," 199.
14. Jacobs, "Interdisciplinary Hype."
15. Carole L. Palmer, Lauren C. Teffeau, and Carrie M. Piermann, *Scholarly Information Practices in the Online Environment: Themes from the Literature and Implications for Library Service Development* (Dublin, OH: OCLC Research, 2009), http://www.oclc.org/programs/publications/reports/2009-02.pdf; Ge, "Information-Seeking Behavior."
16. The 2010 *Horizon Report* lists the need for cross-campus collaboration in response to "the challenges facing the world as multidisciplinary" as one of the four key trends ("2010 *Horizon Report:* Key Trends." January 14, 2010, NMC Words Pressed website, http://wp.nmc.org/horizon2010/chapters/trends).
17. Katy Borner , quoted in John Markoff, "Digging Deeper, Seeing Farther: Supercomputers Alter Science," *New York Times*, April 26, 2011, Late edition (East Coast): D1.
18. Kathleen Fitzpatrick, "The Humanities, Done Digitally," *The Digital Campus* (blog), May 8, 2011, *Chronicle of Higher Education*, http://chronicle.com/article/The-Humanities-Done-Digitally/127382.
19. Kevin Guthrie and Ross Housewright, "Repackaging the Library: What Do Faculty Think?" in "Climbing Out of the Box: Repackaging Libraries," special issue, *Journal of Library Administration* 51, no. 1 (2010), 80, 102, doi:10.1080/01930826.2011.531643.
20. James G. Neal, "Stop the Madness: The Insanity of ROI and the Need for New Qualitative Measures of Academic Library Success" (paper presented at the annual meeting for ACRL, Philadelphia, PA, March 30–April 2, 2011), 427, http://www.ala.org/acrl/sites/ala.org.acrl/files/content/conferences/confsandpreconfs/national/2011/papers/stop_the_madness.pdf
21. Jake R. Carlson and Ruth Kneale, "Embedded Librarianship in the Research Context: Navigating New Waters," *College & Research Libraries News* 72, no. 3 (2011): 167–170.
22. James G. Neal, "The Entrepreneurial Imperative: Advancing from Incremental to Radical Change in the Academic Library," *portal: Libraries and the Academy* 1, no. 1 (2001): 9; James G. Neal, "Advancing from Kumbaya to Radical Collaboration: Redefining the Future Research Library," *Journal of Library Administration* 51, no. 1 (2010), 72–73.
23. Donald G. Frank, Gregory K. Raschke, Julie Wood, and Julie Z. Yang, "Information Consulting: The Key to Success in Academic Libraries," *The Journal of Academic Librarianship* 27, no. 2 (2001): 90.
24. Joan Giesecke, "Finding the Right Metaphor: Restructuring, Realigning, and Repackaging Today's Research Libraries," *Journal of Library Administration* 51, no. 1 (2011): 54–65.
25. Mark A. Puente, "Developing a Vital Research Library Workforce," *Research Library Issues: A Bimonthly Report from ARL, CNI, and SPARC*, no. 272 (October 2010): 5, http://publications.arl.org/rli272.
26. Karen Williams, "A Framework for Articulating New Library Roles," *Research Library Issues: A Bimonthly Report from ARL, CNI, and SPARC*, no. 265 (August 2009): 4–5, http://www.arl.org/resources/pubs/rli/archive/rli265.shtml.
27. In addition to the University of Minnesota, some other libraries where the role of the subject librarian is being reconceptualized are the Digital Librarian Initiative

at Emory, "Emerging Futures of Subject Librarians," http://digitallibrarians.org/node/3389; the Engagement-Centered Model at Ohio State University, http://library.osu.edu/staff/administration-reports/OSUL_Strategic_Plan_Metrics_Status_Report_Je2010.pdf.

28. Edgar C. Bailey, Jr., "Educating Future Academic Librarians: An Analysis of Courses in Academic Librarianship," *Journal of Education for Library and Information Science* 51, no. 1 (2010): 37.

29. Daphnée Rentfrow, "Groundskeepers, Gatekeepers, and Guides: How to Change Faculty Perceptions of Librarians and Ensure the Future of the Research Library," in *No Brief Candle: Reconceiving Research Libraries for the 21st Century*, papers from a meeting convened in Washington, DC, February 27, 2008, CLIR Publication no. 142 (Washington, DC: Council on Library and Information Resources, 2008), 64.

30. A good example is the Mentoring Program at New York University Division of Libraries. The program is an integral component of the dual master's degree program, which is jointly administered by Long Island University's Palmer School of Library and Information Science and New York University's Graduate School of Arts and Science: http://nyu.libguides.com/dualdegreementoring.

31. Matthew P. Long and Roger C. Schonfeld, *Ithaka S+R Library Survey 2010: Insights from U.S. Academic Library Directors* (New York: Ithaka S+R, 2010), http://www.ithaka.org/ithaka-s-r/research/ithaka-s-r-library-survey-2010/insights-from-us-academic-library-directors.pdf.

32. James G. Neal, "Prospects for Systemic Change across Academic Libraries," *EDUCAUSE Review Magazine* 46, no. 2 (March/April 2010), 10–11, http://www.educause.edu/library/ERM1129

33. Rentfrow, "Groundskeepers, Gatekeepers, and Guides," 60.

34. Anthony J. Fonseca and Van P. Viator, "Escaping the Island of Lost Faculty: Collaboration as a Means of Visibility," *Collaborative Librarianship* 1, no. 3 (2009): 81–90; Robert Tomaszewski and Karen I. MacDonald, "Identifying Subject-Specific Conferences as Professional Development Opportunities for the Academic Librarian," *Journal of Academic Librarianship* 35, no. 6 (2009): 583–590.

35. For additional examples see, Brenda L. Johnson, "Transforming Roles for Academic Librarians: Leading and Participating in New Partnerships," *Research Library Issues: A Bimonthly Report from ARL, CNI, and SPARC* no. 272 (October 2010): 7–15, http://publications.arl.org/rli272.

36. Clifford Lynch, "Digital Libraries, Learning Communities, and Open Education," in *Opening Up Education: The Collective Advancement of Education through Open Technology, Open Content, and Open Knowledge*, ed. Toru Iiyoshi and M. S. Vijay Kumar (Cambridge, MA: MIT Press, 2008), 104–118.

37. SPARC, "SPARC Launches New E-Forum for Subject Repository Development and Success," news release, March 30, 2011, http://www.arl.org/sparc/media/11-0330.shtml.

38. Jessica Adamick and Rebecca Reznik-Zellen, "Representation and Recognition of Subject Repositories," *D-Lib Magazine* 16, no. 9/10 (2010), doi:10.1045/september2010-adamick.

39. "About," Cambridge World Shakespeare Online website, http://cwso.blogs.brynmawr.edu (accessed February 8, 2012).

40. Jeremy R. Garritano and Jake R. Carlson, "A Subject Librarian's Guide to Collaborating on E-Science Projects," *Issues in Science and Technology Librarianship*

57 (Spring 2009), http://www.istl.org/09-Spring/refereed2.html.

41. Andrew Colgoni and Carolyn Eyles, "A New Approach to Science Education for the 21st Century," *EDUCAUSE Review* 45, no. 1 (2010): 1–4, http://www.educause.edu/library/ERM1017.

42. Erica Blust, "SU Interdisciplinary Research Group to Present Poster Session on Theme 'Journeys of Interdisciplinary Observation,'" news release, April 5, 2010, Syracuse University, http://www.syr.edu/news/articles/2010/interdisciplinary-research-group-04-10.html.

43. Anne M. Fields and Karen R. Díaz, *Fostering Community through Digital Storytelling: A Guide for Academic Libraries* (Westport, CT: Libraries Unlimited, 2008); Ohio State University, Digital Storytelling, http://digitalstory.osu.edu/.

44. Rebecca Federman, "What's on the Menu?" *Cooked Books* (blog), April 23, 2011, http://cookedbooks.blogspot.com/2011/04/whats-on-menu.html.

45. Alexis Mainland, "Study the Menus But No Orders, Please," *New York Times* (blog), April 27, 2011, http://query.nytimes.com/gst/fullpage.html?res=9902E7DB103BF934A15757C0A9679D8B63.

46. More on Shannon Bohle and this project available at "Shannon Bohle," Virtual Excellence Awards 2011, May 26, 2011, Association of Virtual Worlds, http://awards.associationofvirtualworlds.com/shannon-bohle.

47. Phoebe Acheson, "Reacting to the Past," *Classics Librarian* (blog), February 18, 2011, http://classicslibrarian.wordpress.com/2011/02/18/reacting-to-the-past.

48. Mark C. Carnes, "Setting Students' Minds on Fire," *Chronicle of Higher Education*, March 6, 2011, http://chronicle.com/article/Setting-Students-Minds-on/126592.

49. Megan A. Norcia, "Out of the Ivory Tower Endlessly Rocking: Collaborating across Disciplines and Professions to Promote Student Learning in the Digital Archive," *Pedagogy* 8, no. 1 (2008): 91–114.

Teaching Research across Disciplines: Interdisciplinarity and Information Literacy

Maralyn Jones

> The human mind does not think in disciplines.
> *~Renate Holub*

Introduction

As this volume shows, interdisciplinarity is an increasingly large part of twenty-first-century universities at both the faculty and undergraduate levels. Researchers in fields from the sciences to the social sciences and the arts and humanities are making use of theories, methods, and sources from other fields to enrich their own understanding and to grapple with problems that are simply too complex to understand with the tools of a single discipline.[1] Beyond the explicitly interdisciplinary fields such as area studies, ethnic studies, gender and women's studies, and environmental and resources studies, interdisciplinary approaches are used in such traditional disciplines as literature, history, anthropology, political science, public policy, and public health.

Interdisciplinary research is more challenging than researching in a single discipline because of the fragmentation of scholarly information and the difficulty of gaining sufficient understanding of the methods, tools, and theories of multiple disciplines. Librarians who provide research instruction for students doing interdisciplinary assignments need to develop a specific skill set for this work. This chapter is intended for librarians asking themselves, "How should I teach interdisciplinary research to maximize critical thinking and information literacy?"

Theories of Interdisciplinary Research
Definitions of Interdisciplinary Research
A favorite activity of interdisciplinary scholars is attempting to define interdisciplinarity and to parse the different degrees of disciplinary in-

tegration among types of interdisciplinarity.[2] At the undergraduate level, the usual model involves a single student using methodologies from multiple disciplines to investigate a social phenomenon or problem.

Lisa Lattuca, a prominent scholar of interdisciplinarity, and her colleagues identify different types of interdisciplinary teaching:

- Disciplinary courses informed by other discipline(s)
- Courses that link disciplines
- Courses that cross disciplines
- Courses without a compelling disciplinary basis[3]

What all definitions share, however, is the idea that interdisciplinarity attempts to integrate insights from multiple disciplines to address a compelling problem that defies explanation by a single discipline.

Goals of Interdisciplinary Research

Several writers have developed schema that include goals for undergraduate interdisciplinary research. In *Interdisciplinary Writing Assessment Profiles*, Wolfe and Haynes put forward a rubric for student interdisciplinary writing that provides specific criteria that librarians can teach to.[4] A sample from this work demonstrates how germane the library research session is to excellence in interdisciplinary writing:

1. The problem or issue under investigation has been clearly stated.
2. The scope of the problem is clearly defined.
3. "Textual" evidence is cited to support major assertions.
4. Theory or theoretical principles are used to support major assertions.
5. Primary sources are included.
6. Sources include more than 25 percent recent publications, dated within the last five years of the project's completion.
7. A range of (more than one) perspectives from within the (at least one) discipline are included.
8. Identifies how at least one term is used differently in different disciplines within the context of the problem.
9. Identifies how different disciplinary terms are used to describe similar concepts.

In *Interdisciplinary Research: Process and Theory*, Allen Repko devotes considerable attention to the goals of interdisciplinary research for students.[5] His definition of research is broad, including library research as only one step in the process. Repko's goals overlap considerably with the ACRL *Information Literacy Competency Standards for Higher Education*[6] (henceforth, "ACRL *Standards*"). Table 9.1 highlights points of similarity between Repko's Integrated Model of the Interdisciplinary Research Process[7] and the ACRL *Standards*.

Table 9.1. Comparison of Interdisciplinary Research Model with ACRL *Standards*

Integrated Model of the Interdisciplinary Research Process	ACRL Information Literacy Competency Standards
A. Drawing on interdisciplinary insights	**The information literate student...**
1. Define the problem or state the focus question	...determines the nature and extent of the information needed [Standard 1].
2. Justify using an interdisciplinary approach	
3. Identify relevant disciplines	... determines the nature and extent of the information needed [Standard 1].
4. Conduct a literature search	... accesses needed information effectively and efficiently [Standard 2].
5. Develop adequacy in each relevant discipline	... accesses needed information effectively and efficiently [Standard 2].
6. Analyze the problem and evaluate each insight into it	... evaluates information and its sources critically and incorporates selected information into his knowledge base [Standard 3].
B. Integrating insights and producing an interdisciplinary understanding	**The information literate student ...**
7. Identify conflicts between insights and their sources	... uses information effectively to accomplish a specific purpose [Standard 4].
8. Create or discover common ground	... uses information effectively to accomplish a specific purpose [Standard 4].
9. Integrate insights	... evaluates information and its sources critically and incorporates selected information into his knowledge base [Standard 3].
10. Produce an interdisciplinary understanding of the problem	... uses information effectively to accomplish a specific purpose [Standard 4].

Like the criteria mentioned in Wolfe and Haynes, some of the stages of Repko's model map closely to topics that librarians usually address in library instruction for any students. From Repko's model, "Define the problem or state the focus question," and "Conduct a literature search," would typically be addressed in any library research session. Likewise, the first seven 'interdisciplinary' writing skills identified by Wolfe and Haynes correlate well with the usual content of library instruction sessions.

Repko and Wolfe and Haynes also point out content specific to interdisciplinary research that librarians do not always address, for instance Repko's "Identify relevant disciplines" and the final two criteria from Wolfe and Haynes ("Identifies how at least one term is used differently in different disciplines within the context of the problem" and "Identifies how different disciplinary terms are used to describe similar concepts.") Just as in the ACRL Standards, other research expectations mentioned by these writers would normally be the responsibility of faculty to teach, rather than the librarian.

Elements of Disciplines

Students of interdisciplinary topics need to know what a discipline is. According to Tanya Augsburg, the author of an influential textbook on interdisciplinarity, a discipline is distinguished by fifteen elements:

- Basic concepts | Leading theories
- Modes of inquiry (or Research methods)
- What counts as a problem
- Observational categories
- Representational techniques
- Types of explanation
- Standards of proof
- Ideals/ethics/objectives
- Assumptions and world views
- Disciplinary perspective
- Seminal texts/books
- Major thinkers
- Major practitioners

- Professional academic associations
- Leading academic journals[8]

Without the footing in a discipline that knowledge of at least some of these elements provides, students cannot hope to do more than superficial research, which is the major criticism of interdisciplinary research. While librarians and faculty are familiar enough with the structure of academic disciplines and publishing to be aware that every discipline has such elements, students are novices and need to become aware of these elements to get their research off to a good start. We can be fairly certain that most students could not list more than a few of these defining elements for a single discipline, much less for each discipline they might try to incorporate into their research. Explicit awareness of the common features of disciplines will help students compare and contrast material from different disciplines more effectively. Though neither faculty nor librarians could know the names of leading journals, thinkers, theories, and methodologies in all fields, librarians can teach students effective strategies to find this information.

In *Creating Interdisciplinarity*, Lisa Lattuca claims, "One of the most distinctive and binding aspects of a disciplinary community is the language it employs."[9] In fact many scholars describe the process of learning to do research in multiple disciplines as "becoming bilingual." Augsburg neglects to include disciplinary language as a defining element (though is it included in other elements), a serious omission, since knowledge of discipline-specific terminologies, both language used by practitioners and controlled vocabularies used in library catalogs and databases, is essential to every effective researcher.

Developing effective search terminology is particularly challenging for interdisciplinary students.[10] Undergraduates typically start searching using the first words that come into their minds and use the simplest keyword search options. These strategies exacerbate the problem of too many or irrelevant search results, leading to frustration and poor research. It is both difficult and important for the librarian to teach students the use of controlled vocabularies in databases and catalogs where possible. Different tools, of course, use different vocabularies, or none at all: LCSH, self-defined descriptors, or thesauri created by disciplinary authorities, such as professional organizations. The possibility that similar concepts or problems are assigned different terminology in different disciplines is also confusing. Students also need to learn strategies for narrowing searches in databases without field-delimited searching, such as the basic or keyword search function in many databases and Google Scholar.

Academic librarians wisely place disciplinary language as among the most important elements for students to learn, something essential to doing effective research. For students, academic research requires learning more than two research "languages," because not only must they learn multiple disciplinary terminologies, but also the language of library research.[11] This creates an added impediment to student interdisciplinary research.

Disciplinary Adequacy

Scholars of interdisciplinary studies agree that no individual can attain mastery of all relevant disciplines, and some argue that it is beside the point to even wish to. In some conceptions of interdisciplinarity, research is done by groups of specialists or scholars, each of whom does have mastery over a discipline or subspecialty. Other scholars and undergraduate students more commonly undertake individual research projects and aim simply for "adequacy" with the relevant disciplines.

Possibly the most challenging part of interdisciplinary research is learning to frame questions. Student researchers need both to frame questions in ways appropriate to the disciplines they are working with and to synthesize these in interdisciplinary ways.[12] As novice researchers, students also have problems with topic selection because "what faculty would regard as the 'holes' in the literature that a research question might address, are not obvious to [students]."[13] While students can find models in the disciplinary literature for appropriate questions, it is more difficult to conceive of interdisciplinary questions. Repko mentions three criteria for good interdisciplinary questions:

- They should be open-ended and too complex to be addressed by a single discipline.
- They must be researchable.
- They must be verified using appropriate research methods.[14]

It will be helpful for students to keep these criteria in mind as they do their research, since the quality of research will clearly affect the nature of questions students can answer.

For interdisciplinary students to achieve disciplinary adequacy, they need to learn at least the basic assumptions, methodologies, theories, and so forth discussed by Augsburg. In most programs of interdisciplinary studies, students select courses over a period of years that focus on "a unifying problem, issue, theme or topic called an 'Area of Concentration'"[15] so by the time they start writing their senior theses, they have been introduced to the basics of social science disciplines. However, students taking a single interdisciplinary class will not have had this preparation and will have to acquire adequacy in multiple disciplines quickly, making this an important goal of library instruction.

Interdisciplinary Research and Learning

Interdisciplinary research projects are the quintessential "student-centered learning environments" referred to in the ACRL *Standards*. When students investigate topics using their own unique choices of disciplinary methodologies, librarians have the perfect opportunity to use "problem-based learning, evidence-based learning, and inquiry learning … thereby increasing their [i.e., students'] responsibility for their own learning."[16] For example, since interfaces, terminology, and other features of research tools differ, understanding the underlying similarities is difficult for students. As instructors, librarians need to find ways to use these differences as teaching opportunities.

According to learning theory, moderate mental conflict or confusion stimulates the assimilation of new ideas as people struggle to resolve their confusion. Some scholars theorize that interdisciplinary research is thus more conducive to developing critical-thinking skills than is research founded in a single discipline.[17] Repko quotes Myers and Haynes as saying that interdisciplinary students engage in more reflection than other students, which stimulates learning,[18] but Lattuca et al. argue that it is the combination of interdisciplinarity and constructivist pedagogy, or active learning techniques, that results in greatest student learning.[19] Librarians should capitalize on the innate conflict between different disciplines to cultivate opportunities for learning, using active learning techniques when possible to allow students to construct their own understandings.

Educating Ourselves

When working with faculty in preparation for an instruction session, the librarian would do well to determine out how much disciplinary integration is expected of students and how the faculty will assess whether and to what degree integration has been achieved. In addition, reading even one or two texts on the philosophy of interdisciplinary research will enable librarians to better understand the goals of the faculty and better design instructional experiences and materials to meet these goals. Tanya Augsburg, Lisa Lattuca, and Allen Repko all provide excellent overviews.

Librarians embarking on teaching interdisciplinary research may want to familiarize themselves with ACRL standards produced for specific disciplines. As of this writing, ACRL's websites list these specific standards:

- Anthropology and Sociology—http://www.ala.org/acrl/standards/anthro_soc_standards
- Psychology—http://www.ala.org/acrl/standards/psych_info_lit
- Science and Engineering/Technology—http://www.ala.org/acrl/standards/infolitscitech
- Political Science—http://www.ala.org/ala/mgrps/divs/acrl/standards/PoliSciGuide.pdf
- Literatures in English—http://www.ala.org/acrl/standards/researchcompetenciesles

These standards give examples of the tools, methodologies, and fundamental texts of the discipline that can be useful for the librarian as well as students. An ACRL wiki gives information on standards for additional disciplines.[20]

Librarians have good reason to feel confident in their skills and problem-solving abilities when collaborating with faculty and students in interdisciplinary research since general reference and instruction librarians are used to "living without the comfort of expertise."[21] The frequency with which academic librarians are required to research in unfamiliar fields and with unfamiliar academic terminology makes them more conversant with the problems of students beginning inter-disciplinary research than are most faculty.

Instructional Strategies
Identifying Relevant Disciplines
We have seen that interdisciplinary research requires knowledge of disciplines. Since many library databases are discipline-oriented and library websites often rely on disciplines as an organizing principle for finding databases, library instructors need to steer students to useful databases by helping them choose disciplines relevant to their topics. While there are a number of excellent, large multidisciplinary data-bases (JSTOR, Web of Science, EBSCO's Academic Search prod-ucts, CSA Illumina, and ProQuest's Research Library among them) that should be searched, they often will not suffice for difficult, ob-scure, or more advanced research topics. Beyond the multidisciplinary databases, which not all libraries license, the disciplinary databases loom as terra incognita for most students, yet in-depth research may require students to use these narrower, and often more difficult, tools.

The library instruction session may be the only opportunity stu-dents have to consider the gaps in their disciplinary mental maps. A good warm-up activity in class is to ask students to brainstorm a list of all disciplines that might be relevant to their topic or problem; this could be an individual exercise or done as a class with a sample top-ic. Usually students have no difficulty identifying which disciplines could be relevant once the idea is presented to them.

Another good introductory activity is to ask students if they are familiar with the research methodologies of the disciplines they plan to use, or the major theories, or the types of evidence that are valid. If they are not, ask them to spend five minutes trying to find that infor-mation and then discussing what they did and how it worked. While most will not be able to answer those questions, simply raising them alerts students to the gaps in their knowledge. This is where instruc-tion in Augsburg's elements of disciplines will show its value. It can be most effective to start instruction by making students aware of holes in their own knowledge.

Continuing in this vein, the librarian can ask students to browse the library's list of databases organized by subject. After students have determined the disciplines they plan to use, have them select the databases they think would be best for their topic and ask them to note why they chose each. Class discussion of the selected databases can help point out that even databases in the same discipline will contain different kinds of information: scholarly, news, professional or popular, secondary, primary, and so forth. This is a way to open students' minds to different sources of information and to explore library resources beyond the tools they typically use. This common active learning strategy is effective because it teaches students how to find additional resources they may need as they consider using alternate disciplines in their work. To make this information stick, recommend that students note the names of the databases they plan to use, since they will not otherwise remember them. It is also a good practice to explain the difference between the vendor name, which is much more visible, and the database name.

In an instruction session for a whole class, it is helpful for the librarian to know the students' topics ahead of time in order to consider which disciplines are most relevant and which databases will be most useful to demonstrate or have students work with. Students with related topics can divide up the work of exploring the relevant databases and share their insights with each other or to the whole in class in a small-group exercise.

Reference Tools

A common mistake when exploring a new discipline is in reading one's first article or book and assuming that it represents the mainstream viewpoint of that discipline. When instructing students to search for books and articles on their topics, one goal should be to enable them to identify fundamental works and major theories, helping them achieve disciplinary adequacy. This instruction is not typically necessary for undergraduates in traditional disciplinary fields, but it is essential for interdisciplinary students. Some useful exercises [or approaches] include the following:

- Use a subject-specific encyclopedia or reference work. Important writers and significant concepts or theories will have individual entries as well as bibliographies. It's helpful to mention that these kinds of sources are often faster than web searching and are more authoritative.

- Find published topical and disciplinary bibliographies. Inter-disciplinary students find bibliographies useful as an efficient way to find the seminal works in a field quickly. Beware of bibliographies published on the Web unless the author has verifiable expertise in the field.
- Search for review articles on the discipline.
- Check for book titles or significant authors in a catalog. Seminal works can sometimes be identified by the multiple editions published repeatedly over many years. Seminal authors' names may appear as both author and subject.
- Find the number of times an item has been cited. Google Scholar is a good beginner's tool for this, and more familiar to students than the traditional citation indexes and databases, which, however, are more comprehensive.
- Suggest students ask the faculty member for advice on significant works or writers. The personal referral is faculty members' own preferred method of finding sources in unfamiliar disciplines.

It is also worth pointing out to faculty and students how useful *Wikipedia* can be as a starting place for learning about a discipline. A convenient time to do this is while conducting a library session in an electronic classroom, where students don't have immediate access to the reference collection. Here are a few ideas for using *Wikipedia* in an academic setting:

Direct students to a Wikipedia article in the scholarly style; the one on Max Weber (viewed on March 12, 2011) is a good example:

1. Have students use the View History link to see the pattern of edits to the article, when they were done, who did them, and so forth, for a sense of areas of dissent and controversy in the article.
2. Have students try to find an article cited in the References section of the *Wikipedia* article. Negotiating broken and erroneous links is part of the learning experience, as is finding a Google Book preview and its link Find in a Library.
3. Point out the footnotes. Some *Wikipedia* articles are actually copied from encyclopedias (which may be out of date) with or without credit.

4. Plagiarism activity: Have students explain why there are footnotes for paraphrases and nondirect quotes in the Max Weber article.

Search Strategies

After students have informed themselves about the disciplines they will use, they can start to research their topics. As students interrogate sources from several disciplines, the problem of finding too many potential sources grows exponentially. Interdisciplinary students, even more than other students, are liable to identify more books, articles, and other research materials than they can effectively read or use. For them particularly, the problem is one of selection of the most relevant sources, rather than discovery. For this reason, helping interdisciplinary students formulate sufficiently narrow searches is essential to their success and their time management.

Active learning strategies are central to teaching interdisciplinary research, as we have shown, because no lecture can cover the plethora of potential research tools. Students must learn to teach themselves how to proceed in their research. Books and articles that present ingenious and effective ideas for in-class learning activities constitute a literature in itself, too large to cite here. But without trying to summarize specific teaching techniques, it is safe to say that activities should focus on the principles and methods of narrowing searches and evaluating sources for relevance and disciplinary orientation, even if that means less time is spent on identifying the greatest number of databases or tools.

Using Sources

How should students know what types of information will be valid for their research, given the differences in research questions and in how disciplines use evidence?

The previous work students have done in learning about disciplines should prepare them to assess the validity of evidence. Library instruction should also provide guidance on understanding the validity research results for different disciplines. For example, when teaching the use of multidisciplinary databases like JSTOR, ask students to determine the disciplinary orientation of a particular article. Pointing out clues in the bibliographic and metadata, such as the title of the journal, the departmental affiliation of the authors, descriptors and subject headings, the abstract, and the article's research methodology helps students see that they need not read every article to decide if it is useful.

The work of Joseph Bizup is very useful when helping students select, read, and consider how to use sources. Bizup created a research model called BEAM,[22] an acronym derived from Background, Exhibit, Argument, and Method. Bizup suggests that *any* source can be used in one of four ways in scholarly writing: "*Background* for materials a writer relies on for general information or for factual evidence; *Exhibit* for materials a writer analyzes or interprets; *Argument* for materials whose claims a writer engages; and *Method* for materials from which a writer takes a governing concept or derives a manner of working."

Bizup notes that traditional designation of sources as primary, secondary, or tertiary can confuse students: "A reference librarian at my institution noted that students often become perplexed when they learn that materials considered primary in one discipline may be considered secondary in another. They become perplexed when classifications they had taken as absolute turn out to be context-dependent."[23]

Using the BEAM framework is an effective means of helping students sort out the most useful materials from the mass of search results by guiding their reading of sources from the start towards how they will use the sources in their writing. Because the terms in BEAM are discipline-neutral, they encourage students to use sources in whatever way is required by the particular disciplinary methodology or combination of methodologies they may be using at the time:

> BEAM has a number of other advantages as well. First, it is more ecumenical than the standard nomenclature, not only because it emphasizes function but also because its terms possess a grammatical flexibility the standard terms lack. Like the standard terms, the terms in BEAM can be used as adjectives to modify some general noun like *source* or *research*, but they can also be used as nouns themselves. Therefore, while both nomenclatures suit disciplines such as history or English, BEAM also suits disciplines in which researchers do not customarily refer to their materials as *sources*. BEAM is clearly applicable to literary criticism, but it can also be applied to primary work in the sciences.[24]

Conclusion

Interdisciplinary research assignments demand library instruction that emphasizes the teaching of research concepts rather than the use of specific databases or tools. Interdisciplinary faculty do not necessarily have well-developed mental models of student research goals, since their own research typically focuses on no more than a few disciplines with which they are extremely familiar. The instruction librarian may well be the first to try to make these goals explicit to faculty and to students. To the degree that librarians familiarize themselves with the elements of, and information literacy standards for, specific disciplines, with the goals of interdisciplinary research, and with the expectations of faculty for students to integrate the insights of multiple disciplines in their research, librarians will better be able to design library instruction sessions that equip students to meet those expectations.

Academic librarians are well positioned to support interdisciplinary research for undergraduate students. Experienced instruction librarians using the principles of information literacy are already teaching in ways that support interdisciplinary research. By understanding the types of evidence and research questions appropriate to the relevant disciplines and employing pedagogy that elicits higher-level thinking skills, librarians can design instructional material and experiences that focus on concepts rather than tools and that highlight the differences between disciplines.

Librarians must discuss carefully with faculty members the nature and extent of interdisciplinarity expected of students and how that will be assessed. Library instruction is an opportunity to clarify and make explicit for students the nature of scholarly research in different disciplines and how to succeed in achieving a truly interdisciplinary understanding of a complex problem while becoming competent researchers.

Notes

1. Gail Dubrow, Eric Tranby and Char Voight, eds., *Fostering Interdisciplinary Inquiry: Proceedings from a Conference* (Minneapolis: University of Minnesota, 2009), 31.
2. Daniel Franks et al., "Interdisciplinary Foundations: Reflecting on Interdisciplinarity and Three Decades of Teaching and Research at Griffith University, Australia," *Studies in Higher Education* 32, no. 2 (April 2007): 169–174; , 2; Julie

Thompson Klein. *Interdisciplinarity: History, Theory and Practice*. (Detroit: Wayne State University, 1990).

3. Lisa R. Lattuca, Lois J. Voight, and Kimberly Q. Fath, "Does Interdisciplinarity Promote Learning? Theoretical Support and Researchable Questions," *Review of Higher Education* 28, no. 1 (Fall 2004): 26.

4. Christopher R. Wolfe and Carolyn Haynes, "Interdisciplinary Writing Assessment Profiles," *Issues in Integrative Studies* 21 (2003): 126–169.

5. Allen F. Repko, *Interdisciplinary Research: Process and Theory* (Thousand Oaks, CA: SAGE, 2008).

6. Association of College and Research Libraries, *Information Literacy Competency Standards for Higher Education* (Chicago: ACRL, 2000), 8–14.

7. Repko, *Interdisciplinary Research*, 142.

8. Tanya Augsburg, *Becoming Interdisciplinary: An Introduction to Interdisciplinary Studies*, 2nd ed. (Dubuque, IA: Kendall Hunt, 2006), 117.

9. Lisa Lattuca, *Creating Interdisciplinarity: Interdisciplinary Research and Teaching among College and University Faculty* (Nashville, TN: Vanderbilt University Press, 2001), 29.

10. Julie Thompson Klein and William Newell, "Strategies for Using Interdisciplinary Resources across K–16," *Issues in Integrative Studies* 20 (2002): 142.

11. Necia Parker-Gibson, "Library Assignments: Challenges That Students Face and How to Help," *College Teaching* 49, no. 2 (2001): 67.

12. Repko, *Interdisciplinary Research*, xiv.

13. Parker-Gibson, "Library Assignments," 66.

14. Repko, *Interdisciplinary Research*, xiv.

15. "Learning Initiative," University of California Berkeley College of Letters and Science, accessed 11/5/2010, http://ugis.ls.berkeley.edu/isf/major.php?page=learning_initiative.

16. Association of College and Research Libraries, *Information Literacy Competency Standards*, 5.

17. Lattuca, Voight, and Fath, "Does Interdisciplinarity Promote Learning?" 1.

18. Repko, *Interdisciplinary Research*, 42.

19. Lattuca, Voight, and Fath, "Does Interdisciplinarity Promote Learning?" 24.

20. "Information Literacy in the Disciplines," ACRL wiki, accessed March 12, 2011, http://wikis.ala.org/acrl/index.php/Information_literacy_in_the_disciplines.

21. Lattuca, *Creating Interdisciplinarity*, 133.

22. Joseph Bizup, "BEAM: A Rhetorical Vocabulary for Teaching Research-Based Writing," *Rhetoric Review* 27, no. 1 (January 2008): 72–86.

23. Ibid., 74.

24. Ibid., 72-86.

Research Centers, Collaborative Data Initiatives, and Centers of Excellence: Extending and Applying Interdisciplinary Research and the Role of the Library

Johann van Reenen and Kevin J. Comerford

Introduction

This chapter looks at current trends in and benefits of centers of excellence and research centers and institutes in general, how such organizations stimulate and conduct interdisciplinary research, and how this work can be supported and enhanced by research and academic libraries. When we talk about "centers," we mean centers of excellence, research centers, and research institutes. What counts as a center of excellence? We make the assumption that all research centers and institutes are based on excellence and a focus on specific major challenges above and beyond what one would find in a traditional academic department or research environment. With such specific foci, all centers have clearer scientific, intellectual, and economic impacts and are able to attract the best researchers in their fields. To address major challenges, one assume there is more complexity and thus a need for more interdisciplinarity. We will expand on these assumptions later.

We review current trends in the formation of interdisciplinary centers and examples in the areas of digital humanities, nanotechnology, and high-technology materials and those supporting the business community and governments. We explore what drives the formation and expansion of centers, such as topical and emergent issues (global climate and energy), support for high-level graduate research, helping with the increasing funding and infrastructure challenges, the rise of data curation and integration, and the concomitant informatics imperative. Examples of library involvement with specific projects are provided, such as DataONE for global environmental research data systems, e-research centers, knowledge portals, and data storage, re-purposing, and reusing issues.

Centers existing in traditional research and academic environments face challenges to engage successfully in collaborative and inter- and intradisciplinary work. Research libraries can help overcome such barriers and should develop library-based services in support of centers of excellence and interdisciplinary work. Some of the barriers we discuss in greater detail below include career impacts of collaborating outside one's field; higher time investments; publishing and tenure issues; cultural obstacles; barriers to collaborative teaching; different use of language, knowledge, and research systems and methods between interdisciplinary partners; and funding and infrastructure support for cross-, inter-, and intradisciplinary research collaborative projects. We review technology that enables cross-, inter-, and intradisciplinary research.

We believe librarians can make a difference in all the above areas and conclude with ideas for universities and their libraries to encourage the growth and success of centers of excellence and expand the support of cross-, inter-, and intradisciplinarity on campus. We provide examples of organizational development strategies.

The Rise of Centers, Institutes, and Incubation Initiatives Based on Interdisciplinary Research

The "Research Centers and Services Directory" covers over 15,900 university-based and other nonprofit research facilities in the United States and Canada.[1] Large-scale interdisciplinary research institutes and centers generally form outside the academic units and conduct full-time research, usually focused on long-term interdisciplinary problems. Centers of excellence (COEs) are also common in industry, where they are valued as drivers of competitive innovation; our chapter focus on COEs in academic and research settings.

COEs are essential for universities as economic drivers and often sustain a state's competitive advantage through statewide leadership. Nationally recognized programs in areas of strength serve as the platform for world-class centers of research, which in turn boast remarkable intellectual talent and attract public and private investment. Private investment groups generally look to COEs for inventions to build into businesses, creating jobs and economic prosperity. An essential principle for COEs is to create a reputation for fast, flexible, quality education and training programs. More and more, they strive to lead collaborative and coordinated national or statewide education and training efforts to build a competitive workforce in a global economy. Of importance to libraries, most COEs act as brokers of information and resources related to their targeted industry and research focus for industry representatives, community-based organizations, economic development organizations, community and technical colleges, and other universities. COEs are also formed based on national strategic directions. A recent case in point is the university–Homeland Security cooperative COEs that "bring together leading experts and researchers to conduct multidisciplinary research and education for homeland security solutions. Each center is led by a university in collaboration with partners from other institutions, agencies, laboratories, think tanks and the private sector."[2]

How does a center become a COE? The literature is poor on this topic. US government COEs are "created throughout the federal government in all domains to signify expertise important for elevating the significance of the product or service that is provided."[3] The same report discusses how such COEs are designated, accredited, and certified, and provides the most useful definition: "A center of excellence is a premier organization providing an exceptional product or service in an assigned sphere of expertise and within a specific field of technology, business, or government, consistent with the unique requirements and capabilities of the COE organization."[4]

Intellectual, Global, and Financial Drivers for Cross-, Inter-, and Intradisciplinary Research Centers

Centers of excellence and research centers have become the measure of success and reputation for research-intensive universities. Carnegie Mellon University, for instance, advertises that it has "more than 100 research centers and institutes, addressing a broad range of interests and industries… where Carnegie Mellon students and faculty are working to solve real-world problems."[5] At our own institution, the University of New Mexico, there are over fifty institutes and research centers (excluding those in the health sciences and law). There are many emerging and compelling issues that drive the formation of new centers and institutes. Some of this decade's evolving or maturing trends are discussed below to illustrate the "multiplier" effect of centers.

Digital humanities: In recent years, it has become clear that there are, especially in the humanities, limits to the one-person-one-project research model if the aim is to address large-scale issues, find unique insights, and generate significant grant monies. This has given rise to many digital humanities initiatives and centers. Spiro describes the impetus for these emergent centers:

> Humanities scholars are valued for bringing critical understanding to large amounts of data. In collaboration with computer scientists and librarians, humanities scholars devise methods to mine large humanities databases, coming up with new questions and insights that cross disciplinary and linguistic divides. Humanities (and digital humanities) centers help to coordinate much of this activity. Through efforts by leading scholars and scholarly organizations, tenure and promotion guidelines have been broadened to recognize a wide range of work, including scholarly multimedia, online dialogues, and curated content.[6]

The Consortium of Humanities Centers and Institutes provides good examples of centers formed and based on specific projects. Many of these subsequently grow to support innovative cross-disciplinary research and integrate such research into teaching. The Council on Library and Information Resources (CLIR) conducted a study of thirty-two digital humanities centers.[7] The study describes the nature and characteristics of these centers and their maturation from singular projects to multitiered programs that grew through building capacity with more donations and grants and developing programs designed to engage larger publics. Becoming magnets for additional funding is one of the driving forces for the creation of the center. Mature centers generally sponsor a wide range of activities, including collaborative research groups, scholarly conferences and symposia, and fellowship programs.

Nanotechnology and high-technology materials: The national focus on the potential of nanotechnology to revolutionize many fields of study resulted in numerous centers formed at universities. By the nature of this work, nanotechnology centers are multidisciplinary. The US National Nanotechnology Initiative, for instance, continues to focus on the establishment and development of multidisciplinary research and education centers devoted to nanoscience and nanotechnology, recently reporting that "NNI agencies have developed an extensive infrastructure of more than 60 major interdisciplinary research and education centers across the United States."[8]

Research centers in support of the business community and government: In a recent study of how academic libraries are coping with smaller budgets and limited resources during the current economic recession, Nicholas et al. found that in both the United States and the United Kingdom, libraries are actively seeking various alternative avenues of cooperation for both the provision of services and the acquisition of collection materials.[9] Moreover, it appears that many library institutions feel that in the current economic climate, the only way that they can maintain leading-edge services is through collaboration: "Sustaining momentum will depend increasingly on co-operation across the sector."[10] One area that libraries and academic institutions have recently found to be a viable area of expansion is in the dissemination of business and economic development information. The California Community Colleges Centers of Excellence initiative is one such example of collaboration between academia and the business community.[11] The CCC Centers of Excellence provide research and information services to state community college curriculum planners on current regional economic conditions, business outlook, and workforce-demand data. The mission of the center is to help match California's business and industry labor needs to community college vocational training programs to help ensure that college graduates can make an easy transition from school to the workforce. This program clearly demonstrates how multidisciplinary research centers can play an active role in the community.

While many initiatives like the CCC Centers of Excellence maintain their own library collections or research resources and develop their own outward-facing customer services, many others have historically relied on academic libraries for their professional expertise in collection management and development.[12] In northwestern Ohio, a case in point is the Regional Growth Partnership's Launch Program. This organization works to attract and promote technology start-up companies to the northwest Ohio region. "In October 2007, Launch approached the business and economics librarians at the University of Toledo's library for assistance in selecting information resources to help inventors successfully transfer new technology from a university lab or home garage to a small business venture. Launch staff were aware of some resources but needed an overview of major business databases and recommendations for a selection of books."[13] University of Toledo business librarians worked with the Launch program for over a year to develop both an in-house Launch program business development library and also a selection of legal and business guide books that would be provided to individual business owners free of charge.

Purdue University Libraries offer another example of how the need for information management expertise has prompted a library partnership with an interdisciplinary research organization. In this case, NASA's Advanced Life Support/NASA Specialized Center of Research and Training (ALS/NSCORT), which is tasked with developing technologies to allow astronauts to live in extreme environments like the moon or Mars for extended periods of time, found that it did not have the skills or funding necessary to create an archiving system for its internal documents and published papers: "Realizing that they did not have the resources, expertise or the infrastructure to archive their research materials on their own, the administrators of ALS-NSCORT approached the Purdue University Libraries for assistance."[14] Because the opportunity would provide library staff with a chance to work closely with a "real-world" interdisciplinary research center, it was decided to provide assistance to ALS/NSCORT, even though the project would consume substantial library time and resources. After an extensive initial needs assessment and the exploration of several possible electronic archiving solutions, the Purdue library staff decided to leverage their Digital Commons institutional repository for the project. Implementation of the project took over fifteen months and involved significant modifications to the repository software, as well as many hours spent by library staff to collect and organize ALS/NSCORT documents for ingest into the repository system. A postmortem on the project by Purdue library staff indicated that not all of ALS/NSCORT's requirements were able to be met and that more experience and research was needed by Purdue libraries before they could embark on another similar project. However, the collaboration was ultimately deemed a success by both organizations.

Other national drivers in the formation of research centers and institutes address the need for creating more return on investment for funding agencies and greater and sustained research impact at national and global levels. At the organizational level, centers support student engagement through research experiences, recruitment of faculty and graduate students, and improved retention, as well as the significant impacts on the community and economic development.

We discuss some of the drivers and their impacts in greater detail below.

Centers as Drivers of Graduate Research Support

Research centers and institutes are focused on research based on local strengths and thus hubs for graduate (and sometimes undergraduate) research opportunities. At most universities, interdisciplinary centers play major roles in graduate funding and rich graduate research experiences, sometimes of international standing. At our organization, the University of New Mexico (UNM), science and technology centers are essential in many graduate programs, as will be seen from the few examples below. Like many research-intensive universities, UNM has IGERT (Integrative Graduate Education and Research Traineeship) grant-funded projects from the National Science Foundation (NSF). The Center for High Technology Materials (CHTM) and the Nanoscience and Microsystems Center (NSMS) IGERT programs train and fund researchers with *interdisciplinary* backgrounds and interests: graduate students at CHTM, and PhD scientists and engineers at NSMS. Students receive not only the necessary research and academic components but also the technical, professional, and personal skills needed to address the global questions of the future. Both programs use innovative curricula and internships, and by focusing on problem-centered training, they give their graduates the edge needed to become leaders in these fields. The NSMS also has an REU (Research

Experiences for Undergraduates) program from NSF that pays for the majority of students' expenses and focuses on the development of strong student-mentor relationships as well as laboratory and research skills. Another intradiscipinary IGERT, the Integrating Nanotechnology with Cell Biology and Neuroscience program, provides fellowships to develop a new cadre of scholars with excellent research skills that prepare them for the challenges of the twenty-first century brought by the nanotechnology and bioengineering revolutions.

Universities capitalize on existing infrastructure in their centers to collaborate with the private sector in providing graduate funding and experiences. At UNM, the Center for Micro-Engineered Materials is an industry-university cooperative research program in materials science research and education that strives to maximize the research performed by faculty. Student experiences are highly leveraged based on our traditionally close collaboration with nearby research scientists from Sandia National Laboratories, Los Alamos National Laboratory, and the Sandia Center for Integrated Nanotechnology. Many universities draw on the strengths of local research organizations and industrial research centers.

International interdisciplinary research is generally organized through networks of centers. The NSF-funded PIRE program (Partnerships for International Research and Education) is a collaborative partnership based at a lead university in the United States. The PIRE at Iowa State University collaborates with UNM and researchers at ten other institutions spanning both the United States and Europe and is also the international component of the NSF Engineering Research Center for Bio-renewable Chemicals. Such programs generally provide international research internship opportunities for graduate and undergraduate students that deepen collaborative research between US institutions and international counterparts. This prepares US students and faculty to work effectively in the global research community by addressing environmental problems created by the US dependence on fossil fuels, such as global climate change, and the search for renewable sources of energy, chemicals, and materials. The UNM Library's Data-ONE project participates in the PIRE's work by focusing on managing the data created by environmental research centers and projects—a compelling new role for libraries (more detail below).

At UNM, based on the graduate student "intensiveness" created by centers, the Office of the Vice President for Research, the University Libraries, and the Office of Graduate Studies, assisted by a grant serving Hispanic students, developed a series of classes on research ethics, research compliance, research grant development, and grant writing, submission processes, and management for graduate students. These classes can be taken in specific sections, resulting in four different certificates, or on an as-needed basis. We believe this is a valuable investment in future US researchers.

Research universities cannot provide quality graduate research in the sciences, engineering, and the digital humanities and social sciences without grant funding funneled through focused research centers. Most of the centers mentioned above at the UNM report directly to one of the authors (van Reenen) and are strongly supported by the library liaison program, grant-writing assistance, services of the research data librarians, and the library's extensive electronic collections. Although this close connection (through a joint appointment) is not generally found at academic libraries, it does not preclude university libraries from developing strong ties to centers and institutes through subject librarians, strongly focused data initiatives, and joint grant-writing activities. Devoting special effort to providing instruction and information services to center- and institute-based students ensures a new generation of researchers who are aware of the benefits of involving libraries and librarians in their projects from start to finish. At our institution, the interdisciplinary nanotechnology and biomedical engineering centers resulted in a total restructuring of the library's science and technology collections development processes and budgets. For instance, individual subject funds were deconstructed to create a single interdisciplinary science and engineering collections budget (journals, databases, monographs/e-books, multimedia, and data sets) that is managed by team of librarians with no disciplinary "favoritism" allowed.

Other emerging global drivers for new research centers include concerns regarding energy and the environment, the promise of data-rich and cyber-enabled research to solve large-scale problems, and the explosion of new digital media and gaming initiatives. Successful examples of the latter where libraries already play important roles are the Digital Media Center at Rice University's Fondren Library and the Center for History and New Media (CHNM) at George Mason University. CHNM has used digital media and computer technology "to democratize history—to incorporate multiple voices, reach diverse audiences, and encourage popular participation in presenting and preserving the past."[15] Libraries in such institutions are using their central location (literally and figuratively) to expand their traditional role as information brokers.

Changing Funding and Infrastructure Imperatives as Drivers for Interdisciplinary Centers

Diminishing state funding for universities requires that research grant funding and income from contracts be ramped up. However, infrastructure is immensely important in the genesis of centers and institutes. Mature centers can build on existing capacity, but updating and building new infrastructure can eat away at institutional income. However, many universities see this as a necessary investment trend. Centers with functional rather than research goals (or providing a mix of both), such as centers for high-performance computing, originated based on the need for a national networked infrastructure. Secondary goals generally include that such centers serve as a basis for long-term partnerships and collaboration among industry, academe, and government and as experimental (generally graduate) education sites. Rockwell explains the importance of centers in creating essential research infrastructure to support many other functions at universities:

> In effect, calling something infrastructure is a way of changing the urgency of its provision and changing the perception of who should fund it and maintain it. It is, in short, a great way to argue that some organization like a university or government should fund something in perpetuity rather than fund it as a grant would for a particular period and group. Calling something cyberinfrastructure distinguishes it from that which only a project needs and which is needed only for the duration of the research.[16]

At UNM, the library is partnering with the high-performance computing center and other IT-intensive units to create a shared collaborative research infrastructure at a central library location, the evolving e-Research Center (eRC), discussed below.

The Informatics Imperative as a Driver for Interdisciplinary Support Systems

Finally, for academic libraries the most important emerging impact of centers is the resulting informatics imperatives. Centers and institutes, especially those focusing on cyber-enabled and data-intensive research, create large amounts of data in need of curation and preservation. This and mandates from funding agencies are resulting in new roles for libraries and new skill requirements for librarians. We will describe three approaches in our organization to respond to these emerging expectations.

DataONE (Data Observation Network for Earth): Researchers at UNM have partnered with dozens of other universities and agencies to create DataONE (see https://www.dataone.org/), a global data access and preservation network for earth and environmental scientists headquartered at UNM that will support breakthroughs in environmental research. This is a $20 million NSF-funded project based within both the Office of the Vice President of Research and the University Libraries. The project is under the direction of William Michener, professor and director of e-science initiatives at University Libraries. Expected users include scientists, educators, librarians, resource managers, and the public through providing easy and open access to a broad range of science data as well as tools for managing, analyzing, and visualizing data. We believe DataONE will be transformative in the speed with which researchers will be able to assemble and analyze data sets and in the types of problems they will be able to address. This initiative and our deeper integration into research activities had a cascading effect on the UNM's Centennial Science and Engineering Library that stimulated a strategic review process to remandate the space as a collaborative e-research center providing sophisticated data management and curation services.

The eRC at the University Libraries:

E-Science, cyberinfrastructure—these ideas are at the heart of the great ambitions and promise of science in the new century. The last several decades of network- and computer-enabled work in science have produced untold amounts of data, leading to the challenge of developing practices to manage and provide access to this data. Along with oceans of data and technology, changes in the conduct and nature of science—notably new collaborative and computational science practices—present both novel requirements and exciting opportunities to succeed in meeting this challenge.[17]

The University Libraries are undertaking a fund-raising effort, working with industry partners, and have hired research data librarians with high-level skills in data management, mining, and visualization to create this interdisciplinary collaborative space and related virtual services. Bedard and van Reenen describe how the eRC is planned to address the challenges presented by significant changes in science and engineering "that are rooted in a deep merging of traditionally unconnected areas of intellectual endeavor and new ways of capturing and sharing research data. The scale of such trans-disciplinary research efforts and the complex nature of the systems and problems being studied often require large collaborative interdepartmental and multi-institutional teams."[18] The most important current initiative is to involve the library and librarians more directly and deeply in faculty research and grant writing and in working at a leadership level with the Office of the Vice President for Research. The article describes plans and activities in greater detail, and we will return to this topic in the section on library organizational development in response to what we call "research immersion activities."

Knowledge Portals in Support of Inter- and Intradisciplinary Research: Librarians can play an important role in working collaboratively with researchers to create databases of digital content, archived data sets, harvested metadata to distributed content, and portals that integrate content and services in cross-disciplinary initiatives. For instance, most academic libraries have collections-of-strength (print, digital, and special collections and archives) that match their university's flagship programs. These provide fertile ground for collaborative projects and grant writing. The University Libraries and our internationally known Latin American and Iberian Institute have partnered on two grants from the US Department of Education's Technological Innovation and Cooperation for Foreign Information Access program. The University Libraries rate in the top five Latin American library collections across all subjects from science and engineering, social sciences, indigenous and women's studies, art and dance, to literature and all the humanities. From 2006 to 2009, the collaboration created the Latin American Knowledge Harvester that provided repository instances (DSpace) at partner institutions in Latin America, such as for the social medicine subproject at the University of Guadalajara (Mexico), the archives of Bolivar (Bolivarium) at the Simon Bolivar University (Venezuela), and a joint project with the Brazilian Institute for Science and Technology Information to harvest digital theses and dissertation metadata. These and other existing repositories were utilized to harvest metadata for an interdisciplinary portal to Latin American academic information that should stimulate more cross- and interdisciplinary research. Currently, in 2010, the collaborators are working on a four-year project to develop the underlying services and information products for a Latin American energy policy and dialog portal, LaEnergaia (see http://laenergaia.unm.edu), that involves scientists, engineers, librarians, social scientists, and humanists and has a strong additional focus on the impact of energy policies on indigenous populations.

Data Storage Issues: The lack of sufficient data storage arose from the initial experiments with data curation. The library, Earth Data Analysis Center, DataONE project, the New Mexico state EPSCoR/NSF project, and others formed a Research Data Storage Consortium to pool funding in support of sophisticated storage technology to archive curated data sets. The purchase is currently underway, and the storage will be installed in the high-performance computing facility with flexible collaborative storage guidelines for members.

Challenges to Collaborative Work, Tools, and Behaviors in Inter- and Intradisciplinary Research

Although cross-disciplinary research collaboration is necessary to achieve a better understanding of how human and natural systems are dynamically linked, it often turns out to be very difficult in practice.[19]

We believe that libraries can play a transformational role in addressing the challenges to collaborative work, tools, and behaviors in inter- and intradisciplinary research. Inter- and transdisciplinarity are evolving in all the major science fields and, as we have seen, also in the humanities. In some fields, such as astronomy, collaboration with other fields has been of long enough duration to spawn new interdisciplinary specializations. We see cross-disciplinary interactions with engineering (for instrumentation), astrochemistry (now an active subfield giving insights into cosmic molecular processes), earth sciences (for planetary studies), computer science (for astroinformatics), life sciences (for astrobiology), and a small but growing field of astrostatistics that advances methodology to address challenges in astronomical data analysis.[20] Libraries should develop collections and services that reflect these subfields and engage practitioners at the emergent phase. The same skill sets that make librarians good facilitators and high-level research "observers" can benefit interaction, activities, and information seeking at the edges where disciplines meet.

By the turn of this century, the potential of cross-disciplinary research to provide fresh insights to sometimes intractable national and global challenges was emphasized by many research organizations and research-funding agencies. For instance, the National Academy of Sciences, funded by the National Institutes of Health and other agencies, commissioned a Committee on Strengthening the Linkages between the Sciences and the Mathematical Sciences.[21] Compared to most people's idea of interdisciplinary collaboration, these fields would seem closely tied, yet they struggle to find common ground and an agreed-upon language that describe their differing approaches to solving problems. The committee came to the realization that in most of the sciences, modeling and simulation are the only "viable complement to theoretical studies, because many problems cannot be addressed experimentally."[22] However, the challenge was how to create successful collaborations both at the teaching and research levels. The case studies described by the report exposed very real and also imagined barriers to cross-disciplinary work. Its findings hold true for most collaboration across the campus, from committee work to collaborative research. The most important challenges from the National Research Council (NRC) report are discussed below.

Career Impacts: Cross-, inter-, and intradisciplinary research and teaching have escalating risks for new practitioners and require new skills to manage the resulting complexity. The NRC report documented "diminished recognition of teaching efforts to delayed or denied promotions. The criteria for hiring and promotion often do not credit or reward those considering cross-disciplinary work as highly as those who keep working within the discipline. Although some researchers might welcome this challenge, it could be a significant impediment to others in the early stages of their academic careers."[23]

Time Investments: Pennington shows the time and effort collaborators need to invest in learning enough about another discipline to establish viable research collaborations.[24] This means that the time from start-up to first publishable result can be significantly longer than for single-discipline research. The NRC report says this is "particularly difficult for junior faculty on the tenure clock. Developing and teaching cross-disciplinary courses is also time-consuming. Even where tenure is not a factor, few departments have a good mechanism for assigning teaching credit for such courses or for advising students from outside the researcher's home department."[25] The authors' own work on such teams also confirmed the popularity of cross-listed and cross-disciplinary courses with students but their unpopularity in the departments involved because of time-on-task issues and discontent about credits generated for each department. University structures needs to change to create the necessary incentives, as will be discussed later.

Publishing and Tenure Issues: Cross-, inter-, and intradisciplinary research may prove difficult to publish in each collaborator's "traditional" outlets, sometimes resulting in the research not being published in the most prestigious, discipline-oriented journals. The NRC report showed that, once again, this is particularly problematic for junior researchers, "who generally must demonstrate contributions to the discipline via publication in respected journals. The multidisciplinary journals *Science, Nature,* and *Proceedings of the National Academy of Sciences* welcome cross-disciplinary papers, but they do not offer a large enough forum for the variety of cross-disciplinary research reports expected in the future. Even for these journals, it is harder to find qualified reviewers for cross-disciplinary research than for discipline-specific research, as few reviewers span fields."[26] Such diminished recognition and the time lags discussed earlier can deter collaborations if the university does not incentivize such work.

Cultural Obstacles to Cross-, Inter-, and Intradisciplinary Collaboration in Teaching and Research: The traditional and prevailing systems encourage and reinforce relationships between researchers within a discipline through departmental meetings and seminars, professional society gatherings, and conferences within the discipline. This may be effective in maintaining partnerships, support, and administrative cohesion within the discipline, but it generally means that a typical researcher may find it hard to find time and opportunities to meet and network with colleagues from other disciplines. We provide an example below of library involvement that may facilitate such interdisciplinary conversations.

Different Language, Knowledge, and Research Systems and Methods: The work of Pennington and of Pennington et al. with collaborative multidisciplinary teams at the University of New Mexico made a compelling case for awareness building[27] followed by workshops for early adopters that address the challenges to understanding disciplinary use of language, appreciation for different methods, and learning enough about another field for collaboration purposes. Most interdisciplinary groups underestimate the efforts required in what Pennington calls the "shared conceptualization problem."[28] In the fast emerging field of e-science in particular, she says, "Generation of common conceptual ground is the key barrier in any collaborative eScience effort, on which all other outcomes depend."[29] Later we will show how librarians can help with creating common conceptual grounds. The case studies from the NRC report also found

> Researchers may need to persist over a number of years in their attempts to communicate a problem to their colleagues in another discipline before there is a common appreciation of the essence of the problem. This may happen because the researchers do not yet understand one another's discipline well enough to fully grasp the depth of the problem, or it may happen simply because the potential collaborators do not understand each other's jargon. Potential collaborators need not be expert in each other's fields, but they must at least understand enough of the other discipline to recognize the contribution it can make to their research problem.[30]

As PI of an intradisciplinary grant, one of the authors (van Reenen) found the same challenges. His NSF cybereducation grant involves collaborators from the library (informatics), American studies,
history, earth and planetary sciences, and civil engineering, who will
be developing a program of study and a course on Women, Work, and
Water based on a set of informatics skills and tools. He found that it
took six months for the collaborators to find a shared understanding of
language usage, research methods, and even the identification of the
core problems and collaborative opportunities they hoped to identify.
Recognizing this, the PI and co-PI decided to spend the first phase,
a whole semester, on training the four teaching faculty in areas they
identified as gaps in their general knowledge of the other fields and
of informatics. This decision and the resultant skill development goals
took trust, honesty, and real courage on everyone's part. The most
important lessons we have learned so far is that strong and trusting
relationships are essential, that they take time to develop, and that
the investments of time and patience needed to make this so are very
much worth the resulting collaborative vigor and rigor! The lesson
that the libraries, in particular, learned from this was that librarians
can build on the trusted relationship built over decades with our customers. This trust can be parlayed into facilitation of cross-, inter-,
and iintradisciplinary collaborative teams and initiatives. Our generally accepted service attitudes and neutrality are greatly appreciated.

**Funding and Infrastructure Support for Cross-, Inter-, and
Intradisciplinary Research Collaborative Projects:** As discussed
above, it takes longer for cross-, inter-, and intradisciplinary collaborative projects to get established, is more time-consuming, is more
expensive in the short term, and requires more shared dedicated infrastructure to bear fruit than discipline-only efforts. These additional
challenges require aggressive grant seeking as well as organizational
support, not just in money but in a clear vision for an interdisciplinary collaborative research organization. Funding agencies have recognized these challenges and are increasingly favoring, and in many
cases requiring, cross-, inter-, and intradisciplinary grant proposals.
At UNM, the Office of the Vice President for Research recognized
the need for special efforts to foster cross-disciplinary collaboration
and ensure competitive interdisciplinary grant proposals. A Research

Collaboration Enhancement Committee was formed to investigate ways to overcome the above challenges. Outcomes from this work will be discussed in the next section.

Technology and Collaboration: Technology can play different roles in research collaboration: as a collaboration enabler or platform, as tools developed for capture, analysis, experimentation, and so forth. Pennington describes technology goals best: "Existing technologies may be applied to new scientific research, or new research on emerging technologies may be demonstrated on known scientific problems. But most often, the goal is to simultaneously conduct research on both science and emerging technologies."[31] One example of a successful interdisciplinary collaboration platform is the EthicShare project (see https://www.ethicshare.org), which brings together researchers in ethics from a variety of fields: bioethics, medical ethics, neuroethics, medical, and life sciences research. EthicShare was originally conceived in 2004 at the University of Virginia, but its ultimate realization required broad collaboration from multiple academic institutions and funding from the Mellon Foundation. The initial EthicShare site was launched in 2008, and though it has been fully operational for some time, it continues to undergo testing, development, and improvement.[32] The concept for the site is to provide a comprehensive online research community—in effect, one-stop shopping about the study of ethics—bringing together all of the information and communication/collaboration resources ethicists require under one virtual roof. EthicShare includes its own document collections, online forums, blogs, and interactive communications tools for site members. A unique feature of the site which makes it particularly useful is a direct interface to PubMed, the National Library of Medicine citation database. EthicShare users can search for scholarly articles in PubMed and save links to items of interest in virtual folders or "libraries" of documents. The ability to integrate personal communications and documents, scholarly publications, web links, and online postings is one of the great strengths of EthicShare that makes it both a collaboration enabler and a research platform.

In addition to more traditional online collaboration resources, the appearance of virtual research environments (VREs) in the last several years bears mentioning as a transformative force for future interdisciplinary research. VREs are an outgrowth of the e-research movement, which strives to foster online collaboration of researchers across geographic and subject boundaries and to make heavy use of Web-based tools and technology in pursuit of scientific investigation. Voss and Procter point to the importance of such tools for interdisciplinary work: "E-research is, by definition, a collaborative activity that combines the abilities of distributed groups of researchers in order to achieve research goals that individual researchers or local groups could not hope to accomplish."[33] A notable characteristic of e-research and VRE initiatives is the use of XML-based workflows to document scientific processes. VRE communities frequently feature collections of these workflows, which are designed to function with one or more workflow engines, such as the open source Taverna workflow management system. The move toward documenting scientific workflows using common technical standards is an effort to promote widespread sharing of research interests across traditional disciplinary boundaries.

The oldest and arguably most popular public VRE site is myExperiment (see http://www.myexperiment.org), which was founded in 2007. A joint project of the Southampton, Manchester, and Oxford universities in the United Kingdom, myExperiment has been funded by the JISC and Microsoft Research. The site boasts the largest public collection of scientific workflows on the Internet and also incorporates more traditional online collaboration tools. myExperiment users can post experiment plans and results, join online research and interest groups, tag content and post comments, and share content out to social networking services like Facebook, Twitter, and Delicious.[34] Veezyon (see http://www.veezyon.com) is another VRE-like site that includes online learning content (such as instructional videos and Flash presentations) as well as the ability to let users create their own online research notebooks. The newest VRE service, is Ojax++ (see http://www.ucd.ie/ojax), a collaborative project at University College Dublin, developed jointly by UCD's School of Library and Information Studies and School of Computer Science and Informatics. The goal of this service is "to help researchers work collaboratively by providing a project management and collaboration interface for research activity conducted using third party tools like Delicious, Gmail and

MyExperiment."[35] It appears that Ojax++ is designed to function as a wrapper service that seamlessly integrates content from other VRE services and social networking sites.

While virtual research environments have done much to advance the e-research movement and promote online and distributed scientific collaboration, it is important to remember that VREs as a technology platform are still in their infancy, and many tools that researchers will need to conduct serious e-research efforts have yet to be developed. Voss and Procter, for example, enumerate the activities that researchers need to perform which should be included in a mature VRE environment, most of which either do not yet exist or exist only in rudimentary form. As a suite of online services, a VRE should allow a researcher to easily perform the following functions:

- Authenticate using an authentication service;
- Communicate and collaborate with colleagues;
- Transfer data;
- Configure a resource;
- Invoke a computation;
- Re-use data and give credit to the original producer;
- Archive output data and runtime data;
- Publish outputs, both informally through blogs or wikis and formally through conference or journal papers;
- Discover what resources are available;
- Monitor the state of a resource or process;
- Maintain awareness of who is currently doing what;
- Find out where particular data has come from and how it was processed (provenance);
- Find out who has access to a resource and what they can do with it (authentication and authorisation).[36]

Other serious questions about VREs regard issues that will not be resolved until they attain a higher level of adoption among researchers and a greater level of technical sophistication. For example, will e-researchers be able to guarantee the online persistence of data or experiment plans and workflows that they share? And when collections of electronic workflows grow into the hundreds of thousands or millions of documents, how will researchers be able to find them and ensure they are authentic? While these and other issues bear watching as VREs develop, suffice it to say that they offer a tantalizing and exciting view into how scientific research will be performed in the future and present new challenges for librarians to structure content for findability and accessibility.

Organizational Development to Encourage Cross-, Inter-, and Intradisciplinarity

Organizational arrangements at the university administration level are critical to fostering cross-, inter-, and intradisciplinary collaborative research. The NRC report also identified the need to rethink organizational structures and create incentives to grow cross-, inter-, and intradisciplinary research and courses. Chapter two focuses on case studies that clearly indicate that the "academic programs described ... demonstrate the important role institutional structures play in the education of both undergraduate and graduate students and in the fostering of communication [and collaboration] between mathematical scientists and other scientists" and improved outcomes when "Mathematical scientists and scientists had the opportunity to interact over long periods of time, generally in a common location. There was often an institutional structure, in some cases provided by a funding agency, to maintain the collaboration during its initial phase."[37]

A task force at UNM came to the same conclusions. The executive summary from UNM's *Report of the Committee on Research Enhancement* focused on goals and key requirements to overcome some of the barriers described above.[38] The recommendations for action emphasized leveraging existing strengths at the university and suggested new administrative incentives and longer-term infrastructure planning to capitalize on evolving national research priorities. The committee consisted of representatives from the university library, high-performance computing, biology, and the long-term ecological research program. The last member was also a research professor whose livelihood was collaborative grant writing. The committee decided to focus on three basic goals:

1. Create a vision for a research environment that motivates and

enables research in this new era of information overload, massive computational ability, and enhanced connectivity;

2. Propose strategies for creating institutional tools, structures, processes, and career pathways that will achieve that vision; and

3. Recommend a path forward that includes the development of an experimental prototype to test these tools and strategies, along with clearly defined evaluation metrics.[39]

It was clear to the committee that UNM needed to plan for an evolving interdisciplinary institutional strategy to keep its research enterprise competitive. Current institutional structures were designed primarily to support disciplinary teaching and research within a network of peers, but were not optimized to support a cross-, inter-, and intradisciplinary research vision. It identified three areas to focus on:

1. Semi-automated methods of putting the right faculty together with the right research opportunities

2. an eHarmony-like service [referred to as "rHarmony"] for research social networking.... This system will blend top-down opportunity priming from the OVPR with bottom-up self-organization from the faculty;

3. Dynamic creation of fluid, flexible, and temporary organizational arrangements for faculty that promotes the growth of new research collaborations;

Support of the above by a persistent infrastructure (facilities, technology and people) designed and dedicated to enable collaborations, both new and existing.[40]

The the Office of the Vice President for Research (OVPR) and the University Libraries (UL) responded to these recommendations as funding and other opportunities allowed. The UL committed to a re-mandated science and engineering library to become a hub for cross-, inter-, and intradisciplinary collaboration and support systems—the eRC mentioned above. The UL also recognized the need for nontraditional skills in future hires. Hires over the last two years brought six new, nontraditional faculty to the library with skills that support e-research collaboration, grant writing, multimedia and other digital archiving, data management and curation, and statistical and informatics teaching and research skills. The OVPR reorganized its services, hiring a Director of Arts and Humanities Research Initiatives and five Faculty Research Support Officers (FRSOs). The FRSOs and the new research data and digital initiatives librarians ("data librarians") meet monthly to share information gathered at the beginning of research projects, mostly by the FRSOs, and in the middle and at the end of projects through publishing and data management activities, mostly by the data librarians. Both groups help with awareness building as new research rules, initiatives, and opportunities arise. The UL also began an aggressive plan for collaborative grant writing with other colleges and the OVPR. Currently there are four ongoing collaborative grants and four more in the pipeline. The FRSO/data librarians group is currently emphasizing awareness building among grant writers about emerging funding philosophies of funding agencies, such as NSF's requirement for a two-page data management plan.[41] The UL also created a research guide to digital data management, curation, and archiving.[42]

An area where the library can be of significant help with one of the challenges described earlier is in scholarly publishing issues affecting inter- and intradisciplinary research output. The current academic reward structure favors "those who evince independent thinking and creativity, so the need to be a sole or the lead author to advance one's career is a fact of life. It is, as well, difficult to have balance in collaborative relationships."[43] A thought-provoking, and possibly controversial, article recently published by Friedman, Whitworth, and Brownstein develops this premise further:

> The limitations of traditional academic knowledge exchange systems such as conferences and peer-reviewed journals result in discipline-based scholarship that is feudal in nature and can only dissipate as cross-disciplinary research expands. The next evolutionary step is democratic online knowledge exchange, run by the academic many rather than the publishing-oligarchic few. Using sociotechnical tools it is possible to implement an academic publishing business model that maximizes the power of "extelligence", or knowledge realized through the collective gifting of information. Such a mod-

el would change the roles of journal editors and peer reviewers from knowledge gatekeepers to knowledge guides, and change the competitive yet conforming behaviors of academic researchers seeking publication to behaviors that reward collaborative activity that engages research communities in the act of knowledge exchange.[44]

Both this article and the NRC report shine a light on the difficulty of finding the best scholarly communication vehicles in which to publish inter- and intradisciplinary research output. Some of the problems, such as who reviews such work and how to describe the collaborative process, tools, and methods, are currently being addressed (shortsightedly in our opinion) by publishers spawning new interdisciplinary journals as we have seen in the case of astronomy discussed earlier.

The three UNM library systems (Law, Health Sciences, and University Libraries), with recent participation from the UNM Press and the OVPR, created an eScholar Innovation Center, which will develop electronic publishing services for the university as well as assist faculty in gaining the skill sets needed to participate in interdisciplinary nontraditional publishing ventures. The center is an interdisciplinary effort in itself, as it draws upon the expertise of software developers, graphic design specialists, legal and intellectual property experts, systems managers, and professional information specialists to provide a holistic menu of services for UNM researchers who are new to open access and electronic publishing. Faculty who utilize the center will find support for everything from manuscript preparation to license negotiation and guidance in navigating federal open access and open data requirements. The eScholar Innovation Center will also provide the technical infrastructure and services to help transform the university's currently print-based scholarly journals and publication into electronic resources which can be distributed online. An important function of initiatives like the UNM eScholar Innovation Center, the Townsend Humanities Lab at the University of California Berkeley, and similar projects is to use the mechanism of electronic publishing to make scholarship more easily accessible across disciplines, and thereby help spur collaboration and fuel interdisciplinary research activity.

If librarians invest in building skills in designing interdisciplinary group learning and facilitation on top of their already strong foundation of information management skills and service attitudes, they can become integral contributors to interdisciplinary e-research. Ultimately, they can help with problem formulation and "co-constructed ideas"[45] for grants. The factors listed by Stokols et al. that affect the success of research teams reads like a list of library services and attitudes![46] They fall in six categories: intrapersonal, interpersonal, organizational/institutional, physical/environmental, technologic, and sociopolitical. Stokols et al. also found that leadership style, team communication, and arranging opportunities for face-to-face contact and creative sessions are very important for all types of research teams. Wenger describes three aspects that are essential in overcoming disciplinary differences and that bring diverse communities together around a common purpose: people who act as brokers, material artifacts such as tools and terms, and orchestrated interactions.[47] He stresses the need for a designated individual on interdisciplinary teams to help with "boundary-crossing" activities. Could librarians move from traditional information brokers to "intradisciplinary research brokers"? Future library research and service initiatives should study how libraries can provide services in these areas to support interdisciplinarity on campuses. The reference interview already contains most of what is needed in, for instance, the data interview.

Continued progress in the development of library-originated interdisciplinary programs and initiatives depends heavily upon the ability of new information professionals to perceive patterns of knowledge and scholarship across disciplinary boundaries and to facilitate collaborative activities between students, faculty, and researchers from varied academic backgrounds. Recognition of the need for new library school graduates to possess interdisciplinary knowledge, skills, and abilities is not a recent phenomenon among library and information science education programs, but the idea has been slow to gain momentum. Aharony and Raban found, for example, that despite a high degree of interest in the interdisciplinary study of the economics of information among Israeli library and information science instructors and students, that very few Israeli LIS programs had any plans to provide formal coursework in this area.[48] However, the international movement to transform traditional library science programs into iSchools has had a positive impact on the development of interdisciplinary training of information professionals. The iSchool Organization (see http://www.ischools.org) was formed in 2005 in part to recognize that "the study of information is interdisciplinary, fed by multiple diverse fields."[49]

Another important development in the field of information science education has been the creation of interdisciplinary informatics programs, which are frequently outgrowths of university library and iSchool collaborations with traditional academic disciplines in the physical and social sciences. Some of these programs have developed from collaborative efforts between a cluster of related disciplines, such as the Interdisciplinary Informatics program at the University of Minnesota (see http://www.informatics.umn.edu), which encompasses "health informatics, computational biology, systems biology, bioinformatics, and physical and computational sciences."[50] Others, like the University of Nebraska/Omaha School of Interdisciplinary Informatics (see http://si2.ist.unomaha.edu), which offers undergraduate and graduate degrees in bioinformatics, information assurance, and information technology innovation, are independent programs directly affiliated with an iSchool. The newly christened Graduate Informatics Certificate Program at the University of New Mexico is somewhat unusual in that it is headquartered in the University Libraries, and courses are taught by professional data and digital initiatives librarians.

Conclusion

The promotion and facilitation of interdisciplinary teaching and research and the formation of centers of excellence, as shown above, are major trends in current academic work and are important drivers of research funding. Results from interdisciplinary research often seem the only hope to solve global problems. Academic libraries have a responsibility to support these trends through how they are organized, how collections and data management services are built, and in the risks individual librarians are willing to take to "reach into" the research process.

Many libraries are reorganizing to capitalize on interdisciplinarity, such as building collections and services around emerging centers such as digital humanities, nanotechnology, climate change, and broad concepts such as e-research. They combine subjects into clusters more representative of real-world experiences. For instance, at UNM, the library combined the Chicano/Hispano/Latino library program, the Latin American studies, and the American studies programs into an Inter-American Studies Library Program (ASLP) that make connections between these areas through a lecture series, exhibits, and actual interdisciplinary courses taught by the ASLP Coordinator.[51] Many academic libraries are developing data management and curation systems for all disciplines and are facilitating interdisciplinary awareness about the opportunities for new types of research made possible by access to many different types of reusable and repurposable data sets.

Librarians have proved over the last two decades that they are skilled at assisting researchers and students with technological readiness. They can also play an important role in providing the basic subject field information pieces that researchers from different fields need to begin to understand each other and that allow them to overcome the difficulties "of achieving shared conceptualizations between disciplines."[52] To capitalize even more on the above trends, some libraries, and most library and information science schools, are developing practical informatics courses and encouraging pure research in utilizing emerging skills and tools. Librarians are taking tentative steps into the data arena by finding ways to immerse themselves more deeply in the research process. This can be done by being a co-investigator, by providing subject information skills, data management skills, and most importantly, e-research collaboration facilitation skills. The last skills are slowly emerging, and the importance of understanding and responding to the difficulties encountered in interdisciplinary collaborations is providing our profession with one of its greatest opportunities. One can imagine a time when there is a librarian on every interdisciplinary research team with the awareness, understanding, and skills so eloquently described by Pennington[53] and Wenger's early understanding of the importance of building interdisciplinary communities of practice.[54]

Notes

1. "Research Centers and Services Directory," Dialog website, http://library.dialog. com/bluesheets/html/bl0115.html (accessed February 27, 2012).

2. "Homeland Security Centers of Excellence," US Department of Homeland Security, http://www.dhs.gov/files/programs/editorial_0498.shtm (accessed February 27, 2012).

3. William Craig, Matthew Fisher, Suzanne Garcia, Clay Kaylor, John Porter, and L. Scott Reed, *Generalized Criteria and Evaluation Method for Center of Excellence: A Preliminary Report* (Pittsburgh, PA: Carnegie Mellon University Software Engineering Institute, 2009), ix.

4. Ibid., 7.

5. "Centers and Institutes," Carnegie Mellon University, http://www.cmu.edu/research/centers.shtml (accessed February 27, 2012).

6. Lisa Spiro, "20/30 Vision: Scenarios for the Humanities in 2030," *Digital Scholarship in the Humanities* (blog), http://digitalscholarship.wordpress.com/2010/11/20/2030-vision-scenarios-for-the-humanities-in-2030 (accessed November 20, 2010).

7. Diane M. Zorich, *A Survey of Digital Humanities Centers in the United States,* CLIR Publication No. 143 (Washington, DC: Council on Library and Information Resources, 2008), http://www.clir.org/pubs/abstract/pub143abst.html.

8. "How Is the NNI Helping?" National Nanotechnology Initiative website, http://www.nano.gov (accessed February 28, 2012).

9. David Nicholas, Ian Rowlands, Michael Jubb, and Hamid R. Jamali, "The Impact of the Economic Downturn on Libraries: With Special Reference to University Libraries," *Journal of Academic Librarianship* 36, no. 5 (September 2010): 376–382.

10. Ibid., 381.

11. California Community Colleges Centers of Excellence, "California Community Colleges Centers of Excellence Brochure," http://www.coeccc.net/media/COE_PDF_brochure.pdf (accessed January 25, 2010).

12. Susan E. Searing, "Meeting the Information Needs of Interdisciplinary Scholars: Issues for Administrators of Large University Libraries," *Library Trends* 45, no. 2 (Fall 1996): 315–342.

13. Julia A. Martin, "A Case Study of Academic Library and Economic Development Center Collaboration at the University of Toledo," *Journal of Business & Finance Librarianship* 15, no. 3–4 (2010): 237-252.

14. Jake Carlson, Alexis E. Ramsey, and J. David Kotterman, "Using an Institutional Repository to Address Local-Scale Needs: A Case Study at Purdue University," *Library Hi Tech* 28, no. 1 (2010): 157-173.

15. "About," Roy Rosenzweig Center for History and New Media, George Mason University, http://chnm.gmu.edu/about/ (accessed November 22, 2010).

16. Geoffrey Rockwell, "What Is Infrastructure?" Wiki philosophi.ca, geoffreyrockwell.com website, http://www.philosophi.ca/pmwiki.php/Main/WhatIsInfrastructure (accessed November 22, 2010).

17. Anna Gold, "Cyberinfrastructure, Data, and Libraries, Part 1: A Cyberinfrastructure Primer for Librarians," *D-Lib Magazine* 13, no. 9/10 (September/October 2007), http://www.dlib.org/dlib/september07/gold/09gold-pt1.html.

18. Martha Bedard and Johann van Reenen, "The E-Research Center: Transforming a Traditional Science Library" (paper presented at the 31st Annual Conference of the International Association of Scientific and Technological University Libraries, West Lafayette, IN, June 22, 2010), http://docs.lib.purdue.edu/iatul2010/conf/day2/1.

19. Art Dewulf, Greet François, Claudia Pahl-Wostl, and Tharsi Taillieu, 2007. "A Framing Approach to Cross-Disciplinary Research Collaboration: Experiences from a Large-Scale Research Project on Adaptive Water Management," *Ecology and Society* 12, no. 2 (December 2007): article 14.
20. Eric D. Feigelson, "Cross-Disciplinary Research in Astronomy," arXiv.org, April 23, 2010, arXiv: 1004.4148v1, http;//arXiv.org/abs/1004.4184 (accessed February 28, 2012).
21. National Research Council, *Strengthening the Linkages between the Sciences and the Mathematical Sciences* (Washington DC: National Academies Press, 2000).
22. Ibid., 5.
23. Ibid., 15.
24. Deana D. Pennington, "Cross-Disciplinary Collaboration and Learning," *Ecology & Society* 13, no. 2 (December 2008): 8; Deana D. Pennington, "Enabling Science and Technology Research Teams: A Breadmaking Metaphor," *EDUCAUSE Quarterly* 33, no. 1 (2010): 1–9; Deana D. Pennington, "Collaborative, Cross-Disciplinary Learning and Co-emergent Innovation in eScience Teams," *Earth Sciences Informatics* 4, no. 2 (June 2011): 55–68, http://www.springerlink.com/content/81156061q1754t00/fulltext.html.
25. National Research Council, *Strengthening the Linkages*, 15.
26. Ibid., 16.
27. Pennington, "Cross-Disciplinary Collaboration"; Pennington, "Enabling Science and Technology Research Teams"; Pennington, "Collaborative, Cross-Disciplinary Learning"; Deana Pennington, Thomas Caudell, Diana Northrup, and Johann van Reenen, *Report of the Committee on Research Enhancement & Transformational Research Collaboration,* executive summary (Albuquerque: University of New Mexico, 2009), http://hdl.handle.net/1928/11606.
28. Pennington, "Collaborative, Cross-Disciplinary Learning," 56.
29. Ibid., 57.
30. National Research Council, *Strengthening the Linkages*, 16.
31. Pennington, Peroanl communication, 2/2/2010.
32. "History," EthicShare, https://www.ethicshare.org/about/history (accessed February 28, 2012).
33. Alexander Voss and Rob Procter, "Virtual Research Environments in Scholarly Work and Communications," *Library Hi Tech* 27, no. 2 (2009): 175.
34. myExperiment wiki, main page, http://wiki.myexperiment.org/index.php/Main_Page (accessed February 28, 2012).
35. Ojax++ web site, main page, http://www.ucd.ie/ojax (accessed May 8, 2012).
36. Voss and Procter, "Virtual Research Environments," 179
37. National Research Council, *Strengthening the Linkages*, 9.
38. Pennington et al., *Report of the Committee on Research Enhancement.*
39. Ibid., 1.
40. Ibid., 2.
41. "Dissemination and Sharing of Research Results," National Science Foundation, http://www.nsf.gov/bfa/dias/policy/dmp.jsp (accessed February 28, 2012).
42. University of New Mexico University Libraries, "Digital Data Management, Curation and Archiving," Research Guides website, http://libguides.unm.edu/data (last updated October 7, 2011).
43. National Research Council, *Strengthening the Linkages*, 16.
44. Robert Friedman, Brian Whitworth, and Michael Brownstein, "Realizing the

Power of Extelligence: A New Business Model for Academic Publishing," *International Journal of Technology, Knowledge and Society* 6, no. 2 (2010): 105.

45. Pennington, "Collaborative, Cross-Disciplinary Learning," 59.

46. Daniel Stokols, Shalini Misra, Richard P. Moser, Kara L. Hall, and Brandie K. Taylor, "The Ecology of Team Science: Understanding Contextual Influences on Transdisciplinary Collaborations," *American Journal of Preventive Medicine* (supplement) 35, no. 2 (August 2008): S96–S115.

47. Etienne Wenger, "Communities of Practice and Social Learning Systems," *Organization* 7, no. 2 (May 2000): 225–246.

48. Noa Aharony and Daphne R. Raban, 2008. "Economics of Information Goods: An Interdisciplinary Subject for Israeli LIS and MBA Curricula," *Library & Information Science Research* 30, no. 2 (June 2008): 102–107.

49. "About," iSchools Organization website, http://www.ischools.org/site/about (accessed February 28, 2012).

50. "UMII Programs," under "Graduate School Fellowships," University of Minnesota Interdisciplinary Informatics website, http://www.informatics.umn.edu/programs.html (accessed February 28, 2012).

51. Suzanne Schadl, curator/librarian, University of New Mexico, personal communication, February 2, 2010.

52. Pennington, "Collaborative, Cross-Disciplinary Learning," 57.

53. Pennington, "Cross-Disciplinary Collaboration"; Pennington, "Enabling Science and Technology Research Teams"; Pennington, "Collaborative, Cross-Disciplinary Learning."

54. Wenger, "Communities of Practice."

Shaping the Future through Interdisciplinary Integration

Craig Gibson

The many paradoxes of interdisciplinarity are evident in the contributions to this volume. The structures of the academy are straining toward integration across disciplines in order to solve transdisciplinary problems and "grand challenges," but most faculty and researchers continue to identify with the norms, research practices, and socialization into the academic profession that they learned in graduate school—meaning they identify with their discipline or their particular academic department or specialty. Interdisciplinary work is sometimes rewarded and recognized, but such recognition is not yet the standard, even though the rhetoric from many university and college administrators calls for breaking down "silos" within higher education institutions in order to address big problems. Knowledge creation itself is simultaneously dependent on disciplinary faculty making connections and learning from each other, which means questioning some assumptions of their own disciplines, while also retaining their own research protocols and methodologies in order to advance more specialized work in those disciplines. In short, interdisciplinarity poses great promise but also great uncertainty for those who look to it as a new paradigm within the academy—a "game changer" it may eventually become, but it is not yet clear how it will become so.

The definitional problem itself for interdisciplinarity, as differentiated from transdisciplinarity and multidisciplinarity, is one difficulty for the academy, and that problem is reflected in several of the chapters in this book. That several of the contributors felt the need to attend to issues of definition, or show taxonomies that make up an intellectual map, is particularly revealing. All of the authors agreed to write on a particular aspect of library programs, services, collections, or engagement with the larger community, in light of emerging trends in interdisciplinarity. Framing the particular "library" issue within the interdisciplinarity context allows the contributors to step back from the standard "library" perspective and draw out wider implications for the library's ongoing significance in a time when traditional library metrics are being questioned. In a way, interdisciplinarity has always been implicit in library processes, standards, classification schemes, and services, even when all of these processes, standards, schemes, and services are mostly attuned to highly granular and discipline-specific methods, data, and knowledge structures. Authors in this volume have identified many problems with the epistemology used by libraries that reflects traditional academic ways of knowing, and have succeeded in linking scholarly communication, digital projects, area studies, classification and cataloging, collection development, and other traditional and nontraditional aspects of library service with emerging ways of knowing throughout the academy.

The future of the academy may not be definitely knowable, but we can see trends and harbingers of change. Greater accountability, greater transparency, more focus on outcomes and the "value proposition," a focus on collaboration with partners within and beyond the institution, and more direct connections in solving big societal problems—all of these have been evident now, with varying degrees of emphasis, for a decade, and their importance is likely to grow. In working with others to shape a shared future, academic librarians will need to identify their unique contributions, which will necessarily focus more on external relationships and metrics rather than traditional, inward-looking ones. The future is likely to see the following:

1. **More creative staffing recruitment and professionalization.** Instead of traditional bibliographers, libraries will recruit knowledge specialists with expertise in technology, data mining, research management, assessment, and scholarly/research-based approaches to teaching and learning. Such creative workforce development will depend on understanding interdisciplinary shifts at a particular institution.

2. **Reorganization of traditional library departments.** The "recombinant library" of which Lorcan Dempsey wrote[1] is becoming a reality, with new structures focused on external (to the library) challenges and problems. Traditional refer-

ence departments, usually location-bound, may become user assistance teams that span digital services, assessment and user research, teaching and learning initiatives, and special formats/collections programs. The service delivery model of such departments will increasingly be mobile and positioned outside library buildings altogether, in places where inter-disciplinary clusters of faculty and students work on projects together. Such cross-departmental expertise is ideally situated to respond to the highly mobile, interdisciplinary faculty member or student of the present, one who has become acculturated to looking beyond the department-based home (or the departmental library, or any library) for assistance.

3. **Extending library programs and services into larger "team" environments within the academy.** The newer options for reorganizing libraries mentioned above will also include an "extension" aspect, where the appropriate librarian in a group can work as a research or teaching/curriculum team member at the campus level. The extension of library expertise into interdisciplinary structures at the campus level will be one indicator of success for the library's strategic future.

4. **Continuing evolution of discovery tools.** The discovery environment, already a focus of librarians, software and ILS designers, and others, is currently very challenging, with provisional solutions for integrating pathways to research, data, and multiple formats for information. It is the perennial problem of discovery tools: precision versus recall with the current generation of such tools shifting the balance toward large, Google-like "recalls," while faculty and students want precise results in order to save their time and focus their attention. Interdisciplinary thinking within the library, with greater attention toward discovery environments that bring together resources, expertise, and links to an expanded view of knowledge, may offer some relief for the continuing discovery problem of too much unfiltered information.

5. **Increasingly flexible knowledge classification.** Cataloging and knowledge classification will become more flexible
   activities in order to foster interdisciplinary research. The
   advent of RDA and the shift from older taxonomies such as
   LCSH will allow metadata specialists to describe resources
   in ways that facilitate interdisciplinary information seeking
   and help students and faculty more readily make connections
   across disciplines and knowledge domains.

6. **A view of knowledge itself.** Library strategic plans increasingly call for the library to become an essential partner in
   research processes, in curriculum design and development,
   and in outreach to partners through the institution and
   beyond, but such partnerships depend on a firm grounding
   in how the libraries can add value in the knowledge creation
   process and sustain attention in a fragmented academy and
   among researchers at all levels who want information delivered to them, with little interaction, and in the most readily
   usable format for them, as they prepare classes, write grant
   proposals against deadlines, or submit course assignments.
   A more integrative view of knowledge, of what disciplines
   contribute to the "intellectual map" of the institution, and
   how questions and challenges of interdisciplinarity create a
   richer overlay of possibilities for the institution, is necessary.
   The library can prepare the foundation for this more integrative view of knowledge through a web presence that shows
   how the library's services, collections, and programs support
   all academic programs, while also demonstrating the connections across knowledge domains throughout the institution—connecting researchers (the VIVO project at Cornell
   is an example) and showcasing the big challenges that the
   institution wants to address. If the library can demonstrate
   that how it organizes itself and its services makes a difference in addressing those big challenges, it will become
   the essential partner that its strategic plan advocates. More
   creative metrics focused on value, impact, and relationship
   building, along with integrative knowledge creation, will be

necessary for the library to develop that large map of knowledge and relationships throughout the institution.

Interdisciplinarity continues to challenge all members of the academic community, even those who are its champions. Libraries may find a new, more explicit and intentional role for themselves in fostering the increasingly interdisciplinary work of researchers, scholars, and students, if they look beyond traditional library structures, norms, and assumptions. Such a role will move resources and expertise to places where scholarly conversations that span boundaries occur—virtually, in blogs or Twitter feeds, or face-to-face, in physical "hubs" for scholars from across an institution who are addressing together some of the "grand challenges" facing society. The library as repository therefore becomes more ubiquitous by positioning itself at those interdisciplinary points of convergence that are ever more visible in higher education.

Note

1.   Lorcan Dempsey, "The Recombinant Library: Portals and People." *Journal of Library Administration* 39, no. 4 (2003): 103–136.

About the Authors

Roberta J. Astroff, MLS, PhD, is head of the Downtown Campus Library at the University of Texas at San Antonio. Her current research focuses on institutional and discursive practices.

Angela Carreño is the Head of Collection Development in the Collections and Research Services unit at New York University Bobst Library. In addition to the masters in library science, she has an advanced degree in Latin American history from The Johns Hopkins University.

Kevin J. Comerford is an Assistant Professor and Digital Initiatives Librarian at the University of New Mexico. Mr. Comerford has extensive experience in digital asset and media management, and is currently engaged in developing data curation, open access publishing, and content management resources at UNM.

Ann Copeland has served as the special collections cataloging librarian at Penn State University since 2001. She has been active in the Bibliographic Standards Committee of the Rare Books and Manuscripts Section of ACRL, and was one of the editors of *Descriptive Cataloging of Rare Materials (Serials)* (Library of Congress, 2008).

Mark Dahl is interim director of the Aubrey R. Watzek Library at Lewis & Clark College. He is a librarian, technologist and administrator with an interest in the future role of the academic library and a passion for the liberal arts.

Evelyn Ehrlich works as subject librarian and administrator in the Collections and Research Services and Public Services units at New York University Bobst Library. In addition to the masters in library science, she has advanced degrees in Jewish Studies and German history from Brandeis University and Columbia University.

Craig Gibson is Associate Director for Research and Education at The Ohio State University, where he is responsible for reference and research services, outreach and engagement, the libraries' instruction program, and departmental libraries. He has been Associate University Librarian for Research, Instruction, and Outreach at George Mason University Libraries and has held other positions in instruction and reference services at Washington State University and Lewis-Clark State College; his current research interests focus on engagement measures for academic and research libraries.

Dan Hazen spent some three decades as the Latin American bibliographer at Cornell, Berkeley, and then Harvard, while also engaging in library projects and consulting assignments throughout the region. He currently serves as the Associate Librarian of Harvard College for Collection Development.

Jean-Pierre V. M. Hérubel, Ph.D. is Professor of Library Science, Humanities, Social Sciences, and Education Library, Purdue University. Among his interests are the history of academic disciplines, disciplinary cultures, disciplinary publication, and historiography. He is the librarian for Art, Anthropology/Archaeology, and Philosophy among other subjects.

Cynthia Holt is the Head of the Collection Development and Preservation Department at George Mason University Libraries and has been involved in collection development work in academic libraries for eighteen years.

Maralyn Jones is a reference and instruction librarian and liaison to the Interdisciplinary Studies Field Major department at Berkeley. In 2011 alone, she taught classes in academic research for more than 1,000 students as well as many individual research sessions, in which she developed the ideas outlined in her contributed chapter.

Daniel C. Mack is Tombros Librarian for Classics and Ancient Mediterranean Studies, Professor of Classics and the Bibliography of Antiquity, and Head of the George and Sherry Middlemas Arts and

Humanities Library at Penn State. His research interests include interdisciplinarity in academia, liaison librarianship in the digital age, ancient Mediterranean religion, and Rome in the age of Caesar Augustus.

Gretchen E. Reynolds, formerly a Social Sciences Liaison Librarian at George Mason University, is now a Research Librarian at the National Intelligence University, located within the Defense Intelligence Agency. The views expressed in this chapter are those of the author and do not reflect the official policy or position of the US Government.

Johann van Reenen is a Professor and Associate Vice President for Research at UNM. He has been active in digital library initiatives and open access scholarship, especially in Latin America. His current interests include collaborative interdisciplinary research support systems.

John C. Walsh is Associate University Librarian for Resources & Collection Management Services with George Mason University Libraries.

Jill Woolums has been an academic librarian at UC Berkeley since 2001, serving primarily in the Education Psychology Social Welfare Library and the California Digital Library. Her primary responsibilities focus on collection development, instruction, website development and research advisory services.

Index